Serving Communities with Courage and Compassion

SERVING COMMUNITIES WITH COURAGE AND COMPASSION

Editors Gabrielle McMullen,
Patrice Scales & Denis Fitzgerald

Connor Court Publishing

Connor Court Publishing Pty Ltd

Copyright © Catholic Social Services Victoria 2020

ALL RIGHTS RESERVED. This book contains material protected under International and Federal Copyright Laws and Treaties. Any unauthorised reprint or use of this material is prohibited. No part of this book may be reproduced or transmitted in any form or by any means, electronic or mechanical, including photocopying, recording, or by any information storage and retrieval system without express written permission from the publisher.

PO Box 7257
Redland Bay QLD 4165
sales@connorcourt.com
www.connorcourt.com

ISBN: 9781922449085

Cover design by Maria Giordano

Printed in Australia

CONTENTS

Preface   Joan Healy RSJ   viii

Introduction   Gabrielle McMullen, Patrice Scales and Denis Fitzgerald   1

Section 1   Serving Communities in a Renewed Church

Francis Sullivan, *Margin Call: The Risk of Integrity*   23

Ursula Stephens, *2020 Mary MacKillop Oration – Mary MacKillop: The Authenticity of Speaking Truth to Power* and Monica Cavanagh RSJ, *Response to the Oration*   37

Sarah Jane Grove, Lisa McDonald and Linda Di Sipio, *Respectful, Impactful Formation for Mission*   59

John Warhurst and Katherine Juric, *Governance for Mission*   71

Gabrielle McMullen with Sheree Limbrick, *Safeguarding Everyone in the Church Today and into the Future*   85

Peter Hudson with Sherry Balcombe, Helen Christensen, Helen Kennedy and Henry Williams, *Makarrata: Healing the Wounds of the Past*   95

Gabrielle McMullen with Trudy Dantis, Denis Fitzgerald, Cath Garner and Lana Turvey-Collins, *The Journey Towards the Plenary Council*   113

Patrice Scales and Joshua Lourensz with Claire Victory and Belinda Clarke, *Building a Strong Future for Catholic Social Services*   129

Section 2 Courage and Compassion in Action

Jocelyn Bignold, Vincent Long Van Nguyen OFM Conv and John McCarthy with Patrice Scales, *Putting Courage and Compassion into Action*   145

Maria Harries and Robyn Miller, *The Centrality and Challenge of Child Safety*   161

Gabrielle McMullen with Helen Burt and Anne Kirwan, *Advancing Dignity and Equality within the Framework of the NDIS*   187

Patrice Scales with Daniel Clements and Deanna Davis, *Restorative Justice: Signs of Hope*   201

Andrew Gardiner and John Lochowiak with Denis Fitzgerald, *Towards Treaties with Australia's First Nations Peoples*   213

Netty Horton with Jack de Groot, Tony Nicholson and Sally-Anne Petrie, *Responding to Homelessness: Building Houses or Creating a Community?*   223

Janene Evans, Cabrini Makasiale, Felicity Rorke and Michael Tonks, *Domestic Violence: Awareness, Prevention and Progress*   233

Section 3 Catholic Social Services Active at the Margins

Denis Fitzgerald with Alana Crouch, Cathy Hammond and Mark Phillips, *Parishes as an Integral Part of Social Services*   253

Claire-Anne Willis with Meagan Giddy and Maryanne Stivactas, *The Mission Alive in Regional and Rural Communities*   269

Bronwyn Lay and Andrew Hamilton SJ, *Ecological Justice: How to Listen to the Cry of the Earth and the Cry of the Poor*   285

Fiona Basile with Farah Farouque, Sam Patterson, Andrew Yule and Barney Zwartz, *Mobilising Media for Mission and Advocacy*   293

Gabrielle McMullen with Janet Cribbes, Jack de Groot and Ursula Stephens, *Collaboration Enhancing the Church's Disaster Response*   315

Debra Zanella, *Mission at the Margins: The Call to Uncommon Courage*   333

Mark Monahan, *Serving Communities with Courage and Compassion – A Reflection*   351

Acknowledgements   360

Contributors   363

Preface

Joan Healy RSJ

It was no ordinary conference. The catastrophic bushfires were still burning in Australia, a country tinder-dry with drought. First Peoples were saying that their land was tortured. Pope Francis was calling us to be aware of the interdependence of all of life, all of creation on this vulnerable planet. It seemed that every crisis had the greatest impact on those who had least. Always the most at risk were the least protected. The context of the time coloured everything.

Participants, leaders in Catholic social services from across Australia and from New Zealand, quickly found that they had much in common. Each was a professional in a particular area of health or community service. They knew the urgency of our times. They had carried the responsibilities of leadership in Church organisations during the shame over revelations of sexual abuse. They readily shared experience.

The three days of the conference gave space and inspiration to consider together the complex issues of our societies and our Church communities. It is good that the presentations from this conference can be released in book form; this wider circle of reflection is needed. The challenges we face require listening, prayer and discernment.

The twin themes of compassion and courage were the focus of two keynote presentations and were echoed in the Mary MacKillop Oration traditionally presented at the conference dinner. They

PREFACE

became background to all plenary sessions, and to the smaller groups which focussed on specific issues. A glance through the chapters of this book shows the breadth of the areas covered.

Francis Sullivan presented the first keynote, "Margin Call: The Risk of Integrity". We were challenged not to close ranks when threatened, but to become a "heart-driven" Church community, professing Gospel values. "Let our broken hearts speak", he said.

Dr Ursula Stephens, in delivering the Oration, explored the responsibility of speaking truth to power, a responsibility that risks consequences. Throughout her life Mary MacKillop recognised truth-telling as a duty. She suffered for it. "How can we too have the courage to speak truth to power and accept the consequences?", Dr Stephens asked.

Debra Zanella offered the final keynote, "Mission at the Margins – A Call to Uncommon Courage". She traced the inspiration of prophets of our time. She emphasised the call to speak out against acts of injustice and the underlying structures that support them. "The time is now", she said.

There was a time in Victoria, around 50 years ago now, when leaders of what we then called "the social apostolate" came together for three days and nights to share faith, professionalism and the lives we were living. In those days, the Second Vatican Council was recent; there was surety and a certain simplicity: "We will proclaim the Gospel in our deeds".

By contrast our time, a half century later, is neither simple nor sure. COVID-19 has complicated it even further. Nevertheless, there is the opportunity of a 'new normal' that this generation will help to shape. Courage and compassion are surely useful foundations.

We who are called to be witnesses to a Gospel way of life and service know full well that ours is a time of complex need and moral dilemma. From the Gospels comes the certainty of the power of love, the compassion that we live, and the truth that we dare to speak. As the poet Christopher Fry wrote, "Affairs are now soul size. The enterprise is exploration into God".[1]

This time is our time.

---

[1] Christopher Fry, 1951. "A Sleep of Prisoner"; accessed at https://someinspiration.com/inspiringstuff/sleep-of-prisoners/.

Introduction

Gabrielle McMullen, Patrice Scales and Denis Fitzgerald

Serving Communities with Courage and Compassion is the fourth book to emerge from the current series of Catholic social services conferences. Over the past decade, the Catholic social services sector has gathered in Melbourne biennially for a conference focused on the mission of Catholic social services and formation for ministry of those in key roles in the sector. The 2020 conference, *Serving Communities with Courage and Compassion*, was held on 26-28 February 2020 at the Catholic Leadership Centre in East Melbourne. Some 280 participants attended sessions across the three days.

Why another book? The conference explored so many aspects of the subject matter – of service, communities, courage and compassion – a written account will enable that exploration to continue, both for those who participated at the time, but also for the many others in Catholic social services and far beyond whose vocation is to engage with these aspects of the human condition. That has been the experience of many who have engaged with the previous volumes in the series,[1] and who have proposed this further publication.

---

1 G. McMullen and J. Warhurst (eds), 2014. *Listening, Learning and Leading: The Impact of Catholic Identity and Mission*. Ballarat: Connor Court Publishing; G. McMullen, P. Scales and D. Fitzgerald (eds), 2016. *Review, Reimagine, Renew: Mission Making a Difference in a Changing World*. Redland Bay, Qld: Connor Court Publishing; and G. McMullen, P. Scales and D. Fitzgerald (eds), 2018. *Hearing, Healing, Hope: The Ministry of Service in Challenging Times*. Redland Bay, Qld: Connor Court Publishing.

Nor are these issues important only to the Catholic social services community. The conferences have been organised by Catholic Social Services Victoria, in partnership with Catholic Social Services Australia, but they have increasingly also attracted attendees from the health and aged care sector, parish ministries and educational initiatives focused on overcoming disadvantage and building personal capacity. For the first time in 2020 we also had five delegates from our Aotearoa New Zealand Catholic Social Services counterpart. Their participation added to the enriching diversity of representation from all Australian states and territories, and from major cities and regional and more remote centres. This richness, in turn, led to broader engagement in many discussions – for example, in a workshop on domestic violence, which included formal New Zealand input, the experience of the two countries was seen to differ considerably.

"It was the best of times; it was the worst of times ..." So, in important ways, is the case today. As we met in February 2020, communities were working on recovery from the devasting bushfires of the 2019-2020 summer and from floods in New South Wales and Queensland. Other parts of the country were still in severe drought and dealing with its economic and social consequences. The potential impact of COVID-19 was just entering our consciousness.

There were challenges too on many other fronts. The recent decades of continuous economic growth had coincided with the entrenchment of disadvantage, including among asylum seekers and the long-term unemployed, and our First Nations peoples had not shared proportionally in social and economic advancement. Compassion is no longer a sufficient response – courage and service are sorely needed.

The Catholic Church over these same decades has been a

INTRODUCTION

continued source of human enrichment, but has failed in important areas, and faces deep challenges. The suffering and the betrayal of trust that characterise the sexual abuse of children will cast a shadow over the Church for many years to come. Smaller and older congregations and fewer clergy have developed alongside a transition in leadership and in the composition of staff and volunteers in many areas of Church ministry. Both secular society and governments take a more distant and questioning approach to many aspects of the Church than was the case not many decades ago. These challenges impact on how Catholic social services, as part of the Church, are able to serve those in need in the community. They also impact on the essence of these organisations, which are increasingly led and staffed by people who are not themselves Catholic but who are dedicated to serving communities with courage and compassion as part of the mission of the Church.

Leadership concerns in society today reach far beyond the Catholic Church. Top down leadership across society is viewed very differently now, with the increased turnover rate of Australian Prime Ministers a stark reminder that effective leadership and the trust of the people are no longer necessarily associated with those in positions of authority. There is a deep sense that compassion and courage need to be applied across society if the community is to be well served.

Despite those challenges, amongst those gathered at the conference there was a strong feeling of optimism for the future. We heard many instances of how Catholic social services were evolving, in response to the 'signs of the times', to serve communities and to continue the ministry of Jesus in diverse and powerful ways across Australia. Stories of "courage and compassion" were frequent.

Intent of the 2020 Conference

In its planning, the 2020 conference committee identified a number of aims that it sought to achieve:

- to empower both those in governance roles and those 'at the coalface' to take the mission of Catholic social services forward;
- to present case studies of how Catholic social services are serving Australian and New Zealand communities in order to share experiences, learn from one another, and promote innovative and best practices in our ministry of service;
- to provide an occasion of formation for those in governance and service roles, those who are Catholic and those who are not, to deepen their ability to contribute to the mission of Catholic social services;
- to recommit jointly, as conference participants, to the mission of Catholic social services and to return renewed and hope-filled to continue ministries of service.

The concept of 'formation' is important here. Formation goes beyond the acquisition of knowledge, or the building of new skills, important as both of these are for everyone working in community service. It reaches to the development of the heart, of a deeper understanding of why such service is needed, of what interior disposition is called for to sustain a commitment, and of how to nurture that understanding and commitment and share them with colleagues and others with whom we need to cooperate.

In the Catholic tradition, this commitment is a response to the Gospel call to love of neighbour, informed by reflection on that call in light of the experience of the Church over the years. That has resulted in a body of Catholic social teaching which makes paramount the principles of respect for the dignity of each person,

INTRODUCTION

the centrality of solidarity in working for the common good, and the importance of allowing each person and each part of society to work as part of an organic whole where support is given where it is needed and no-one seeks to dominate another. Formation in the Catholic social services environment involves exploring the elements of this tradition.

In designing the program, the conference committee sought to build in strong engagement by the delegates. Thus, the program included opportunities after plenary lectures and panel presentations for 'audience' participation. Each attendee could register for two of the interactive workshops. Times and spaces were provided to encourage informal exchange between conference participants. This interactive dimension strengthened the formation potential for participants. A conference can be a feast of information, but formation requires that this input be digested, and reflected upon. Interaction is a catalyst for this absorption. So too does a written account facilitate this deeper engagement. On the day, an inspiring presentation, such as that by Francis Sullivan in his opening keynote, can rouse the spirits of a gathering, but deeper reflection is significantly assisted by an opportunity to return to the words of the oration, to savour them, and to consider closely what implications they might have for one's own personal or organisational response.

When the conference committee debriefed after the event and reviewed the breadth of the attendees' ministries, the quality of both the presentations and the delegates' participation in the program, and the evaluations received from delegates, we were confident the conference aims had been extensively achieved. Participants felt 'nourished' for the demanding ministry that awaited them in the year ahead. One participant with decades of experience in Catholic ministries said that she has never been to a conference that was so right for the times.

With such findings, how could we not work to make the rich

'palette' of conference contributions available to a wider audience? Through a reading of this book, you can also be a judge of whether the conference met its expectations. As you make your way through the following chapters, do you find yourself being engaged and challenged, reflective, optimistic and hopeful?

*****

The following sections of this Introduction present an outline of each chapter of this volume and capture the conference content under three broad themes which emerged:

- Serving Communities in a Renewed Church,
- Courage and Compassion in Action,
- Catholic Social Services Active at the Margins.

The closing section of this Introduction then summarises those elements of the conference where we took time to "Celebrate the Service of Communities", to celebrate the contributions of Catholic social services to the Church and society, and to give thanks to God for the many blessings on our services.

Serving Communities in a Renewed Church

Francis Sullivan's chapter, **Margin Call: The Risk of Integrity**, calls on Catholic organisations and those within the Catholic social services sector to reflect on, and reconsider, what it means to provide services to the most disadvantaged and disenfranchised groups in our community. Are we up to the challenge of becoming authentic and responding in a radical fashion to the call of the Gospel? Sullivan challenges us to take the risk of living our values, to find unity across differences, and to be advocates for economic justice. He finally reflects on his own spiritual journey on the Camino de Santiago where he leaves the *Royal Commission into Institutional Responses to Child Sexual Abuse Final Report* at the crypt of St James ... and makes a hasty retreat!

INTRODUCTION

Ursula Stephens, in her **Mary MacKillop Oration** at the conference dinner, "Mary MacKillop: The Authenticity of Speaking Truth to Power", contemplates that speaking truth to power is often dangerous and may have consequences for the speaker. That danger, however, did not stop Mary MacKillop. Stephens' seven lessons learnt from Mary MacKillop are helpful principles for all of us in understanding how the inspirational Mary MacKillop can guide our lives and the mission of our organisations.

Sr Monica Cavanagh RSJ, in her response to the Mary MacKillop Oration, reflects further on Mary MacKillop's determination to speak truth to power, in particular to the Catholic hierarchy and clergy within Australia and in Rome, and on Mary's personal growth in her faith, and acceptance of leadership. Cavanagh asks us: As a person working in Catholic ministry, "how am I being called to be the heartbeat of God's love?"

In **Respectful, Impactful Formation for Mission**, Sarah Jane Grove, Lisa McDonald and Linda Di Sipio explore several examples of formation experiences. Each formation experience, they say, will differ depending on the purpose and the 'audience' for whom it is intended. Grove illustrates the importance of respecting the individual's world view, creating a sense of shared mission and articulating the Catholic identity of the organisation. McDonald's example focuses on formation for board members, the critical importance of having a board formation strategy, and growing and nurturing the board in its spiritual leadership role. Di Sipio discusses "imaginative contemplation" as a way of praying with our imagination. This practice uses passages from scripture as an opportunity for individuals to align their own stories with those of the Gospels and to foster personal connections in identifying with biblical characters and events.

The **Governance for Mission** chapter examines two different perspectives on governance – the often-unique challenges facing governance boards in Catholic organisations, and a practical perspective on due diligence responsibilities of these boards. John Warhurst highlights the complexity and diversity of Church governance bodies and, more than ever, the need for accountability, transparency and inclusiveness in governance practice. Directors of governance boards would also be wise to read Katherine Juric's practical contribution on the need for directors proactively to seek an understanding of risk associated with the operation of their organisations. Due diligence is a key legal duty for officers of organisations, and workplace health and safety falls squarely within the responsibilities of directors. Be prepared to take a risk framework checklist to your next governance board meeting.

More than at any time in its history in Australia, the Catholic Church is being challenged to show its commitment to the ongoing protection and safety of children and adults in its care. Catholic Professional Standards Ltd (CPSL) was formed in 2017 as a response by the Church to the findings of the Royal Commission into Institutional Responses to Child Sexual Abuse. In **Safeguarding Everyone in the Church Today and into the Future**, Sheree Limbrick, CEO of CPSL, recounts progress in the work of CPSL, including the adoption and roll-out of the National Catholic Safeguarding Standards, implementation of the Standards and related training across the Catholic Church, and the first ten audits of Church bodies conducted by CPSL. To have achieved this level of engagement and implementation in the usually slow-moving Church environment is a major achievement in itself and, as this chapter shows, the protection and safety of children is paramount in the role of CPSL and to the future of the Church itself.

Makarrata: **Healing the Wounds of the Past** is a candid, honest and sometimes heart-rending chapter from the conference opening night's forum. Four Australian Indigenous presenters shared personal and professional insights that cannot help but make each

INTRODUCTION

of us reflect on the struggles for justice and equity of Aboriginal and Torres Strait Island peoples. Beginning with a reading of the "Uluru Statement from the Heart", through reflections on cultural responses, the Stolen Generation and subsequent inter-generational trauma, and the 2020 Closing the Gap Refresh, this chapter proffers a practical and powerful invitation to all Australians to stand in solidarity with Aboriginal and Torres Strait Islander peoples. Readers could find it valuable to answer the four questions at the end of the chapter as a stimulus for driving change in their organisations.

In **The Journey Towards the Plenary Council**, we have a record of Trudy Dantis, Lana Turvey-Collins, Cath Garner and Denis Fitzgerald discussing progress on the three-year journey to the Catholic Church's Plenary Council and ways in which we can continue to participate in the process. Reading this chapter, it is clear that listening, dialogue and discernment have been vital components of this journey. Throughout the chapter, the message is that this is a 'hope-filled' journey – interrupted by the COVID-19 pandemic – that may guide the Church to full renewal and reform, and bring about a Church that is participatory and inclusive. Turvey-Collins issues a message for people to continue to be engaged in the journey, to 'have their say' right up to the Plenary Council itself because, as she says, "we need to get this right".

In **Building a Strong Future for Catholic Social Services** three younger generation leaders share their insights into the future challenges and opportunities for Catholic social service organisations. Clare Victory from the St Vincent de Paul Society, Belinda Clark from CatholicCare Tasmania and Joshua Lourensz from Catholic Social Services Victoria see a strong future towards the flourishing of our society through the unique role that Catholic social service organisations play in providing services and advocating to counter the growing gap of disadvantage in Australia. They urge us to think beyond current funding boundaries, to seek out the most disadvantaged in our society who are missing out, and to look within our own organisations for future leaders. Three case studies exemplify those principles in action. These three inspiring younger leaders offer great hope to the Catholic social services sector.

Courage and Compassion in Action

A bishop, a CEO and a chairperson share their unique perspectives in the chapter, **Putting Courage and Compassion into Action**, on the courage and compassion that operate as daily fixtures in the work of Catholic agencies and those who use their services. Jocelyn Bignold tells of the courage of women who bravely face multiple barriers in leaving family violence to seek employment, often successfully, sometimes not, but always courageously. Bishop Vincent Long, himself a 'boat person' who advocates publicly on behalf of refugees and asylum seekers, urges us to work to change the political narrative from demonisation and fear to a positive message of courage and determination. John McCarthy, as Chair of the Archdiocese of Sydney's Anti-Slavery Taskforce, passionately challenges us to understand modern slavery and human trafficking and our unwitting role in sustaining these hideous practices when we purchase products and services tainted with slave labour. From each of these presenters, a steadfast resolve emerges to improve life opportunities for those striving for a better life for themselves.

At no other time in the history of the Catholic Church has its abysmal performance at protecting children – every community's most precious asset – been so scrutinised, found wanting and now called to account. In **The Centrality and Challenge of Child Safety**, two of Australia's most respected leaders in the family and child protection 'space', put into context the absolute demand for everyone working across the Church and the social services sector to take responsibility for our role in accepting the poor standards of

INTRODUCTION

the past, implementing the highest professional standards around child safety, and changing the culture within our Church to one of compassionate champions for children and young people in our care. After reading this chapter, no-one – at any level of the Church – can claim 'we didn't know', and turn away from this most vulnerable group in our community without taking action.

The voices of both the organisational leader and the client are heard very vibrantly in the chapter on the National Disability Insurance Scheme (NDIS), **Advancing Dignity and Equality within the Framework of the NDIS**. Anne Kirwan led CatholicCare Canberra Goulburn through its role during the NDIS trial period, and then six years of implementing the market-focused, people-centred NDIS in its organisational practice. It has not been an easy journey. And neither is the NDIS journey of the client, as Helen Burt so eloquently highlights in writing of her experience – disappointing, frustrating and deflating, she records, as she negotiated the demands of the new system. Now, however, in her second year of the service, Burt has experienced something that offers to her, as a client, the real transformative experience that the NDIS should be. Some very pertinent points are highlighted in the workshop discussion, not least of which is the key issue of recognising the value of disability care workers.

The earlier a young person 'touches' the criminal justice system, the more likely it is that he or she will have a lifetime in the system. This harsh reality was the sobering fact that formed the basis of the workshop, **Restorative Justice: Signs of Hope**. Any person who believes that that there must be other ways than incarceration of dealing with young people in the criminal justice system will find this chapter insightful, informative and hopeful. Daniel Clements and Deanna Davis, with a wealth of experience in youth justice in city and regional areas, explain restorative justice, and the practical application of restorative practice in group conferencing, in youth justice and other settings. Their thoughtful, compassionate insights help us to understand that there are different ways of 'setting wrongs right' that will help to keep young people out of the criminal justice system, while addressing the impact of their behaviour.

In this powerful chapter, **Towards Treaties with Australia's First Nations Peoples**, Denis Fitzgerald summarises the workshop at which Andrew Gardiner and John Lochowiak discussed the importance of formal treaty arrangements to our First Nations Peoples, and the way in which we can all contribute to those processes. The relationship between treaty and dispossession and disadvantage is powerfully explained, as is the importance, through a treaty process, of finding ways to say 'sorry', of the teaching and learning of Indigenous languages, of education and listening to stories. An elected member of the First Peoples' Assembly, Gardiner urges the Victorian Government to waste no time in forging ahead with a treaty in partnership with the First Nations Peoples. There is a 'call to action' for all Australians to support and bring about treaty for First Peoples. Lochowiak reminds us: "It's in your interest as social service organisations to engage Aboriginal community members and help them to participate in treaty".

As homelessness figures increase, all too sadly, so does housing stock decline, denying the basic right of a 'roof over one's head' to thousands of people. In this chapter, **Responding to Homelessness: Building Houses or Creating a Community?**, Netty Horton summarises the workshop led by Tony Nicholson with Sally-Anne Petrie and Jack de Groot that explored, at a number of levels, the possibilities for providing social housing. The discussion went far beyond homelessness and housing, and delved into the complexities of providing integrated support, employment and community inclusion as a way of allowing every person the right to housing and to flourish and contribute to their communities. Two case studies provide insights into the opportunities and obstacles

INTRODUCTION

in providing social and community housing, and the current and potential role of parishes in providing housing, respectively.

With horrendous levels of domestic and family violence impacting victims and victim survivors, the **Domestic Violence: Awareness, Prevention and Progress** chapter offers perspectives from Victoria, Australia and New Zealand that were presented in a workshop chaired by Felicity Rorke. In a community crying out for effective ways to protect families, Janene Evans looks at the background to the recommendations from the Royal Commission into Family Violence 2015, and subsequent law reform. The New Zealand perspective, described by Sr Cabrini Makasiale and Michael Tonks, is presented with two initiatives which focus on family violence prevention and a parenting education program for fathers, respectively. These are practical early intervention programs responsive to the needs of local people in their communities.

Catholic Social Services Active at the Margins

Declining Mass attendance, an ageing cohort of parishioners and an absence of the young in our churches might lead us to wonder if there is a future for Catholic parishes in the welfare of their parish communities. In **Parishes as an Integral Part of Social Services**, Denis Fitzgerald, with Alana Crouch, Mark Phillips and Cathy Hammond, shows vibrant, responsive social service in action with examples of programs partnering with parishes. Crouch from Centacare Brisbane focuses on its work in managing 128 childcare facilities across the Archdiocese of Brisbane. Two-thirds of these are 'owned' by parishes and the partnerships aim to support families and children, and assist them to become part of the Catholic community in which they live. Phillips and Hammond relate the experiences of CatholicCare Sydney and its initiatives of working with parishes to develop responses to community need, including social housing. They also highlight CCareline, a single portal for contacting all services of CatholicCare Sydney. And a spirited sharing of various partnership experiences that ends this chapter reminds us that, in addition to being fruitful in practice, social service partnerships with parishes are a necessary part of the Christ-centred mission of both parishes and Catholic agencies.

The very real challenges confronting regional and rural communities are highlighted in **The Mission Alive in Regional and Rural Communities**, written by Claire-Anne Willis, from the workshop conducted by Meagan Giddy and Maryanne Stivactas. Giddy and Stivactas, well-versed in the provision of diverse initiatives and programs in regional areas, share practical first-hand experience of providing services in Shepparton in Victoria and Wilcannia-Forbes in New South Wales that directly respond to the needs of the people in those communities. The case studies show the importance of listening to, and working with, the local people; of developing strategic partnerships; and of responding to identified need through a variety of outreach initiatives, including mobile services. Readers will find the work taking place in these regional areas inspiring, and a reminder that listening to local voices is the best way to respond to the needs of communities.

Laudato Si' is the starting point of this chapter, **Ecological Justice: How to Listen to the Cry of the Earth and the Cry of the Poor,** by Andrew Hamilton SJ and Bronwyn Lay of Jesuit Social Services. From different perspectives, they address the topic of ecological justice and the ways in which we are called to hear, listen and respond to the cry of the poor. Lay writes about fostering an ecological culture at Jesuit Social Services, and integrating an ecological justice perspective into all its programs and advocacy. Hamilton reflects that "when we listen to the cry of the earth, we are inevitably drawn to hear the cry of the poor". How might the recent bushfires and COVID-19 pandemic cause

INTRODUCTION

us to reflect on the type of community in which we want to live in the future? Hamilton suggests each of us start by being attentive to the beauty of the world around us, and rally and act against its destruction.

Getting attention in today's crowded and competitive media world is a constant issue for not-for-profit organisations. In **Mobilising Media for Mission and Advocacy,** Fiona Basile reports on the forum that brought together four experienced communications and media specialists to share their experiences of how not-for-profit organisations can maximise the use of the media to publicise, and advocate for, their work and activities. From different corners of media experience, Andrew Yule, Farah Farouque and Barney Zwartz joined with Sam Patterson to provide sound practical advice for dealing with the media. Their advice: offer something of value, develop mutual trust, be an expert voice, offer fresh news and facts, know the outcome you want, put forward your strongest personality on your social media platform. These will help define your media strategy and more than likely give your organisation an improved media profile.

It was a fortuitous time, following months of devastating drought, bushfires and floods across Australia, to have a conference workshop on **Collaboration Enhancing the Church's Disaster Response.** The reflections, experiences and insights of the three presenters, Janet Cribbes, Jack de Groot and Ursula Stephens, now form a powerful chapter that speaks of the impact of disasters on communities, the challenges of dispersing funding aid in a short period of time, and the lessons learned about expectations of politicians, the media and the community in relation to disaster response. Stephens details how recognition of the need for a whole-of-Church response led to the formation of CERA, Catholic Emergency Relief Australia, which aims to provide a strategic, co-ordinated and focussed response to future disasters. In the final discussion, we are reminded that front-line workers, including volunteers, need to be cared for in the aftermath of disasters and the trauma.

In the final keynote address, entitled **Mission at the Margins: The Call to Uncommon Courage**, Debra Zanella reflects on the power of prophets in today's world, the power of prophecy, and the risks of prophecy. The prophets of whom Zanella speaks are not only the prophets of old; these are today's prophets – each of us, our organisations and the people we serve. Zanella writes that, while not everyone is called to be a prophet in the classical sense of the word, we are all called to be carriers of the prophetic message in our time. This chapter comes to life through the names and examples of people she sees as 'prophets', and will entice you to read more of their 'prophet' journeys. Finally, Zanella challenges us by asking: "What will you do, here and now in this world, in our time? Will you simply stand looking in?" Her thought-provoking chapter will inspire us not to stand by, but to be part of the change that is needed in this world and our Church.

The concluding chapter, Mark Monaghan's commentary on the conference, **Serving Communities with Courage and Compassion – A Reflection**, encapsulates the thoughts, the challenges, the barriers, the hardships, the initiatives and the successes that were presented throughout the conference plenary presentations and workshops. In those sessions, Monahan heard the call for a change in how we – the Church and Catholic agencies – do things; to find new ways of leadership and different leadership models and structures; to explore what our mission really could be; to broaden the sense of welcome to every person, not just through words but through actions; and to no longer accept the way things are, but strive for what could be. Are we ready for a new paradigm? One of consultative leadership, that values the voice of the child, people

INTRODUCTION

with a disability, the non-English speaking community member or the volunteer unpacking the dishwasher? This is a 'call to action', a challenge to change ourselves and the culture of our organisations. In conclusion, Monahan inspires us to "keep going, to be brave, to 'stick at it', and to be courageous as we serve our communities with compassion".

Celebrating the Service of Communities

A conference such as *Serving Communities with Courage and Compassion* is also a time to celebrate the contributions of Catholic social services to the Church and society and to give thanks to God for the many blessings on our services. Presentations during the three days together were richly interspersed with liturgies, led by conference liturgy coordinator Peter Hudson, then Network and Member Support Coordinator at Catholic Social Services Victoria. On several occasions, participants joined together to recite the conference prayer:

> *A Prayer for Compassion and Courage*
>
> Compassionate God,
> Your unconditional love for all
> inspires our hearts and empowers our actions
> for those who are most vulnerable.
> May we boldly and humbly serve one another
> and be steadfast in our work for justice for all people.
> Keep our hearts open to the joys and the hopes of our world, and
> our ears ready to hear your call to truth, justice and reconciliation.
> Let us continue to draw inspiration and strength from those,
> like St Mary MacKillop, on whose shoulders we stand.

> We gather here in Jesus' name to be nourished and to move forward together in hope and joy.
> Amen

The major celebration was the conference Mass for which Bishop Paul Bird CSsR was chief celebrant. He is the Delegate for Social Services of the Australian Catholic Bishops Conference and was an active participant in the conference. The Mass was on the day after Ash Wednesday and Bishop Bird's homily included reflections by Pope Francis on "the great gift we have in the season of Lent". Highlighting that Lent is a time "meant for turning to God and being warmed by God's love", Bishop Bird said:

> Pope Francis often contrasts love with indifference. He sees terrible indifference to the plight of so many who are suffering in our world today. He speaks about the globalisation of indifference. In regard to refugees, for example, Pope Francis laments the indifference that people seem to show to those who have been driven from their homes by war or those who seek to escape grinding poverty. Pope Francis speaks about a better way, the way of compassion. And he seeks to show us the way by giving an example of care for those in need. You might remember his visit to the refugees on the island of Lampedusa in his first days as Pope. He went to be with them, to show them compassion. He went to show them the warmth of love.

The message of the homily resonated with the moving examples of "serving communities with courage and compassion" which we had heard in the conference presentations of the previous days. Bishop Bird said: "There can be a wonderful interplay between the service we offer in our agencies and the liturgy we celebrate at the altar". He illustrated this with a story about Mother Teresa told by

INTRODUCTION

the English journalist Malcolm Muggeridge in his book, *Something Beautiful for God*:[2]

> Malcolm Muggeridge observed that Mother Teresa and the Sisters always started their day with prayer. They would attend an early morning Mass in their chapel. Then they would go out into the city streets. There they would find the sick and the dying. Some of these people had no homes. They would be suffering and even dying on the side of the road. The Sisters would do what they could to give them comfort.
>
> One morning, as they were preparing for their work, Mother Teresa spoke to the Sisters. She referred to the Mass they'd been to that morning and she also referred to the tasks that lay ahead of them that day. She said, 'This morning, Sisters, we were at Mass and we saw how reverently the priest held the Body of Christ at the altar. Today, in the streets, we'll meet the sick and dying. We must likewise hold them reverently, for they too are the Body of Christ'.

The homily reminded us powerfully of the essence of Catholic social services. As he concluded, Bishop Bird prayed for our ministry: "May we grow in reverence for Christ as we meet him in those who are in need. May God grant us the grace to serve them with courage and compassion".

---

[2] Malcolm Muggeridge, 1971. *Something Beautiful for God.* New York: Harper & Row.

SECTION 1

Serving Communities in a Renewed Church

Margin Call: The Risk of Integrity

Francis Sullivan

As we commenced the Catholic Social Services conference, we recognised the original inhabitants of the land on which we were meeting and its elders, past, present and emerging.

I noted that we also gathered as custodians of the collective ministries of religious orders, dioceses and faith-inspired organisations seeking to bring charity, justice or both to the needy, the marginalised and the often forgotten.

Whether overtly or not, this is done in the name of the Church. Even more so it is inspired by the example of Jesus. It is very much an intentional activity, a moral exercise. We specifically seek to instil a virtuous culture within the haphazard and perilous places where poverty and disadvantage dwell. Good works by good people for the good of others – not a bad gig!

But, importantly, for us it is also a Catholic gig – one where there are many Catholic identities, yet motivated and sustained by the same spirit, the same founding story portrayed in the Gospels which is the subject of ever deepening understanding and application.

It is within that light that I provide my thoughts. I do so not as an expert in the delivery of social services, but rather as a fellow traveller who has reflected fairly deeply, particularly over the last six years or so, on the ramifications of the Gospel for the Catholic Church in contemporary Australia.

I offer these reflections from a perspective of hope and optimism. I sincerely believe that the desire to bring about justice and wellbeing for others is intimately motivated and sustained by God. That is what faith in action means to me and I suspect many in Catholic agencies hold the same or a similar sense of how this work in which they are engaged is actually a faith-based and inspired endeavour. It is not an overt mission for conversion and redemption, nor an organised strategy to demonstrate how caring the Church can be. Rather it is an extension, a natural consequence, of heartfelt and clear-headed commitment to do something in the face of need, suffering and destitution.

I also believe that we need to be realistic about the place of Catholic social services in the broader theatre of Australia's welfare and community services sector. Where once it was a foundation of the evolving safety net, it now makes a somewhat niche contribution within a wider and more comprehensive government and other non-government services network.

So, there are likely to be debates over the essential, if not crucial, contribution Catholic-based services provide to the community and the necessity or otherwise for their continued support from governments, policy makers and funders of all descriptions. I do not propose to solve that ever-brewing issue. What I do want to concentrate on has more to do with the identity of this ministry, its relationship to the public perception of the Church and the need for an enlivened spirituality that both sustains us and motivates our engagement with the realities of life.

Margin Call

The title of my presentation is quite deliberate. In the financial world a margin call occurs when the value of an account has fallen below agreed levels. At that point additional capital is required to restore the value of the account. If the trader does not deposit funds into the account then assets are sold regardless of their previous market value. The upshot is a depleted investment, with the investor's reputation damaged, and its future clouded.

I put it to you that this is not too far from the situation we currently find ourselves facing in the Catholic Church. Through gross mismanagement and blatant deception, the institutional Church has squandered the goodwill of the overwhelming majority of its members. It has debased the value of the Church in the broader community. This has added fuel to the fire over the relevancy of the Church to modern day life.

Just as depressing is when some in positions of authority and influence in the institution remain on a course that holds little hope for any correction in the near term. You can still hear senior Church personnel deluding themselves that the crimes of child sexual abuse, cover-ups and obfuscations are things of the past; that the good works of the Church, in schools, community services and health, will restore its public standing; and that the public critics and cynical media are part of a broader 'anti-Church' agenda in a post-Christian world. This 'blindness' risks becoming pathological and will only see the institution further erode its value and any real sense in the community at large of the Church being a social asset and force for good.

Throughout the years of the Royal Commission into Institutional Responses to Child Sexual Abuse,[1] some would lament that there was little attention paid to the extent of good works undertaken by the Church across our community, works of social service, healthcare, pastoral support and education. Some now fear that those works will be tainted by the loss of trust that the community holds for the institution in general. Others despair

---

1 The Royal Commission into Institutional Responses to Child Sexual Abuse ran from 2013-2017; see *Final Report* at www.childabuseroyalcommission. gov.au/final-report.

at the 'brand damage' that the revelations of the scandal have brought.

There seems to be some substance to this fear. For example, we hear these days of a hardening attitude in government bureaucracies towards Catholic organisations. There have been instances where Catholic organisations have not been included in government initiatives without any stated reason or have been warned that their tax-exempt status is under threat. These organisations have no direct link with the sex abuse scandal but now they are in line to bear the consequences.

That said, I believe the bigger concern is the risk that leaders will 'circle the wagons', seek to regroup and then substantially continue on without any significant change. And that change is primarily about our heart.

Have we the capacity to let our broken hearts speak? Can we dare to be different? To accept humbly that our way of seeing things, reacting to things, proclaiming things, needs to change? Are we too captive to an arrogance born of certainty and institutional longevity? Have we stopped hearing the cries of the poor, the oppressed, the misunderstood and the strange ones? Have we become part of a system where meeting needs is wrapped up in a self-serving ideology of social action and importance?

These are confronting questions, but necessary none the less. They arise from the type of self-analysis that comes with spiritual discernment, supposedly a mainstay for any ministry.

They are also prompted by the prophets of our times. Those who have courageously unsettled our comforts, questioned our intentions and stretched our imaginations. They are the people who have risked their lives for a world that at least could be better for others, let alone for themselves.

They are the brave hearts who dared to speak truth to power, who wore the rejection and the scapegoating of an institution in denial. They are the free spirits who have stood proudly in the face of prejudice and discrimination knowing all too well that 'fitting in' was the price for acceptance and harmony – a price too high, too often, which they have refused to pay.

Identifying the Issues

First and foremost, we need consensus on what a Church and, in turn, Church-run social services, are on about. In a society that regards religion as just another lifestyle choice at best, we need to resist trying to 'pump air into old tyres' that have run their course. We need to dream of an engaged, vibrant and relevant Church where these features are reflected in its outreach and, more importantly, in its manner, disposition and basic humanity. We need to change the terms of engagement. If the Church is not primarily missionary, then it will become ossified as a propositional institution, out of touch and out of time.

The sex abuse scandal made it abundantly plain that when the institution is threatened it tends to close ranks, manage its risks, and not act and speak out of its heart but strategise out of its head. Only a heart-driven Church will have any chance of relating beyond its increasingly narrowing base.

Secondly, the scandal revealed just how far from 'victim-friendly' the institution really was. It was rare to hear of occasions where victims were believed rather than tolerated; to hear where victims were assisted to make their case rather than interrogated in order to be found wanting; to hear where the Church authorities were transparent and pastoral rather than cautious and reliant solely on legal and insurance advice. It was also rare to learn of the frequent cases where the Church authority sought confidential compliance from victims rather than overt reporting to the police. Only a Church that walks along with victims and risks becoming a victim with them can resonate the spirit of Jesus and the dream of the Gospel.

Thirdly, the glaring lack of moral leadership during the scandal not only speaks volumes about the potential to be disconnected from our basic reason for being, it also warrants 'major surgery' as to who gets to participate in the governance of the Church. Unless we break the shackles of entitlement and cronyism and become inclusive and more representative in our decision-making, we risk losing any hope of renewal and reform.

Yet, maybe not unsurprisingly, we still find the same model of administration and the same culture of clerical entitlement controlling the management of the institution. Doing more of the same should not be the answer. There is, however, every indication that the fear of loss of control will continue to ward off sensible power-sharing between clergy and laity, the promotion of women into governance roles, and the democratising of administrative functions, such that local parishes and communities are trusted to design and oversee ministries to meet very local needs. That challenge lies very much before us and we should not let it fall to those inside the Church bubble. Instead we need to agitate for the change we identify, to speak confidently of its benefits and to insist on a seat at the tables that matter.

The Risk of Integrity

As the second aspect of the chapter's title states, can we take the risk of integrity? Are we up to the challenge of becoming authentic and responding in a radical fashion to the call of the Gospel?

The underlying notion of Catholic social thought is liberation. It calls for a new mindset that unlocks the structures of oppression, both within ourselves and for others. It asks us to wake up to the attitudes and behaviours that enslave, oppress and dehumanise. Most importantly, it compels us to ask whether we are part of the problem or the solution. To be part of the solution is to take the risk of living our values.

Seeing disadvantage and injustice is not merely an intellectual exercise. It requires us to stand up for those too weighed down and silenced by oppressive systems and cultures, ostracised by self-interested forces, belittled through selfish agendas and discarded by self-serving movements. It challenges us to own our values even in the face of fear, uncertainty and intimidation.

It definitely compels us to take sides – in a power imbalance we need to see life from the underside, to identify who is losing out, who needs our influence and capabilities to come their way. It means living with hope that the law of the jungle, of 'the mob', of the *status quo*, of the 'way things are done around here', of the owners of opportunity and chance do NOT determine what is right, just and decent.

Moving to the Margins
Others will more eloquently outline what radical steps are required to meet people at the margins. They may well quote Pope Francis as he implores the Church to be at the margins and in the messiness of life.

Here I want to pick up on two aspects of moving to the margins. One goes to the dogmatic and social policy position and attitude of the Church, the other to the level of engagement we need with the macro-economic and social context of our community.

Ours is a comfortable, quite conventional Church. We are very much a part of the socially conservative infrastructure of society; upholders of traditional values, lifestyles and conventions; watchdogs for social order. Our asset holdings across dioceses, hospitals and education and community service settings implant a Catholic footprint the envy of any land and capital speculator.

They also engender a conservative, cautious instinct that makes responsiveness and flexibility difficult to deliver.

We bleach the Gospel of its radical nature and we tame its spirit to fit our narrow vista. This is a conditioned response, a confected culture of self-protection and self-promulgation. I think we are called to be so much more – not mere subjects of an institution or the expectations of an organised religion, but rather active participants in stretching our sense of Church and ministry into frontiers where others stay disengaged from difference or, even worse, fight against it.

We need to adopt a spirituality that is non-dualistic, person-centred and humble – one that readily holds what may first appear as opposites in a creative tension; one that pays attention to the surprises of life, its twists, turns, torments and torpor that lead to awakenings of the Divine in ordinary ways. This is a spirituality where silence speaks louder than words, and where love compels acceptance and confusion and risks the loss of identity and transformation into a new creation.

From this disposition I put it to you that there is a call to go to the existential margins as much as there is the imperative to be at economic and socially impoverished places. Poverty does have a postcode, but not just spatially. The dignity and wellbeing of people are coming under significant threat.

I would like to reflect on this threat in the area of gender identification. The despair and despondency some people experience as they seek literally to be themselves in communities where prejudice and religious fundamentalism make them outcasts or worse must be eradicated. It is not enough for churches to spruik platitudes and empty rhetoric over the challenges confronting people of same sex attraction, gender dysphoria or trans-sexual orientation. Respect and loving embrace should come with no strings attached.

To be truly 'catholic' is to find unity across differences. It is to acknowledge that everyone is being made in the image of God. We are unfinished products, glimpses of the divine, symphonies aching for the crescendo!

Our tradition speaks of the blueprint for life as being an unfolding of revelation for everyone; that their deepest yearnings, their longings for love and acceptance, are not found in confected personality or rigid compliance to external expectations, even obligations. Rather, it is in giving primacy to the particular expressions of being human, valuing them as graced gifts, before we seek to corral people into the constraints of commonality and convention.

The 'signs of the times' are calling the Church to rediscover within its tradition this more pastoral approach. For too long we have adopted a 'one size fits all' approach to human sexuality and intimacy. The upshot has been alienation and despair, particularly for young people courageous enough to seek an authentic and honest lifestyle in the face of heavy social conservatism and prejudice, often with the voice of the Catholic Church ringing in their ears.

So much energy has been directed to bolstering static notions of human nature and their rigid understandings of what are orthodox lifestyles and moral choices that we have demonised individual freedoms and rights in the process. Little wonder people lose interest and begin to question how seriously the Church listens to the evolving revelation of its times.

A further boundary beckons in the field of economic justice. It is coming up to 30 years since the Australian Catholic bishops released their economic critique *Common Wealth for the Common Good*.[2] It was a bold and far-reaching statement challenging the

---

2 Australian Catholic Bishops Conference, 1992. *Common Wealth for the Common Good: A Pastoral Statement on the Distribution of Wealth in Australia*, North Blackburn, Victoria: Collins Dove.

economic *status quo* and the political settlement over economic rationalism and market-driven policy. It sounded the call for the poor, the victims of income inequality and the evolving underclass in our society. It was an important and necessary intervention in the public debate.

Our times shout out for a similar siren call. Debates rage over the levels of income inequality. They are usually joined by ideologues on both sides. But taking the side of impoverished and disenfranchised people is not an option for Gospel-inspired organisations. It is a mainstay of the mission.

So, it comes with the territory that we need to be advocates for economic justice. This, in turn, means being economically and sociologically literate and, most importantly, confident in the application of Catholic social thought.

The Church, and Catholic social and human service groups in particular, must not vacate the field of public debate and policy making. We have a voice that others can use. We have a tradition of economic thought that seeks a just distribution of wealth and opportunities. We need once again to lean into public discourses that are deliberately crafted to appeal to the comfortable at the expense of the suffering. We must not shy from critics who seek to put the Church in its place. Our place is alongside those who suffer, are impoverished and face the perils of life on their own. Our voice needs to echo the pleas of the silenced.

Our True Heart

This is our true heart – one open, non-judgemental and compassionate; one that hears the cries of the poor, the downtrodden and the forgotten.

Our hearts have been broken and it is good that they have. For only broken hearts can hear the word of God. Only soft hearts can sense the echo of the Spirit. Only open hearts can move the mountains between people, across communities and within the deeper imaginings where violence and hatred fester.

These days we are blessed by prophets of honesty and hope – these are the victims of abuse, and advocates for the fullness of life. Whether they have visited us from the scandal of abuse, or whether they tentatively live amongst us eager for our awakening and embrace, they deserve our heartfelt respect and we their forgiveness.

Conclusion

After the conclusion of the Royal Commission I embarked on the Camino to Santiago. I deliberately chose a route that would last 40 days. The biblical imagery and the ancient purpose of the pilgrimage very much shaped my intent for the post Royal Commission time.

In days past the pilgrimage was undertaken as a journey of absolution, a time for confession and even atonement. I very much felt the need to spend time shedding my role with the Truth Justice and Healing Council[3] and also acknowledging the way that experience had shaped me and my understanding of my faith journey.

You are encouraged to bring something from home with you as you walk the Camino. Whether it is a stone or keepsake, it is to be a symbol of something you want to let go of or give particular reverence to. I chose to carry in my backpack the final report of the Commission into the Catholic Church.[4] That report detailed the statistics of the people abused within the Church as obtained from

---

3 Francis Sullivan was Chief Executive Officer of the Truth Justice and Healing Council, which was established to co-ordinate the Catholic Church's response to the Royal Commission into Institutional Responses to Child Sexual Abuse.
4 Royal Commission, op. cit. n. 1, Vol. 16, *Religious institutions*, Book 2.

official Church records. I wanted to carry the report out of respect for the individuals whom those statistics represented. I did not carry the report as some kind of penance, more as a labour of love.

From the very outset of the Royal Commission I felt strongly that the bravery of those abused was the only impetus that would lead the Church to truthfulness and integrity in the scandal. As I approached the cathedral in Santiago, I reflected on the work of the Truth Justice and Healing Council and the dedication of its staff to seek transparency and accountability in and by the Church for the good of those abused. I also felt that the victims should be honoured in such a prominent place for the Catholic world as the cathedral in Santiago had become.

So, I entered the cathedral in time for the pilgrims' Mass. It is a moving and almost other worldly experience, an assembly of the sorrowful, the expectant, the bemused and the exhausted. A collective of seekers uncertain of the journey's end despite arrival at its destination. So much like the experience of victims where closure seems elusive and words often are empty and pointless.

Once the Mass was concluded I sought a spot to place the report. The cathedral is heavily guarded, especially near prominent places like the altar and tabernacle. As it happens, most pilgrims queue to ascend the stairs behind the main altar to embrace the statue of St James. As luck would have it, I found the stairs to the crypt empty of pilgrims. In the crypt are the bones of St James encased in a silver casket behind iron bars. Pilgrims can kneel before the casket and leave holy cards or coins. I took my chance. I managed to get the report through the bars and tossed it towards the casket. Happily, the report landed face up in front of the casket, a fitting place. I took the 'money shot' and quickly made myself scarce!

Then I wrote this poem as a testament to what I felt was part of the sacramental experience of my arrival in the cathedral.

MARGIN CALL: THE RISK OF INTEGRITY

As a wreath these names I lay,
remembered as prophets, not prey.
Muted cries now loud and far
scandalise abuse of power.

Lightly laid, no exhausted thump,
proud to serve and stand beside
courageous souls,
though some have died.

Resolute for truth to tell,
beyond complicity and denial.
Too many this private hell
for decency to resile.

Here they lay as votive flames.
Virtue moans without redress.
Incensed embers these precious names,
struck for justice to impress.

2020 Mary MacKillop Oration
Mary MacKillop: The Authenticity of Speaking Truth to Power

Ursula Stephens

Introduction

There is an ancient Greek word for someone who speaks truth to power – *parrhesiastes*. Mary MacKillop provides an excellent example of a *parrhesiastes*.

Speaking truth to power is dangerous and usually has consequences for the speaker. Such danger did not stop Mary MacKillop – throughout her life she recognised truth-telling as a duty. What can we learn from her courage and determination? How can we too have the courage to speak truth to power and accept the consequences?

The concept of "speaking truth to power" is a contested one. There are those, like the American philosopher and social critic, Noam Chomsky, who are dismissive of the notion. He asserts: "power knows the truth already" and is busy concealing it. It is the oppressed who need to hear the truth, not the oppressors.[1] That view is endorsed by Václav Havel, the Czech philosopher, playwright and first President of the Czech Republic, who wrote in his *Power of the Powerless* essay about the struggles in his own country:

> The post-totalitarian system touches people at every step, but it does so with its ideological gloves on. This is

---

1 Terry Eagleton, 3 April 2006. "The Truth Speakers", *New Statesman*; accessed at www.newstatesman.com.

why life in the system is so thoroughly permeated with hypocrisy and lies:

- government by bureaucracy is called popular government;
- the working class is enslaved in the name of the working class;
- the complete degradation of the individual is presented as his ultimate liberation;
- depriving people of information is called making it available;
- the use of power to manipulate is called the public control of power, and the arbitrary abuse of power is called observing the legal code;
- the repression of culture is called its development;
- the expansion of imperial influence is presented as support for the oppressed;
- the lack of free expression becomes the highest form of freedom;
- farcical elections become the highest form of democracy;
- banning independent thought becomes the most scientific of world views;
- military occupation becomes fraternal assistance.

Because the regime is captive to its own lies, it must falsify everything. It falsifies the past. It falsifies the present, and it falsifies the future. It falsifies statistics.[2]

Havel wrote this in 1978 and went on to lead the Velvet Revolution that finally toppled communism in Czechoslovakia in 1989. It worries me how much this resonates with Australia today.

---

2 Václav Havel, October 1978. *Power of the Powerless*, p. 9; accessed at https://s3.amazonaws.com/Random_Public_Files/powerless.pdf.

Our advocacy work needs to be with the oppressed as much as the oppressors. So, what does speaking truth to power really mean, and why does it matter?

Consider the following from Kathryn Harrison's *The New York Times* review of Laurel Thatcher Ulrich's book, *Well-Behaved Women Seldom Make History*. She wrote: "Much of what is characterized as female behaviour is a matter of voice – of a woman insisting she be heard: paid, not only attention, but also the respect due to a being as fully human and necessary as a man".[3] This made me think of Mary MacKillop. She would have been seen in many quarters as 'misbehaving', at least according to the expectations of the bishops and leaders with whom she had so much trouble, while pursuing her earnest and faith-filled mission of service to the poor. She gained respect for her courage and persistence against many odds. Fr Paul Gardiner SJ describes these at length in his book, *Mary MacKillop: An Extraordinary Australian*[4] – she certainly was that.

I would like to outline the lessons I think I have learnt from Mary MacKillop. I was very privileged to be in Rome for her canonisation. That grace-filled, wonderful experience of witnessing the ceremony, then meeting Pope Benedict XVI and him thanking me personally for my faith were life changing.

The First Lesson from Mary MacKillop is to Hold on to Your Faith

Faith in God's will and his love for us is what empowered Mary MacKillop. It gave her, as it can give us, the ability to lift our eyes above the drab landscape of what is and imagine what could be.

---

3 Kathryn Harrison, 30 September 2007. "We're No Angels", *The New York Times*; accessed at www.nytimes.com/.
4 Paul Gardiner, 1993. *Mary MacKillop: An Extraordinary Australian*. Newton, NSW: E. J. Dwyer/David Ell Press.

Her faith was constant at the beginning and the end of her life's journey, as it should be for all of us. In the words of Karl Rahner, she tells us: "Go forth from the heart and centre of your own being in order that you may find your own heart".[5]

Faith inhabits her every step along the way – it enabled her, as it enables us, to keep going, keep hoping, keep believing and keep trying. Without a deep core of belief, we cannot sustain our resolve against the tide of opposition that will come our way. We have seen this in the aftermath of the child abuse scandals, the fall-off in numbers of people participating in the sacraments, the complete loss of trust in the institutional Church, not just here in Australia, but around the world.

Faith matters because not only is it your sustenance in hard times but also your compass, as we know it was for Mary MacKillop. Faith is the ability to perceive what cannot be seen – yet. In the New Testament we read: "Faith is the substance of things hoped for and the evidence of things not seen" (*Hebrews* 11:1).

With faith, you are able to move forward even when the path is uncertain and the way dark, because your faith impels you with the belief that something better or more worthy lies ahead. As organisations, if we were without faith, what would make us any different to any other organisation? Without the principles of Catholic social teaching underpinning our very existence, many of us might never do anything of consequence, because we would lack any reason to dare the uncertainty that always comes when we seek change from the way things have always been.

Mary MacKillop has shown us through her life's work and her

---

5 Karl Rahner SJ, cited in Yvonne Harte, 2019. "A personal reflection on the contemporary relevance of devotion to the Sacred Heart of Jesus"; accessed at www.sosj.org.au/wp-content/uploads/2019/06/Feast-of-the-Sacred-Heart-2019.pdf.

legacy that people who effect great change are, and will always be, people of faith: faith and great vision are inextricably linked in the human soul. She experienced many "dark nights of the soul" (St John of the Cross) questioning herself and her faith. At times she was angry with God but, as Gardiner tells us:

> Mary MacKillop revered people in holy orders, and respected all authority as a derived expression of God's will. But she had problems when prelates extended their jurisdiction *ad libitum* or neglected the directives of higher authority. She endeavoured to resolve those difficulties not only justly but with undiminished respect and unaffected charity.[6]

Mary MacKillop trusted God completely and, as we know, God does not make mistakes. He does not give up on any of us, and we should not give up on him. Despite the humiliating circumstances she endured through the Adelaide Commission of 1883, which culminated in her expulsion from Adelaide, Mary MacKillop simply trusted to the power of truth. The end result was to see her deposed as Mother General and her control of the Sisters of St Joseph usurped.

The Second Lesson from Mary MacKillop's Life is the Importance of Choosing Your Own Course

To walk the path of your own choosing, you must be certain, as Mary was, deep within yourself, that it is the path you have truly chosen to walk. Along the way there will be many distractions, many voices trying to divert you, many fingers that point in accusation, trying to move you onto a different path.

Whenever Mary encountered opposition, what kept her going in pursuing her vision was the deep and certain conviction that

---

6 Gardiner, op. cit. n. 4, p. 6.

God was her leader. She must follow her own choices, wherever they might take her – her advice: "We must pray that God may direct us to do what will please God most and tend to the common good".[7] And as we know, it led her to excommunication because of the ecclesiastical battles she encountered, as she determined to maintain the independence of her Sisters and stick to her path. Again, Gardiner describes her thus: "She aimed to defend human dignity and human rights against the many public forces that were directed against them".[8]

Do you remember the story of the desert fathers, when Abbot Lot said: "Father, as far as I am able, I keep my little rule and my little fast and my prayer, meditation and contemplative silence ... what more should I do?" And Abbot Joseph rose and stretched his hands towards heaven and his fingers became like lamps of fire: He said: "Why not become bigger – all flame?"

This is the challenge for us too, because we are pretty much like Abbot Lot 'keeping our little rule'. We try to be good, prayerful, honest, decent, moral, generous and sincere as we go about our daily lives. We too need to ask: What more should I do? We too need to become bigger. Mary MacKillop's answer would be: "Never see a need without doing something about it".[9]

Mary's MacKillop's Third Lesson for us is to Rise above the Limitations of Others!

Her experience was of others constantly trying to place limitations on her. This is just as much an inevitability for us today. We operate

---

7 6 December entry in *St Mary MacKillop Daily Thoughts Perpetual Calendar*. The quote is from 1 December 1881; accessed at www.sosj.org.au/wp-content/uploads/2017/08/12631.pdf.
8 Gardiner, op. cit. n. 4, p. 27.
9 Mary MacKillop, 1871; accessed at www.sosj.org.au/may-her-motto-be-our-inspiration/.

in an environment where guidelines, standards, regulations, rules and practices abound in public administration, in Church practices, in society.

We need to respect authority and trust in institutional arrangements, but not to be blind to the interests being served by them. Their vital purpose is to maintain control, to limit the horizon, and thereby limit achievements. This means, like Mary, we often need to be boundary riders, not always to acquiesce to the limitations placed on us. Rather, her example was to challenge them. This is where we need Mary's courage, because we know that those who seek to limit our achievements are those who often lack the courage or perseverance to choose a similar path. Maybe their motives are centred in the unsettling sense of their own lack of direction, or belief in themselves. If they can hold you back, it helps them feel better about remaining in the comfort of mediocrity. Perhaps our aspirations may be a threat to the *status quo* – for whatever reason, it is up to us to find the strength and inner vison, as Mary did, to resist these limitations.

Gardiner describes the "Cusack affair"[10] where the school master, in anticipation of a visit from the school inspector, juggled roles and switched the children Mary and Annie had been teaching, to claim their teaching success as his own. When the story got out, the school master sacked Annie, and Mary was blamed for the whole business. Mary wrote: "For four months this storm raged – and I stood alone ... God permitted a very bitter enemy to rise up against me, who said such things of me that all I cared most for, turned against me".[11]

---

10 Gardiner, op. cit. n. 4, p. 51.
11 Ibid.

The Fourth Lesson that Mary MacKillop has for us is to Persist against Opposition

After Archbishop Patrick Francis Moran arrived in Sydney in 1884, following his role as the ecclesiastical agent in Rome for the Australian bishops, he investigated claims made about Mary and the Josephites and actions taken against them by the Bishop of Adelaide. The truth was revealed, not by Mary MacKillop, who understood that revealing the whole truth would be so potentially damaging. She sought guidance from Archbishop Moran on how much he wanted to know: "Were I to write everything and your Grace have to use the same officially I might have to add much more to his already heavy sorrows than I wish".[12] And truth eventually did prevail. The rest, as they say, is history.

Opposition to ideas that bring about change is inevitable. As I said, maintaining the *status quo* is a very comfortable position for others, but to be a change-maker, we need to question and challenge the 'rules' and understand whose interests they really serve.

Take, for example, the current climate change debate and the Government's ideological position on climate change. Any criticism of the *status quo* is met with derision, legal repressions for whistleblowers, unjust opposition, even downright intimidation of journalists. That experience is mirrored in the public calls for abandoning the Indue 'cashless card'[13] rollout to all welfare recipients and to the treatment of asylum seekers and refugees.

We have to learn to persist in our resistance to this injustice, to refuse to be cowed into giving up on what we know is wrong, and

---

12 Ibid., p. 319.
13 For information on the Indue cashless card, see www.dss.gov.au/families-and-children/programmes-services/welfare-conditionality/cashless-debit-card-overview.

to call out the interests being served. As Mary reminds us: "In our unity under God lies our strength".[14]

Mary MacKillop's Fifth Lesson is that We Must Speak up for Justice

Many of the rights and opportunities we take completely for granted were first championed by trailblazers like Mary MacKillop. In 1873 correspondence to Monsignor Kirby in Rome,[15] she spoke of:

- the indifference of secular government towards the poor,
- a self-indulgent society that mitigated against the welfare of the family and children,
- the problems of a Church that lacked the personnel to cope with the needs of its people,
- Australia as a dangerous place for Catholics,

speaking truth to power and knowing exactly what she was doing. The more Mary was unwilling to be treated unfairly, the less she was able to sit idly by while others were being treated unfairly. She had her vision and her plan to achieve it.

Her example provides us with a sense of urgency and commitment to do the same. So many of the issues resonate as strongly now as they did then. We often quote the Beatitudes when we speak of social justice. But as Mary MacKillop fully understood, and so must we, the Beatitudes are not a recipe for getting on with the work. Rather, they state the various situations in which we might find ourselves:

- To live in the non-competitive way of the 'poor in spirit'.

---

14 Sheila McCreanor (ed.), 2016. *Mary MacKillop 1873 – One Year of an Extraordinary Life*. Hindmarsh, SA: ATF Press, p. 30.
15 Gardiner, op. cit. n. 4, p. 127.

- To experience the sadness of those who 'mourn' because of the circumstances in which they find themselves.
- To be meek, gentle and unselfish rather than profit-driven.
- To have a passionate commitment to justice.
- To hunger and thirst that things will be made right as a loving God would want them to be.
- To exercise mercy and to be a peacemaker, like a 'pacemaker' for the hearts of others, to help them live better lives.

Mary dedicated her life to God, through her ministry to the poor, and entrusted her safety and success to His infinite goodness and desire.

Mary MacKillop's Next Lesson is to Insist on Integrity

Speaking truth to power is about having a willingness to tell the truth no matter what. While John the Evangelist rightly says: "The truth will set you free" (*John* 8:32), we know that telling the truth can make you very unpopular. Mary knew, however, that popularity is not the main thing: integrity is.

It is Mary MacKillop's courage and strength, key themes of the 2020 Catholic Social Services conference, that bring us back to the concept of *parrhesia*. The French philosopher and historian, Michel Foucault,[16] described *parrhesia* as when a speaker expresses his personal relationship to truth and risks his life because he recognises truth-telling as a duty to improve or help other people (as well as himself). In *parrhesia*, the speaker uses his freedom and chooses frankness instead of persuasion, truth instead of falsehood or silence, the risk of death instead

---

16 For further information, see Michel Foucault, October – November 1983. "The Meaning and Evolution of the Word 'Parrhesia': Discourse & Truth, Problematization of Parrhesia – Six lectures given by Michel Foucault at the University of California at Berkeley"; accessed https://foucault.info/.

of life and security, criticism instead of flattery, and moral duty instead of self-interest.

We can substitute 'she, her, hers (and herself)' for the above and recognise that by death Foucault meant not only literal death but also a large personal loss such as one's personal or professional reputation – then we have an excellent description of the courage of Mary MacKillop. There is much more to explore in this challenge to speak truth to power.

A Final Lesson from Mary MacKillop is to Understand Your Own Power and How to Use it

Mary MacKillop understood her own power and how to use it. She understood the risks of what she was undertaking. Through her leadership and her ability to inspire, because of her passion, her decision-making skills, her compassion, her insight and her integrity, she has created a lasting legacy in the works of the Sisters of St Joseph and, of course, in her elevation to sainthood by the Catholic Church.

So now is the time for each of us to ask ourselves: do I have Mary MacKillop's courage and convictions to speak truth to power? –

- to persist and confront those who hold important positions, whether in government, business or religious institutions,
- to demand a moral response to a problem,
- to endure the criticism of the institutional Church and hold on to the truth that is our faith in action,
- to advocate both to the oppressors and to the oppressed,
- to be bigger – all flame.

Mary Mackillop believed that she was blessed by God, *because* of her life. That is what we need to be too, not just happy that God is *in* our lives. This is such an important difference.

Our loyalty and commitment to our faith, to political parties, to our community networks, to our families, can cause us to disbelieve or turn away from the truth of what is happening all around us. It can be easier and safer to see only what we want to see. There are many challenges confronting us as a nation, as a Church and as a community of good souls.

So, I leave you with a thought from Mary MacKillop: "God wants an heroic love from you".[16] I wish you the strength and courage to be as heroic as Mary MacKillop.

---

16 27 February entry in *St Mary MacKillop Daily Thoughts Perpetual Calendar*, op. cit. n. 7. Quote is from a 26 February 1872 letter of Mary to Flora MacKillop; the birth of John MacKillop, Mary's brother, was on 27 February 1845.

Response to the Oration

Monica Cavanagh RSJ

In delivering the 2020 Mary MacKillop Oration, Ursula Stephens addressed an important topic in the life of the Church and society at this time, "the authenticity of speaking truth to power". Her address resonated strongly with me and inspired this response.

On the day I received the title of the 2020 Oration, I opened the most recent *Global Sisters Report* e-newsletter. It had an article by Nancy Westmeyer entitled "Love cures the misuse of power" which aligned with the message of the Oration:

> The misuse of power is out of control. Perhaps it has always been so, but this misuse is becoming more and more public. The consequences of bullying, lies, sexual abuse, corporate mismanagement and greed, political gerrymandering, the use of inferior materials in construction, countries annexing land that belongs to other countries, the lack of respect for the innate dignity of each person – we read in the newspaper, hear it on the radio and TV, experience it in our neighbourhoods, churches and our cities, and feel it in our hearts.[1]

If we were to do what the Oration outlined and act courageously, to speak truth to this power, our world would be a different place.

Recently we commemorated the 75th anniversary of the atrocity

---

[1] Nancy Westmeyer, 17 February 2020. "Love cures the misuse of power", *Global Sisters Report* e-newsletter; accessed at www.globalsistersreport.org/news/spirituality/column/love-cures-misuse-power.

of the Holocaust, a total misuse of positional power. At the same time, we have heard many stories of victims of the holocaust exercising their personal power in the life of people – for example, Etty Hillesum whose words and expression of love brought hope to her fellow travellers.[2]

I have just finished reading a book, *Last Stop Auschwitz*, in which the author, Eddy de Wind, writes of love being the force that sustained hope for him within the death chambers of Auschwitz. Towards the end of the book he tells the story of a woman survivor, Roosje, who comes to a moment of realising that she had to stay alive: "I was lying in the pit among the murdered women, but I was still alive. Then I felt that something changed inside me. I had to stay alive. I wanted to live to tell all of this, to tell everyone about it, to convince people that it was true".[3] She needed to do this for all those whom she had seen killed. This woman used her personal power to speak truth and this is what those in Catholic social services are called to do every day.

In the words of Nancy Westmeyer, we are called to "build up a loving force that counteracts the misuse of power", whether that be by "speaking up for someone being trashed by gossips" or "advocating for someone in a health care facility or for a homeless person seeking housing" or welcoming a refugee.[4]

Mary MacKillop brought an explosion of God's love to the great needs of her time in Australia. She saw the needs of those afflicted and she heard God speaking to her in the words of *Isaiah* (40:1):

> Who will comfort my people? Who will wipe away their tears?

---

[2] For biographical information on Etty Hillesum, see www.amisdettyhillesum.com/Anglais/biography.html.
[3] Eddy de Wind, 2020. *Last Stop Auschwitz*. London: Transworld, p. 193.
[4] Westmeyer, op. cit. n. 1.

RESPONSE TO THE ORATION

And who will heal the broken hearted? Who will bind up wounded souls?

Mary responded with human hands, human eyes and human touch:

- I hear the cry of your people, as she sat with the widow of a man who committed suicide.
- I know the hunger of your poor, as she reached out to the boy with no shoes.
- I share the pain of the broken, as she shared her lunch with a homeless man.
- I feel the shame of those who fail, as she welcomed Scotch Bella, a female prisoner, into the Sisters' care.

Affirming the dignity of those forgotten, shunned, ignored is the antitheses of the misuse of power. Mary urged her Sisters to "use every means at their disposal to bring others to life".[5] Today her life urges us to do the same.

In light of the Oration, we might ask, is my heart big enough to respond as she did when we hear the cries of so many people broken by unjust systems, languishing in natural disasters, fleeing violence and war? Where in today's world do we need to be an explosion of God's love? Where in my current situation am I called to be a breath of God's love? As a person working in Catholic ministry, how am I being called to be the heartbeat of God's love?

Mary never lost sight of her vision "to seek God in the care of the little ones of His flock"[6] and "to seek first the poorest most

---

5 Letter: Mary MacKillop to Sisters, 12 March 1899 in *Mother Mary's Circulars to the Sisters*. North Sydney: Sisters of St Joseph of the Sacred Heart, 1976, p. 193.

6 Letter: Mary MacKillop to her Mother, 21 August 1867 in Sheila McCreanor (ed.), 2004. *Mary MacKillop & Flora: Correspondence between Mary MacKillop and her Mother, Flora McDonald MacKillop*. North Sydney: Sisters of St Joseph of the Sacred Heart, p. 18.

neglected parts of God's kingdom".[7] This too is your call, women and men serving in the Catholic social services today.

The Oration shared how Mary's courage and determination certainly got her into some trouble. It also brought great blessings and hope for the children whom she chose to serve, and for those living at the fringe of Australian society. Her heart was moved with compassion as she spoke her truth to Monsignor Tobias Kirby in Rome of the conditions facing the Church in Australia in the 1870s. What was needed here in Australia would be out of place in Europe was her observation. Her courage and persistence against the odds and her perseverance in the face of adversity were evident in so many ways throughout her life. Her experience in Queensland with Bishop James Quinn and Fr Julian Tenison Woods are examples of such adversity. She writes to Sr Andrea Howley, one of her confidants: "Among the worst things I have to endure is when I have to see Bishops and Priests and in the cause of our loved work, have to hold out against all their arguments and threats".[8]

After some scathing remarks in the local Brisbane paper about the Sisters, she wrote regarding Bishop James Quinn: "From my heart I forgive Bishop Quinn the wrong he is trying to do to me through the agency of his paper, but this does not prevent my seeing that justice to a certain extent is done to the Institute".[9]

She also chastises Fr Woods who refused to speak with her on her visit to Brisbane, after he stirred up trouble among the Sisters in Queensland:

> I write to you as a duty ... Why if you had such charges to make against me, why did you remain over a week in

---

7 Letter: Mary MacKillop to Sisters, 6 March 1900 in op. cit. n. 5, p. 204.
8 Letter: Mary MacKillop to Sr Andrea Howley, 10 June 1871 in Paul Gardiner, 1993. *Mary MacKillop: An Extraordinary Australian*. Newton, NSW: E. J. Dwyer/David Ell Press, p. 214.
9 Ibid., p. 224.

Brisbane and not come to see me about them, and why did you rather speak to the Sisters about things so calculated to destroy their peace and to make them think ill of their Superiors? ... If you have a grievance against me, tell it to myself but not to the poor sisters.[10]

There are many occasions when we find Mary speaking truth to power. I will cite just two more. She writes to Bishop Laurence Bonaventure Sheil prior to her excommunication when he advised her that he was going to change the rule which he had previously approved, citing that he wanted there to be lay Sisters and choir Sisters – a change that went right against her value of respecting the dignity of all and that would put the Sisters under the direct authority of the local priest. She wrote: "I cannot in conscience see the rule altered and remain still a sister. If you choose to alter the rule, I feel I must take the alternative that you offered and leave the Institute until it may please God to give me in some other place what my soul desires".[11]

When women received the right to vote in Australia, Mary wrote to the Sisters urging all the Sisters to have their name on the electoral role and to take responsibility for finding out who were the most suitable candidates. She concludes by cautioning: "Every so-called Catholic is not the best man".[12]

Speaking truth to power comes at a cost. For Mary MacKillop, it did not come without its difficulties. It impacted on her health, her relationships and her emotions. Despite such stresses she did

---

10 Letter: Mary MacKillop to Fr Woods, 12 September 1879 in Gardiner, op. cit. n. 8, p. 221.
11 Letter: Mary MacKillop to Bishop Sheil, 10 September 1871 in Sheila McCreanor, 2011. *Mary MacKillop and a Nest of Crosses: Correspondence with Fr Julian Tenison Woods 1869-1872*. North Sydney: Sisters of St Joseph of the Sacred Heart, p. 259.
12 Letter: Mary MacKillop to Sisters,16 July 1903 op cit. n. 5, p. 219.

not let any obstacle deter her from acting with courage. In the words of Joan Chittister, she let "nothing deter the Jesus life in [her], knowing that however [her] efforts end, the resurrection is surely on its way".[13] Mary MacKillop learned how to walk into her fear trusting in her good God that all in the end will be well.

Perhaps this capacity to speak truth to power was a family trait. At the time of Mary MacKillop's excommunication, we have this wonderful letter of her mother Flora to Bishop Sheil. I love Flora's response to this reality:

> Need I say that the telegrams that have issued from time to time in the papers caused me and other friends great pain and anxiety. We would not give credence to their correctness, being under the impression that only notorious sinners would be so dealt with. That my ever-good child, could be such, would be hard for me, or for her many numerous friends in Victoria to believe.
>
> Before taking any steps in this matter to clear my child's character I deem it my duty as a Catholic to beg of your Lordship to let me know her real crime ...
>
> The great sin of her life, in my opinion, has been leaving me, and putting herself under your Lordship's protection, but as I gave my reluctant consent, I will not now reproach her.
>
> I appeal to you ... to clear her. This is surely not too much to ask of your Lordship as their Spiritual Father, and more particularly as we are assured that the cry of the Widow and Orphan was never raised to the Great Father of All without being heard.[14]

---

13 Joan Chittister, 26 February 2018. "A choice of directions"; accessed at www.joanchittister.org/word-from-joan/2-26-2018/choice-directions.

14 Letter: Flora MacKillop to Bishop Sheil, September 1871 in Bernadette O'Sullivan, 2012. *Flora Mackillop: A Truly Blessed Mother*. Strathfield, NSW: St Pauls Publications, pp. 103-104.

RESPONSE TO THE ORATION

The Oration rightly identified that what was central to Mary MacKillop's life was her faith. Mary wrote that all is "done in God and for God".[15]

She was a woman of deep faith and big heartedness. In the depths of her heart, in her inner being, she knew that she was the beloved of God and this flowed out into her encounters with people, whether with friend or stranger whom she also recognised as the Beloved of God. Even in her darkest moments she could say: "When I could not see my way God kept my heart full of trust".[16]

Mary's commitment to restoring dignity to the lives of the poor and underprivileged was a natural expression of her spirituality and is a distinguishing feature of her work. Those working in Catholic social services and serving those most disadvantaged in our society are called to keep the challenge of the Gospel at the heart of their ministry of service. Like Mary MacKillop, let the love of God fill your heart and from this sacred core deep within you, let love flow to those whom you serve, whether pleasing or unpleasing.

The Oration referred to the importance of choosing your own course. At a certain moment in Mary MacKillop's life she comes to the realisation that she has a responsibility for the leadership of the Sisters. Prior to this she was dependent upon the wisdom and insight of Fr Woods. In a letter written to Fr Woods in April 1870 she writes:

> It seems to me now that our good God gave me great graces for the position to which He has called me. I see them all and I see how shamefully I have wasted them. My own dear Father Woods, there is some strange, almost

---

15 Letter: Mary MacKillop to Sisters, 12 July 1881 in op. cit. n. 5, p. 106.
16 Letter: Mary MacKillop to Sisters, 28 June 1874 in op. cit. n. 5, p. 74.

wonderful change in me for which I cannot account. It urges me too, to say such strange things to you and to return to them over and over again though it may be at the cost of giving you pain.[17]

From here on in, we see the growth in Mary's leadership and her capacity to choose the course set out for her. She had the ability to listen to the voice of God speaking in and through her life. Her belief that she must be tuned into whatever the will of God required of her guided her throughout her entire life. She writes to the Sisters in 1907: "Our hearts must be burning with zeal and courage in the service of our God. ... It may sometimes be dark and full of many windings, but a beautiful, bright light shines at the end of this path and a few more windings will bring us to it".[18]

Mary took the heart of what the Church is called to be, a sign and instrument of God's love, into the lives of the people. She chose to use her personal and positional power as an expression of love. She chose courage over comfort and took the honourable action no matter what others thought. Her humility taught her again and again that it was God's work and we are participants in that mission.

Like Mary MacKillop and in the words of Sr Doris Klein CSA, "we stand on the edge of our hopes and dreams and we ask in trust to be led and supported by a Love and Energy much larger than we can imagine. We ask to walk here in courage and integrity, as we attempt to discern the voice of God amid the cacophony of our doubts and fear".[19]

And in the words of Wendell Berry, poet and farmer, from his

---

17 Letter: Mary MacKillop to Fr Woods, 6 April 1870 in op. cit. n. 11, p. 60.
18 Letter: Mary MacKillop to Sisters, 10 March 1907 in op. cit. n. 5, p. 242.
19 Doris Klein, 2001. "Risk the Sacred Journey" in *Journey of the Soul*. Oxford: Sheed and Ward, p. 105.

novel *Hannah Coulter*, which capture well the centrality of love for Mary MacKillop, remember:

> Love is what carries us
> For it is always there,
> Even in the dark, or most in the dark,
> But shining out at times
> Like gold stitches in a piece of embroidery.[20]

May you go forth knowing that God indeed wants a heroic love from you.

---

20 Wendell Berry, 2004. *Hannah Coulter – A Novel*. Berkeley, CA: Counterpoint, p. 51.

Respectful, Impactful Formation for Mission

Sarah Jane Grove, Lisa McDonald and Linda Di Sipio

The work of Catholic services and agencies reflects the diverse characteristics and needs of our society and how our Church can contribute to responding to our times and culture. Formation experiences themselves can be just as varied. Defining the concept of formation and its place in bringing alive a mission culture, through inspiring, inclusive and meaningful formation experiences, can seem challenging at times.

The critical nature of formation for ministry was addressed in a workshop entitled "Respectful, Impactful Formation for Mission" at the 2020 Catholic Social Services conference. It was presented by three mission leaders from St Vincent's Health Australia (SVHA):

- Dr Lisa McDonald, SVHA Group Mission Leader,
- Linda Di Sipio, Mission Education and Formation Lead at St Vincent's Hospital Melbourne,
- Sarah Jane Grove, Mission Integration Manager in the St Vincent's Hospital Sydney Network.

This chapter, which reflects their presentations, highlights three elements for consideration in offering meaningful formation experiences:

- Formation as an Opportunity for Reflection, Staff Engagement and Nurturing a Catholic Culture,
- Formation for Boards and Senior Leaders,
- Imaginative Contemplation as a Tool for Formation.

Formation as an Opportunity for Reflection, Staff Engagement and Nurturing a Catholic Culture

Sarah Jane Grove

Formation experiences can serve to affirm and socialise a staff member in support of their particular role, and to engage them at a deeper level in the Catholic culture in which they have chosen to work. The type of formation experience and the level of participation and engagement will be influenced by the degree of comfort and openness of staff to the process of formation. As such, the purpose and place of formation within an organisation need to be clearly articulated by leaders of the professional community. With this knowledge and an invitation to respond in a manner that is authentic to them, staff will appreciate and respect the purpose of formation, as a feature of the organisation's Catholic cultural identity.

The composition of staff in Catholic professional communities has become increasingly secular in its nature, with many unfamiliar with Catholic tradition and rituals. The diversity of our staff is of great value, offering many perspectives as we seek to connect with others, to be inclusive in our collective work. Our challenge is balancing respect for the individual's world view against creating a sense of shared mission and articulating the Catholic identity of the organisation.

Providing the opportunity for staff members to personalise Catholic values in the context of their professional role and reflect on their experience of the shared mission, both affirms the individual as well as developing a sense of collaboration across the organisation more broadly.

Consider the following invitation to staff:

Our Mission, Your Story

RESPECTFUL, IMPACTFUL FORMATION FOR MISSION

How have you experienced our mission in recent times – to respond to those in need, particularly the most marginalised and vulnerable in our society?

Where do you see people bringing to life our shared values of (compassion, justice, integrity and excellence) in our community here at (Catholic agency)?

This type of reflection, guiding staff on how their expertise and commitment aligns to their organisation's intention and mission imperative, can be formative. Formation experiences when planned thoughtfully and effectively can be impactful and contribute to developing a culture whereby the understanding of the mission is dynamic. Formation experiences can also serve as a useful framework and tangible approach to support staff to engage more deeply with the language of mission and the stated values of the organisation.

Different work contexts will benefit from approaches that reflect staff structures and needs and the characteristics of the organisation. Formation is more likely to be respectful, meaningful for their colleagues and impactful, when formal leaders and facilitators of formation take the time to observe the work culture and listen to the perspectives and experiences of staff to inform their practice in offering formation.

The lives and attributes of saints and historical figures in the ministry have long been connected with Catholic organisations and communities. The celebration of a relevant saint or revered leader in our tradition can be a formative experience when these cultural stories are considered in our own context. In his Apostolic Exhortation *Gaudete et Exsultate,* Pope Francis reminds us that besides those saints and martyrs whose lives were "an exemplary imitation of Christ", there should also be praise for "the middle class of holiness"[1] – that is, that holiness is found in those living in our midst, reflecting God's presence. Pope Francis calls us to see the holiness of those around us, in the places where we find ourselves, including our workplaces.

A gathering where a saint's feast day is the focal point can open up pathways for staff reflection regarding the value of their role, their connection with colleagues, and the unique gifts they contribute to the team with which they work. Leaders might also take the opportunity to make a connection between the life's work of the saint and the work focus of their team, along with offering affirmations, by naming the strengths of their staff and their collective successes. Such an interpersonal style of leadership and willingness to reflect back to a team can be highly impactful. This approach can also be extended to sharing a meal and creating other joy-filled occasions towards fostering a workplace environment that reflects our Catholic tradition and cultural values.

Formation for Boards and Senior Leaders
Lisa McDonald

From time to time, it comes as a surprise to board directors newly appointed to a Catholic organisation, that what will be required of them is spiritual leadership. Most will have been drawn to the role in which they now serve because of an excellent organisational reputation, key alignment with their values, or the prospect that the skills they bring are necessary for the success of the entity. Most will not have theological or ministry qualifications (and they are not a necessity). As they step into their role, the breadth and beauty of the *ministry identity* of the organisation comes into view, along with a deepening awareness of their own special responsibility to lead from the mission perspective.

---

1 Pope Francis, 2018. Apostolic Exhortation: *Gaudete et Exsultate*, Sections 5 and 7, respectively; accessed at w2.vatican.va/.

An organisation does well to view new directors and leaders through an appreciative lens and with gratitude and reverence for the life experiences they bring and their openness to sharing their gifts with the ministry. Our valuing of them is reflected in the quality of the formation experiences in which we invite them to participate. Formation of boards and senior leaders enriches them in their capacity to draw upon the 'wingspan' of our mission in their leadership, in turn leading to better decisions in the spirit of the great Vatican II document *Gaudium et Spes* where the faithful are encouraged to "scrutinize the signs of the times and interpret them in the light of the Gospel".[2]

At SVHA, we offer this definition of formation which has informed our policy and practice, including for senior leaders, since 2016:

> Formation is a process of socialisation into the SVHA community in the context of who we are, who we serve and who we strive to be for the purpose of building up the community and carrying on our Catholic teachings and traditions. It is a deepening of our understanding both personally and communally of our identity, traditions and our responsibility in continuing the healing mission of Jesus. Formation is a process of the head, heart and hands intended to help SVHA staff to find meaning in what they do and how they serve in the spirit of Mary Aikenhead Ministries. It acknowledges and respects that people come to SVHA with their own story, skills and expertise. It is also adapted to the specific needs and experience of those for whom it is provided.[3]

---

2 Second Vatican Council, 1965. *Gaudium et Spes: Pastoral Constitution on the Church in the Modern World*, Section 4; accessed at www.vatican.va.
3 SVHA, 2015. *Formation for All Policy*, revised October 2018. Sydney: SVHA.

One of the great privileges of my role as SVHA Group Mission Leader is having carriage of preparing a Formation Plan for our Board Directors each year. This usually comprises six sessions of two hours in length and the goal of each formation experience is three-fold:

- to nurture the directors' own spirituality,
- to provide relevant content in a reflective format which will help them in their governance,
- to guide the group in experiencing how they work together in the wider context of our mission.

Preparation for each session is highly intentional. I had heard it said that you cannot lead people without loving them and I think the same is true for preparing respectful, impactful formation for mission. Our regard, our compassion and our care for board directors and senior leaders must be a focal point as we prepare their formation experiences. We do this by seeking to know what they are curious about, what concerns them, and what their hopes are for their contribution to the ministry, with these insights as touchpoints for discernment, and planning accordingly.

In the lead up to the session we show our regard for senior leaders by choosing facilitators and content presenters thoughtfully. Presenters have a better chance for their content to 'land' in a fruitful way if they too have an understanding of the individual board member's interests along with the wider context of the governance responsibility that they carry.

The session itself should be hosted with heart! For us that means a warm atmosphere created by a generous welcome, ample time for reflection and dialogue, an ear attuned to the leading influence of the Holy Spirit, and a venue which allows participants to be comfortable. There is something to be said for concluding a session well too. Gracious summarising of key themes, genuine appreciation for time spent together, and a simple blessing are key 'tools of the trade' in this regard.

It is wise, even after the session, perhaps even months or years later, to refer back to it and to build on it with subsequent formation experiences. We certainly should employ evaluation on a regular basis, but more than this we should look for the impact our formation efforts have on senior leaders personally and professionally and on the direction and achievements of the organisation.

By way of example, one session employing this holistic approach and prepared for the board directors of SVHA was titled "Listening and Responding as a Catholic Ministry in Light of Clerical Sexual Abuse". Here is how it transpired.

Listening and Responding as a Catholic Ministry in Light of Clerical Sexual Abuse

We warmly welcomed one another and guests, including a survivor of sexual abuse and his wife and an executive leader from a school whose leadership in this area is widely commended.

We then commenced by acknowledging the traditional owners of the lands on which we were gathered. This is always a feature of our formation experiences not only for the primary reason that it honours Aboriginal and Torres Strait Islander peoples and their ownership of land, but also because it situates our experience in a wider, sacred context.

We next read a reflection chosen because of its resonance with our session topic. It was from the book *Tattoos on the Heart* by author Greg Boyle SJ which commences with the words:

> Success and failure, ultimately, have little to do with living the gospel. Jesus just stood with the outcasts until they were welcomed or until he was crucified – whichever came first.[4]

---

4 Gregory Boyle, 2011. *Tattoos on the Heart: The Power of Boundless Compassion.* New York: Free Press, p. 172.

The focal point of our time together came next. Within SVHA works a very authentic man, who bravely agreed to share his story of clerical sexual abuse with the board directors. He asked if his wife might also join our session to be a support person for him. He shared with great courage and the directors reciprocated with full attention and care. Every person in the room was greatly moved, disturbed and compelled by his story. As he concluded, the chair and the CEO came up to our guest to thank him and actually hugged him, a gesture which our guest later described as quite healing.

Mindful of the responsibility of leaders of Catholic ministries to contend wisely with the issue and consequences of clerical sexual abuse, we next heard from an executive leader of St Patrick's College in Ballarat which is respected for its courageous, survivor- and victim-informed response.

Throughout the session, people were free to offer a thought or ask questions. We closed prayerfully and gently. We checked in on our guests afterwards.

SVHA is now working on its own response, informed by the formation session we experienced.

Imaginative Contemplation as a Tool for Formation
Linda Di Sipio

Frances Sullivan in his keynote address at the Catholic Social Services conference promoted the importance of formation in Catholic organisations. He was asked, "What do you understand by the term formation?" He paused and responded:

> When I first became a father, I was given the name 'father'. I did not know what this meant but, as I have grown and my children have grown, I have come to understand what is meant to be a father. I see formation in this way. When working for a Catholic social service, we grow in hope

that the experiences had in the workplace help shape our understandings of what it means to work for a Catholic organisation.[5]

The room was deeply moved by his response. Significantly, his story intersected with my own and I felt engaged by this intimate revelation. This 'encounter' provided a thread into my workshop presentation which invited participants to engage in an imaginative contemplation experience of a Gospel passage. "Imaginative Contemplation", a way of praying with our imagination, is far from fantasising.[6] It is a dynamic activity that enables a story to speak to us.[7] Contemplating passages from scripture provides an opportunity for individuals to align their own stories with those of the Gospels and to foster personal connection in identifying with biblical characters and events.[8] The opportunity to use imaginative contemplation with stories from the Bible does not impose a Catholic worldview on individuals, so it suits environments, like contemporary Catholic healthcare or community services, which have a pluralised 'audience'.[9]

Formation at St Vincent's Public Hospital Melbourne takes on a variety of dimensions. Underpinning many of the experiences is the fact that stories have the potential to anchor us in purpose.

---

5 Frances Sullivan, in discussion following his Catholic Social Services conference keynote address, 2020. "Margin Call: The Risk of Integrity", which is reproduced in this volume.
6 Francis D. Alvarez, 2015. "Ignatian Contemplation in the Classroom: Fostering Imagination in Scripture Study" [online pdf]; accessed at www.religiouseducation.net/papers/rea2015-alvarez.pdf.
7 Paul Ricoeur, 1995. *Figuring the Sacred: Religion, Narrative and Imagination*. Minneapolis: Fortress Press, p. 10.
8 Michael Paul Gallagher, 2001. *Dive Deeper: The Human Poetry of Faith*. London: Darton, Longman and Todd Ltd, p. 20.
9 Linda Di Sipio, 2019. "Teacher Readiness: A Pedagogy of Encounter" in Michael Buchanan and Adrian-Mario Gellel (eds), *Global Perspectives on Catholic Religious Education*. Singapore: Springer, p. 193.

An example of a SVHA formation program is "Inspired to Serve". It is a two-hour program which all staff members are expected to attend at least once. The program, through a range of activities and experiences, seeks to build a connection between the work of staff and the 'Big Christian Story' of the Sisters of Charity. Participants are invited to 'peer into' the story of their foundress, Mary Aikenhead, and the Sisters of Charity and understand how their purpose was underpinned by Gospel stories.

A recent study conducted at a Catholic girls' school looked at staff engaged in a series of imaginative contemplation experiences. The study showed that guided dialogue and contemplative experiences had the potential to create an openness to teacher formation through the development of safe and trusting learning communities which, in turn, contributed to collegiality and further teacher collaboration.[10] The study's findings have subsequently been transferred into a healthcare setting. Thus, staff at St Vincent's Hospital are given ongoing encouragement to make sense, through their lived experience and storytelling, of their own personal values in the context of the SVHA values. The use of imaginative contemplation provides a tool to grapple with such questions and subject matter in a way that invites participants to enter into deeper learning as "a community in learning".[11] This approach is particularly helpful when participating in a process of change.

The community in learning is guided in the imaginative contemplation first by reading the chosen scripture passage. A second reading of the text is then accompanied by a music score with a similar theme as well as visual stimuli in the form of artwork or a film clip. After exposure to the passage and supportive material,

---

10 Ibid., p. 200.
11 Michael T. Buchanan, 2020. "Teacher Education: what Australian Christian schools need and what higher education delivers", *International Journal of Christianity and Education,* 24(1), 102.

participants are invited to express their personal contemplative experience using a variety of artistic media of their choice. An integral part of the session is the space to share and dialogue with each other on the contemplative experience.

The example used at the conference was the Gospel story of the Gerasene demoniac at *Luke* 8: 26-37. The guided instructions for contemplation were:

- picture the face of the demon when Jesus confronts the demon,
- picture the face of Jesus when he confronts the demon,
- picture the face of Jesus when he meets the man from Gerasene,
- picture the reactions of the family of the man from Gerasene when he is no longer possessed and he returns to them.

The Gospel story was adapted from *The Message* translation of the Bible.[12] The accompanying soundtrack music was composed by Edward Sheamuir for the film *Mother and Child*. The music score tracks were "Elizabeth Alone" and "Elizabeth's Letters". The visual stimuli were taken from the St Vincent's Hospital Melbourne Art Collection.

Conclusion

Formation experiences can be varied in their duration, style of facilitation and the extent to which people are invited to participate actively. The point of commonality is that these opportunities seek to nurture an awareness of the head, heart and hands elements that we bring to our work and of right relationships with others, as we move through life together with God's grace.

Ultimately, formation seeks to create opportunities for staff to be affirmed and empowered to be present and contribute to their

---

12 Eugene H. Peterson, 2002. *The Message: The Bible in Contemporary Language*. Carol Stream, IL: NavPress.

own 'community' of compassion. This chapter has explored how formation experiences will differ depending on their purpose and the audience for whom they are intended. It is our hope that the provision of these illustrative models of effective formation experiences will assist others in planning for impactful and respectful formation. Formation for ministry is critical for the future of the Catholic sector and, in our experience, with careful planning, accessible formation offers a powerful way of ministries engaging with their professional communities.

Governance for Mission

John Warhurst and Katherine Juric

The 2020 Catholic Social Services conference included a workshop entitled "Governance for Mission". The critical role of effective governance of Church ministries has been a focus across the biennial conferences organised by Catholic Social Services Victoria in conjunction with Catholic Social Services Australia.

The 2020 workshop was presented in two parts: the first considered principles of good governance with particular reference to Catholic ministries, and the second provided a case study of governance risks and dangers in practice. This chapter captures the content of the workshop and its presentations by:

- Professor John Warhurst AO, member of the Catholic Church's Governance Review Project Team and Chair of Concerned Catholics Canberra Goulburn – "Challenges in Governing Contemporary Catholic Ministries"; and
- Katherine Juric, Risk Consultant for Catholic Church Insurance Limited – "Work Health and Safety as a Governance Obligation in Catholic Social Services".

Challenges in Governing Contemporary Catholic Ministries
John Warhurst

Introduction
This chapter has drawn on my membership of the Governance Review Project Team and my long experience as a member of

boards and advisory councils in both episcopal and congregational settings. Part one of the chapter reflects the former and part two the latter.

Church Governance in Flux

Catholic Church governance in Australia suffers from considerable dilemmas. The clue to these problems within the Church comes in the challenging recommendation of the Royal Commission into Institutional Responses to Child Sexual Abuse that it should review "the governance and management structures of dioceses and parishes, including in relation to issues of transparency, accountability, consultation and the participation of lay men and women".[1] In so recommending the Royal Commission noted with some approval the approaches to governance of largely lay-led Catholic health, community services and education agencies. This situation suggests the undoubted complexity of Church governance practices.

The big picture shows that governance of the Catholic Church is in flux within agencies, sectors and dioceses and at the national level. There is so much change underway that it is difficult to follow. Some of this change within Church governance has been driven by state regulatory and funding demands, while some is a consequence of the challenging new situation in which the Catholic Church finds itself.

Many of the big national agencies, like Caritas Australia and Catholic Social Services Australia (CSSA), for both of which I have served at board level, are rethinking their governance structures. Incorporation is now common across Church agencies.

---

1 The Royal Commission into Institutional Responses to Child Sexual Abuse, 2017. *Final Report*, Vol. 16, *Religious institutions*, Book 2, Recommendation 16.7, p. 682; accessed at www.childabuseroyalcommission.gov.au/final-report.

The governance of diocesan Catholic education across Australia is being reshaped significantly. Some dioceses have embarked upon new approaches to consultative governance of their own affairs, like synods and assemblies, leading into the Plenary Council 2020[2] at which governance may be a major theme. The Association of Ministerial Public Juridic Persons, with eleven members including bodies like Edmund Rice Education Australia, has emerged as a strong third peak body in the Church alongside the Australian Catholic Bishops Conference (ACBC) and Catholic Religious Australia (CRA). Catholic Professional Standards Ltd, set up in 2017, has taken responsibility for oversight of new child safety systems. Simultaneously, the ACBC has undertaken a drastic restructure of its staffing, funding and governance. Most recently, following the 2019-2020 bush fire emergency, a new body, Catholic Emergency Relief Australia, emerged to play a potential 'whole-of-Church' coordinating role in future disaster recovery. More governance changes will almost certainly follow.

There are really two distinct though over-lapping parts to the official Church in Australia, within which the Catholic community exists. First, there is the core 'official' diocesan/parish segment and, second, there are the associated schools, hospitals, aged care facilities and social service, international aid and development agencies, many of which are associated with religious orders and congregations.

The second part of the Church, largely lay-led and often largely funded by state and Federal governments, has inevitably and irresistibly been drawn into operating under civic governance rules and guidelines. Most do so now with enthusiasm. But the first part of the Church has until now strongly resisted any such

---

2   For background on the Plenary Council 2020, see www.plenarycouncil.catholic.org.au.

incorporation of civic governance standards, which, as revealed by the Royal Commission, has been to its detriment.

The Royal Commission report predicted that changing the future governance and culture of this first part of the Church would be predicated upon learning a lot from the second part. Significantly, the acceptance by the ACBC and CRA leadership of the Royal Commission recommendation led to the setting up of the Implementation Advisory Group (IAG) in 2018 and then its subsidiary, the Governance Review Project Team (GRPT).[3] The first test will come when the GRPT report is considered initially by those holding Church authority in May 2020 and ultimately when it is discussed by the Plenary Council Assembly. Action rather than just words is required.

The lessons of secular good governance are clear and long-standing. They include the introduction and monitoring of mechanisms for accountability, transparency and inclusiveness. The GRPT report has reiterated the desirability of such civic standards in diocesan and parish governance. These are largely absent as yet, and, in some cases, resisted by those bishops and priests in charge and/or dismissed as deriving from 'aggressive secularism'.

That is why making a strong theological case for good governance principles is absolutely necessary if change is to happen. That case is a strong one, based on high levels of overlap between civic and canonical governance. Perhaps the one civic principle seemingly most absent in ecclesial thinking and practice is transparency, though the Code of Canon Law (Canon 1287, §2) does encourage Church financial administrators to "render accounts to the faithful concerning the goods which the faithful have given to the Church". Such accounting must be public and made widely available for transparency to be realised.

---

3 For background on the establishment and work of the IAG, see www.catholic.org.au/responseandprevention.

The relevant ecclesial principles include subsidiarity, highlighted by Pope Francis in his *Letter to the People of God*[4] in August 2018, and stewardship, a strong element of his encyclical letter, *Laudato Si'*.[5] Another essential principle of good Church governance, synodality, seeks the active participation of all members of the Church in the processes of discernment, reflection, consultation and co-operation at every level of decision-making and mission.

Synodality and discernment have been accepted as the foundational elements in the processes governing the Plenary Council and these principles are already built into the governance processes of many Church and agency boards.

The Church must not just talk about good governance but implement it, and that is the responsibility of those individuals with leadership and governance roles across the Church. In dioceses and parishes, the individuals who exercise formal authority are bishops and priests, respectively.

Boards and Advisory Councils

My own experience has taught me that Church governance is complex and varied. There are diverse structures and diverse membership of Church boards and councils, although, with exceptions like CSSA which includes some elected directors from member agencies, most are appointed and dismissed by bishops or religious superiors. The leadership style of the appointed chairpersons I have encountered has varied from the highly consultative to the autocratic, from hands-on to inaccessible due to work demands. Good governance can be compromised.

---

4 Pope Francis, 20 August 2018. *Letter to the People of God*; accessed at www.vatican.va/.

5 Pope Francis, 2015. Encyclical Letter, *Laudato Si': On Care for Our Common Home*; accessed at w2.vatican.va/.

The Composition of Boards

The composition of boards is crucial to their performance. The boards with which I have been associated have all been professional, hard-working and with diverse membership. The usual composition has been made up of appointees with relevant practical expertise, together with a range of skills in the law, finance and economics, public policy and government, education, fundraising and community relationships, media and communications, theology and Church experience, among others.

These boards take gender balance seriously and work towards achieving it. The women board members with whom I have worked have invariably made a powerful contribution and, within the Church, their presence is particularly important given its official male character. The boards do tend to be disproportionately Anglo-Celtic and elderly, demographics which should be addressed.

The talent pool for boards is shrinking as Church attendance shrinks. The net should be cast as wide as possible to include members from other Christian denominations and other faiths. This raises the question of how 'mainstream Catholic' Church boards should be regardless of expertise. Episcopal boards can be especially sensitive in this regard. As chair of a Nominations Committee, I have experienced the rejection by a bishop of a Catholic nominee for being insufficiently 'Catholic', meaning they were judged non-practising in the accepted sense.

Best Practices

As board members we are challenged to be true to our responsibilities. It is also worthy of note that, while being experienced professionals, we are largely unpaid volunteers with limited opportunity allowed for professional formation as directors. Adequate formation is a serious matter.

The support of the senior leadership team, led by the Chief

Executive Officer (CEO), is crucial to good governance and, importantly, the CEO must be allowed to lead the organisation. The board must balance its support for and trust in the management of the CEO with judicious advice and criticism. The same applies to relations with other senior leaders responsible for mission, programs, human resources, finance, communications, audit and risk. The board must independently make it its business to know what is going on deep within the organisation in accordance with good governance principles while not interfering in administration. How to achieve such 'deep knowledge' can be a sensitive matter.

In Church agencies the board must support the CEO in dealing with the Church hierarchy in a way which is respectful without being unduly deferential. The culture of the Church, that is day-to-day practice, is crucial to allowing good governance to flourish by going beyond mere adherence to Church and state rules and regulations.

Dangerous Situations

There are dangers to which board members should be alert. These include the following:

- Governance at arms-length causing boards to be unaware of the true state of affairs in areas like human resources, inter-personal work-place relations and 'sick' organisational cultures. This can happen equally in secular and Church organisations, as the Royal Commission into Misconduct in the Banking, Superannuation and Financial Services Industry has shown, but our Church values should prevent such dysfunction or at least protect us from the worst examples of it.
- Mission imperatives being balanced appropriately with financial prudence and even survival. The margins are narrow in many government-funded programs and most governments

try to take advantage of not-for-profit organisations. Mission-driven programs can be run at a loss but there must be a limit to this, especially in situations where capital assets are being run down.

- Political conservatism of Church leaders impinging unduly on the mission of agencies to advocate for the most vulnerable. Institutional self-interest can get in the way of radical advocacy and such conservatism will not only come from Church leaders, but from within boards and senior leadership teams.

Conclusion

Governance should never be relegated to the margins because it is seen as a dry subject. Good governance is crucial to being both true to the mission and effective as Church agencies. Good governance in contemporary Catholic ministries, working in ever-changing environments, is especially challenging.

Work Health and Safety as a Governance Obligation in Catholic Social Services

Katherine Juric

Amidst the many aspects of governance facing boards of Catholic social services and of other ministries, risk management is a high priority as it encompasses all aspects of operations. This contribution seeks to highlight some key responsibilities and make practical suggestions as to how these may be fulfilled, through a lens of workplace health and safety (WHS), as a risk consideration.

Due Diligence for WHS

Following a 2019 review of harmonised WHS legislation across Australia, many jurisdictions have either passed or are in the process of establishing new offences for industrial manslaughter, as well as the abolition of the right to access directors and officers insurance to pay fines for serious offences.[6] In this context, where regulators may more readily base prosecutions on the more serious offence of reckless conduct (as opposed to the lesser charge of general negligence), directors and officers must pay close attention to how they may personally affect the management of health and safety within their organisations.

Where directors and board members have influence over decisions that affect financial and administrative decisions of the corporation or entity, they may be considered officers. In turn, most board members may be deemed officers. Due diligence is a key legal duty for officers of organisations. Within the context of WHS, due diligence means proactively taking reasonable steps to:

- gain and keep up to date on knowledge of risk matters impacting the social services sector,
- gain an understanding of the organisations' operations, hazards and risks. Consideration must extend beyond the physical 'workplace' or office to wherever and whenever workers are conducting work on behalf of the organisation,
- ensure the organisation has appropriate resources and processes to eliminate or minimise risks. This includes the requirement actively to use resources and implement such processes,
- ensure the organisation has appropriate processes for receiving, considering and responding to risk-related information; and also processes to comply with any other WHS duties relevant

---

6 AICD, 29 January 2020. "States toughen WHS laws with new industrial manslaughter offences"; accessed at http://aicd.companydirectors.com.au/membership/membership-update/states-toughen-whs-laws-with-new-industrial-manslaughter-offences.

to the sector. In the context of WHS, such information includes reported incidents, hazards and other issues,

- double check the adequate provision and use of resources and processes through functions such as audit and review.[7]

Officers should consider the structure of the organisation, the scope of their role, and their influence over decision-making and budgetary spending, in order to establish reasonable steps. In establishing structures to achieve the above, boards need to consider:

- identification of who will formally provide information to the board (such as incident rate, health and safety programs and initiatives), including the method of relaying such information. Advisors need to come with an array of skills to assist in the navigation of complex regulations: WHS, quality, safeguarding, cyber and notifiable breach legislation to name some,

- forming a clear link with operations. Communication must include instruction, clarity and direction to senior leaders around critical risks of interest to the board, for example, where performance improvement notices have been issued by regulators for health and safety breaches. This will help establish confidence that risks are being identified, managed, treated and escalated. Simple methods such as procedures for communication between WHS committees, managers and boards; and robust meeting agendas and templates will provide some of the evidence that boards have enacted their duties,

- methods to drive and support a health and safety culture amongst workers and others engaging with the organisation.

---

7 Safe Work Australia, n.d. "What does an officer need to do?"; accessed at www.safeworkaustralia.gov.au/book/what-does-officer-need-do.

Verification of WHS Management

Accessibility and usability of a Risk Management Framework is essential to governance of WHS risk in the Catholic social services context. The use of simple online platforms and even well-structured shared drives to house policies and procedures for the management of WHS have been used successfully by Catholic organisations. Key objectives of frameworks include outlining a structured process for identifying and managing WHS risks, identifying mechanisms for monitoring and evaluation of systems, and articulating the flow of information between stakeholders.

The use of simple, achievable objectives and targets are evidence of WHS risk management in play. Therein lies opportunity for communication of progress to the organisation and, in turn, driving culture. Examples of WHS objectives and targets for social services may include risk assessments (lead indicator) of key work tasks, and number of incidents (lag indicator). Another key component is a risk appetite statement which serves to evaluate the level of risk that remains once a risk has been controlled. For example, practical training for disability support workers in managing client aggression is standard within the sector. Organisations need to understand what level of risk remains following the training. If it is found that the remaining risk of injury is significant, then the organisation must act further to reduce the risk.

An effective framework cannot be maintained without clear processes for reporting, monitoring and review of performance. Internal risk registers and incident registers should be reviewed on a regular basis at board meetings, and occupy a spot on the agenda. Board reports should provide a short, sharp summary on progress on completion of outstanding actions from incidents, status of critical risks (and incidents, including notifiable incidents) and progress on achievement of objectives and targets. On the topic of WHS auditing and review, Catholic organisations should not be alarmed when audits turn up findings and recommendations (ostensibly 'bad' news). On the contrary, where issues are found, then rectified and the whole process is documented, we provide evidence of a system at work and culture in action. Finally, proactive review of policies and procedures should be scheduled every 2-3 years and link back to the board's agenda.

How Can the Board of a Catholic Social Service Organisation Support and Drive WHS Culture?

Simple and cost-effective measures that boards can encourage in their organisations include:

- staff surveys: these are a point in time or 'pulse' reading of staff awareness of WHS processes and willingness to engage in processes such as incident reporting and risk assessments. Communication on key results and follow-up are essential to ensure the success of staff surveys,
- setting of cultural key performance indicators (KPIs) for operations: leaders could aim to conduct a number of 'safety conversations' with staff per quarter,
- setting the forum for reporting on KPIs: select no more than four KPIs to include in regular board reports,
- setting the requirement for education and awareness: boards can require senior leadership to implement programs around key lines of defence, online learning, social media content and inclusion of WHS-based KPIs in staff performance reviews.

Learnings for Officers Arising from Key Incidents

In the Deepwater Horizon incident of 2010, where an oil rig explosion caused eleven deaths and untold environmental damage, senior managers had undertaken safety conversations with staff hours before, but failed to notice indicators of critical risk in their preoccupation with routine safety, such as slips and falls.[8] This highlights the need for boards and officers to prioritise critical risks and ensure the appropriate flow of information, and demonstrate how WHS management is an example of good risk management in play.

As a further example, consider the case of SafeWork NSW v B & J Benchtops Pty Ltd [2019] NSWDC 674 (18 November 2019). The incident involved a worker manually transferring off-cuts from one bin to another, whilst standing on the raised tines of a forklift that was operated by a co-worker who was not licenced. The worker fell from the tines. The investigation found that safe work method statements were not available for the task, and that the director relied on a business partner (who was on sick leave) to manage health and safety. It was found that the director had acquired responsibility for due diligence, automatically, once he had assumed the tasks and responsibilities of the director role. The director was convicted and fined for the offence. This particular example highlights the need for directors proactively to seek an understanding of risk associated with the operation of their organisations.[9]

---

8 Workplace OHS, 15 March 2011. "Effective safety audits: Lessons learnt from the Deepwater Horizon incident"; accessed at https://workplaceohs.com.au/hazards/hazardous-chemicals/news/effective-safety-audits-lessons-learnt-from-the-deepwater-horizon-incident.
9 OHS Alert, 22 November 2019. "Director inherited due diligence duty, convicted over fall"; accessed at www.ohsalert.com.au/.

Safeguarding Everyone in the Church Today and into the Future

Gabrielle McMullen with Sheree Limbrick

Introduction

The briefing session on "Safeguarding Everyone in the Church Today and into the Future" at the Catholic Social Services conference in February 2020 focussed on the work of Catholic Professional Standards Ltd (CPSL), its roll-out of the National Catholic Safeguarding Standards for protection of children, the status of audits of Church entities, and engagement of Church authorities with CPSL processes. The briefing was also an opportunity to provide an outline of measures to protect vulnerable adults as part of the Safeguarding Standards framework.

In the session, Denis Fitzgerald interviewed CPSL Chief Executive Officer Sheree Limbrick and the following chapter, written by Gabrielle McMullen, distils that interview.

CPSL has developed a statement of acknowledgement with which it commences meetings and other gatherings. It was proclaimed at the start of the interview and, in turn, opens this chapter:

> CPSL acknowledges the lifelong trauma of abuse victims and survivors and their families; the failure of the Catholic Church to protect, believe and respond justly to children and vulnerable adults; and the consequent breaches of community trust.[1]

---

1 CPSL, n.d. "Who We Are"; accessed at www.cpsltd.org.au/about-us/who-we-are/.

About Catholic Professional Standards Ltd

CPSL was formed in response to the findings of the Royal Commission into Institutional Responses to Child Sexual Abuse.[2] It was established by the Australian Catholic Bishops Conference and Catholic Religious Australia but operates independently of the Church. CPSL is committed to fostering a culture of safety and care for children and vulnerable adults by developing and implementing the National Catholic Safeguarding Standards.[3]

CPSL audits compliance with these Standards, holding the leaders and members of Catholic organisations accountable for the safety of children and vulnerable adults who come into contact with the Church and its works. These include Catholic dioceses, congregations and institutions providing education, health and aged care, social and community services, pastoral care and other services. CPSL publicly reports audit findings and provides education and training in respect of the Safeguarding Standards.

Establishing CPSL

CPSL commenced operations almost three years ago. At the Catholic Social Services conference in 2018, Limbrick was invited to make a presentation as the new CEO of the then new company, Catholic Professional Standards Ltd. At the 2020 conference she was able to report significant progress with the roll-out of CPSL. She highlighted that CPSL's first focus was the development of the Standards which were officially adopted by members of the company, namely the Australian Catholic Bishops Conference and Catholic Religious Australia, and were published in May 2019.

---

[2] *Final Report of the Royal Commission into Institutional Responses to Child Sexual Abuse*; accessed at www.childabuseroyalcommission.gov.au/final-report.
[3] Further information on the National Catholic Safeguarding Standards is provided below and at www.cpsltd.org.au/safe-church/.

Importantly, CPSL was able to work with the Royal Commission into Institutional Responses to Child Sexual Abuse in the last six months of its existence and before it published its Final Report.[4] CPSL also worked with the Human Rights Commission, which took the recommendations of the Royal Commission with regards to what constitutes a child-safe organisation and turned them into the National Principles for Child Safe Organisations.[5] The National Catholic Safeguarding Standards take the National Principles and effectively contextualise them for the Church in Australia. The Standards also allow CPSL to perform one of its other functions, which is to audit Church organisations in relation to their safeguarding practices.

Limbrick noted a couple of important aspects of the framework. These Standards are not just to be applied by parts of the Church that are considered to be working actively with children; they are designed to be adopted by everyone in the Church. However, how the Standards are applied varies depending on whether or not an individual is actively working with children. There is a minimum set of requirements that apply irrespective of whether you are a very small congregation, perhaps not working with children or with more retired members than active members, or a volunteer-run organisation, or a large national healthcare or education ministry, or an Association of Christ's Faithful.[6]

The Standards essentially focus on four areas: leadership and improvement; engagement with children, families and communities; the people involved in Church entities (making sure the right people

---

4 *Final Report of the Royal Commission*, op. cit. n. 2.
5 The National Principles and material on child-safe organisations can be accessed at https://childsafe.humanrights.gov.au/national-principles.
6 Under the Code of Canon Law, groups of the baptised, clerical and/or lay, who come together with a common purpose and apostolate are referred to as Associations of Christ's Faithful.

are in given roles, with the right knowledge to perform their role); and Church bodies' systems and processes to support the protection of children. Their focus is on prevention while also giving guidance on how to respond when concerns or poor behaviours are evident within an organisation.

The First CPSL Audits of the Catholic Sector

In the lead-up to the launch of the Standards in May 2019 and since then, CPSL has trained over 1,000 people across the Australian Church in relation to implementation of the Standards and the audit process. These include bishops, congregational leaders, chief executives, vicars general and parish volunteers – it is quite a broad cross-section of people. By the end of February 2020, CPSL had completed ten audits. Six reports had been published, all of which are available on the CPSL website. In mid-2020, twelve months after auditing commenced, CPSL was aiming to publish a report on the trends, gaps and strengths that had emerged.

In 2020 CPSL is also looking to increase its engagement with a range of Church stakeholders through the audit process. For example, in a diocese, the audit team visits a range of parishes and talks to parish councils, parish priests, parish secretaries and safeguarding officers. In 2020 CPSL will make a concerted effort also to engage with families and with children, as well as staff and volunteers working across the diocese. The same applies to audits of religious institutes – if an audit team is going into one with active ministries, team members will seek to meet with representatives from across the ministry as well as religious institute members in order to broaden stakeholder engagement.

In terms of implications for the social services sector, CPSL's principle is not to duplicate what already exists in terms of government regulation or oversight. For this reason, broadly speaking, education, social services, and health and aged care have not been CPSL's primary focus. Rather it has been working with parts of the Church and ministries that do not have the same external oversight.

However, the events at St Kevin's College in Melbourne that came to light in February 2020 have led CPSL to prioritise the work on mapping what CPSL calls "inter-operability". Limbrick explained:

> This term essentially means: What's the gap? What's the gap that remains after what your social services might currently need to report to government, conscious that you're reporting on multiple levels across multiple funding channels? Are there things that the Catholic Standards require of you that no government regulator is going to look at?
>
> This is so we can start to audit these ministries – we have commenced mapping in education and will then move to other sectors. Some of this will link in with our work in relation to vulnerable adults. At this stage, we imagine that we'll start actively auditing social services in 2021.

CPSL's Impact on the Catholic Social Services Sector

Prior to her current role, Limbrick was Deputy CEO of CatholicCare Melbourne. Given her knowledge of the Catholic social services sector, Fitzgerald asked her: "What impact and difference on the ground have you seen with the establishment of CPSL?" Limbrick responded:

> This is a very interesting question, and it's very hard to measure. There are four things for me in thinking about where we are today.
>
> The first is not to underestimate the significance of having the Standards adopted in the first place, given the normal

pace of change in the Church. We took less than two years to have a set of pretty robust and specific requirements adopted and agreed to across the Church. This process was predicated on an ongoing conversation, which had obviously started a long time ago and was definitely alive during the life of the Royal Commission, but which has now shifted to prevention and what can be done to protect children in the here and now.

The second factor for me is engagement. We now publish a report on our website about which entities are engaging with us and CPSL's processes: who has been involved in training, who is working towards an audit, and when those audits are scheduled. As I travel the country, I find the depth of understanding and commitment to making changes increasingly encouraging. While certainly not perfect and perhaps not as fast as I'd like, it nonetheless means that change is happening.

The third factor is increasing awareness of prevention in a really practical sense. In talking recently to other faith groups across the National Council of Churches network, I think that some of the work that we've done has sped up others' capacity to take principles that can often seem quite esoteric and 'airy-fairy', and to say, what does it actually mean to lead a child-safe environment? What does that look like? The work and training that we've done has given people practical tools to do that work.

The fourth factor for me is the advantage of having very clear purpose and governance. CPSL is a company with a board. The board's expectations are very clear and we are executing a very clear purpose, so any distraction or potential to move off track can be dealt with because of the clarity of governance. I think this is critical.

Extending Safeguarding to Vulnerable Adults

CPSL's remit is the safeguarding of both children and vulnerable adults in the Church. When it developed the Standards for children, it had quite an open consultation process. Extensive material was prepared, informed by the Royal Commission, and then CPSL officers conducted a consultation road show around the country.

CPSL commenced work on developing the framework for vulnerable adults in 2019, and this time its process started with the guidance of a very experienced reference group drawn from across the country.[7] This group has members from ministries and various other sectors within the Church as well as expertise from outside the Church. It is guiding the development of a set of standards for the protection of vulnerable adults, doing some of the critical thinking to shape the framework for the standards.

CPSL has again been working with the Australian Human Rights Commission. It is also staying in touch with three current Royal Commissions – at the Federal level, those into Disability[8] and Aged Care[9] and, in Victoria, into the Mental Health System[10] – to make sure that what CPSL develops is in line with the thinking emerging from their work. As with the framework for the protection of children, the framework for adults will relate to both regulated and unregulated ministries of the Church, so preparatory work is looking broadly across those aspects.

In terms of the guiding principles being tested in developing the

---

7 For details of the Vulnerable Adults Reference Group, see www.cpsltd.org.au/news-and-media/vulnerable-adults-reference-group-update/.
8 Royal Commission into Violence, Abuse, Neglect and Exploitation of People with Disability; accessed at https://disability.royalcommission.gov.au/.
9 Royal Commission into Aged Care Quality and Safety; accessed at https://agedcare.royalcommission.gov.au/.
10 Royal Commission into Victoria's Mental Health System; accessed at https://rcvmhs.vic.gov.au/.

framework, the intent is to have a single set of standards. CPSL is not looking at two different sets; the thinking is that the current ten Standards for the protection of children[11] represent the same ten foci that need to be in place at the standard level for the protection of vulnerable adults. CPSL is looking to make sure that the approach is similar to that of the existing Standards: namely rights-focused, trauma-informed and strengths-based.

This rationale has been tested with the reference group and CPSL will consult with stakeholders during the course of 2020. In this instance, CPSL is not seeking to define 'victims', so to speak. Instead these standards, using the language of "protecting vulnerable adults", will articulate that all people engaged in the Church have the right to be safe. Limbrick stated:

> With the framework for children, we say that all children have the right to be safe while acknowledging that there are some children who have other vulnerabilities that put them at further risk. Similarly, there are a range of permanent factors that can put adults at risk, such as disability and age, as well as life risks, such as grief and loss or separation and divorce. There is a range of things that may cause people to be vulnerable, but our preferred approach is to not define whether someone is vulnerable in order to class them as in need of protection under the standards.
>
> We're looking at engaging with those with lived experience of failed protection within the Church. With the earlier Royal Commission, we clearly had a very strong voice from survivors of child sexual abuse and we did some consultation with children before we published the Standards for children. We'll do the same with the

---

11 The National Catholic Safeguarding Standards can be accessed at www.cpsltd.org.au/safe-church/national-catholic-safeguarding-standards/.

Standards for adults in terms of hearing from those with lived experience. We're about to commence a consultation process with services and ministries engaged in these spaces – Catholic social services, the health, aged care and disability sectors, tertiary education, formation centres and others.[12]

In terms of progress, the Vulnerable Adults Reference Group is holding meetings and advising CPSL on some of the design questions: Do the ten Standards also hold true for vulnerable adults? What would an approach of trying to include all adults look like? Is the current framework robust enough to manage both adults and children?

By February 2020, work had commenced on drafting Standard One, which is focused on leadership and governance, and on Standard Four, which is about equity and diversity. Once the framework is considered robust, CPSL will consult with a range of stakeholders and develop a portfolio of guidance material, as it did with the Standards for children. It was aiming to be at this point by mid-2020, which is an ambitious target. It would like to see the second edition of the Standards, covering both children and adults, adopted in the second half of 2020.

Conclusion

Limbrick concluded her presentation with a quote from Robert Fitzgerald AM, who served as one of the Commissioners of the Royal Commission into Institutional Responses to Child Sexual Abuse. She said:

He has left us with many, many pearls of wisdom, one

---

12 Attendees at Limbrick's presentation were given the opportunity to participate in a live consultation survey on the development of the standards with their feedback provided to the Vulnerable Adults Reference Group.

of which I use all the time. He was obviously referring to child-safe organisations but I think it applies to any safe organisation. His advice was as follows: 'I am now convinced that the notion of institutions building a community of commitment, knowledge and conversation at all levels is the only way to create and sustain safe institutions'.[13]

It takes a community of commitment, knowledge and conversation. Noting the strengths of the Catholic social services sector with respect to commitment, knowledge and conversation, the last exemplified by the conference, Limbrick stated: "The conversation about safeguarding has to be continued and it has to be about the rights of our children, our vulnerable adults and everyone within the Church. I encourage you to continue this conversation and to get in touch with CPSL through a range of media, including following us on Twitter".[14]

---

13 Robert Fitzgerald, n.d.; accessed at www.cpsltd.org.au/media/1456/20190521-final-ncss-edition-1-web-version.pdf.
14 CPSL can be followed on Twitter at https://twitter.com/CPSL_Aus.

Makarrata: Healing the Wounds of the Past

Peter Hudson with Sherry Balcombe, Helen Christensen, Helen Kennedy and Henry Williams

The 2020 national Catholic Social Services conference opened in Melbourne on the evening of 26 February 2020 with a forum on Aboriginal and Torres Strait Islander issues. The forum drew inspiration and invitation from the 2017 "Uluru Statement from the Heart" and also focused on the challenges of the Closing the Gap initiative.

Conference proceedings were opened with a formal Welcome to Country and Smoking Ceremony led by Wurundjeri Elder Dave Wandin who invited all present to listen to and embrace the land on which we were gathering for our days of listening and reflecting. Uncle Dave movingly shared how the land on which we were gathering had been a nurturing, celebratory and healing force from time immemorial. His people have listened to and respected the rhythms of the land, waterways and sky for millennia and have been blessed with a holistic sense of wellbeing and care which has flowed through the people in their love for the land and each other. He told those gathered that this sense of spirituality is core to Aboriginal people, goes much deeper than formal religion, and is a legitimate way to make sense of the wonder, beauty and flourishing of all creation. It is a spirit of wellbeing that encompasses all people who walk on this land and its flora and fauna.

In welcoming us to country, Uncle Dave asked us to dwell gently, connected and nurtured, while we sojourned on his people's land. He then invited delegates physically to embrace the smoke rising from a coolamon[1] and to allow its connection to earth and healing to renew them during a time of respectful listening and truth-telling. "Wominjeka", he said; that is "Welcome".

After the scene had been so richly set, conference delegates adjourned indoors to listen with respect to Aboriginal and Torres Strait Islander stories. The opening forum, "Beyond Surviving to Truthfully Thriving: Continuing Our Journey of Listening in Truth and Justice", called us to deepen our commitment to reconciliation. There was a sense among those gathered that we are on this journey of reconciliation together. Part of this journey is the acknowledgement that anything that diminishes the lives of individuals and communities also has a limiting effect on the broader society, and that reconciliation is in the interests of all. No one group can truly flourish if other parts of society are unable to achieve their human potential.

The forum offered a stimulating mixture of personal and professional voices which invited participants to reflect on and engage with the struggles for justice and equality of Aboriginal and Torres Strait Islander peoples. We were privileged to hear from four presenters:

- Sherry Balcombe, an Olkola/Djabaguy woman from Far North Queensland and Coordinator of Aboriginal Catholic Ministry in Melbourne,
- Henry Williams, a Torres Strait Islander man of the Kala Lagaw Ya people and Reintegration Team Leader at Centacare Kimberley based in Broome,
- Helen Christensen, a Tiwi Islands' Miyartiwi woman from

---

[1] A coolamon is "a bowl (a curved wooden tray) which has been used by many Aboriginal tribes, especially by Aboriginal women as a gathering tool"; see www.karlangu.com/stories/32-coolamon.

her mother's side and a Central Australian Anmatjere woman from her father's side, a lawyer and Indigenous Education Officer at Catholic Education Melbourne, and

- Helen Kennedy, a descendant of the Trawlwoolway and Plairmairrener clans from north-eastern Tasmania and CEO of the Victorian Aboriginal Community-Controlled Health Organisation.

Uluru Statement from the Heart

Historical dispossession of land and systematic dismantling of Aboriginal languages and law have had devastating impacts on Aboriginal and Torres Strait Islander peoples. However, this is not the whole story. Aboriginal culture continues to develop and strengthen despite this adversity. This resolve is evident in the 2017 "Uluru Statement from the Heart", which is a powerful and practical invitation to all Australians to stand in solidarity with Aboriginal and Torres Strait Islander peoples. Opening the forum, the "Uluru Statement from the Heart" was read boldly for the assembled delegates by Balcombe. The statement concludes with this invitation:

> In 1967 we were counted, in 2017 (and onwards) we seek to be heard. We leave base camp and start our trek across this vast country. We invite you to walk with us in a movement of the Australian people for a better future.[2]

This is the call of *makarrata*, an Aboriginal ceremonial ritual symbolising the restoration of peace after a dispute, an occasion of two parties coming together after a struggle to heal the wounds of the past. Its core message acknowledges that something wrong has been done and together we now seek to make things right. In the

---

2 For further information about the March 2017 "Uluru Statement from the Heart", see https://ulurustatement.org/.

spirit of *makarrata*, forum participants then listened to the 'voices' of Williams and Christensen, who shared some of their story of cultural awakening and struggle.

Surfacing from the Deep: Cultural Responses to Indigenous Experience

Williams encouraged delegates to keep an open mind in relation to what he would share with them as he spoke from the heart as a Torres Strait Islander man. Referring to the title of his presentation, "Surfacing from the Deep: Cultural Responses to Indigenous Experience", Williams said that he felt its imagery captured the struggle Indigenous people experience as they are exposed, through their various stages of life, to contemporary society. For all involved, these are deep-rooted and traumatic experiences and present a variety of cultural responses and outcomes. He emphasised that Aboriginal and Torres Strait Islander people bear the scars of intergenerational dispossession, injustice and oppression but that they are trying sensitively to move the rest of Australia forward to acknowledge past wrongs. They are trying not to point the finger in accusation and admonishment but to remain neutral and develop understanding of how we can approach this reality together as Australians.

From his own culture Williams shared two areas where there is a need for greater sensitivity and understanding in relation to the deep-rooted Indigenous sense of connection and responsibility to family. We all suffer from grief and loss in many ways, he said, but these are particularly challenging for Aboriginal and Torres Strait Islander peoples who have to deal with bereavements in extended families. Many relatives are considered to be brothers and sisters rather than a series of first or second cousins. Indigenous peoples' deep sense of grief and loss is felt in many ways and from a series of perspectives: familial, individual, cultural and Indigenous. He had heard reference to how cultural depression can be described as "a cold of the soul". He felt this imagery captured some elements of the Indigenous cultural struggle insofar as an untreated cold can lead to more serious issues of health and wellbeing. Williams saw this cultural malaise as a form of black and white systemic confrontation. To highlight this point, he spoke of the tensions he experiences within his own organisation in relation to leave entitlements versus cultural and family responsibilities and, more broadly, individual security versus respect and maintenance of clan culture.

When looking at cultural obligations there is also the issue of an individual living away from home, out of country. Williams presented himself as an example of that as a Torres Strait Islander man living and working in Broome. When it comes to cultural obligations, tombstone unveilings are an important part of Torres Strait culture and have been from time immemorial. When a relative dies, there are the immediate funeral expectations, but there is also the obligation to have a tombstone opening three years after interment of the deceased. A tombstone unveiling provides a 'platform' not only for celebrating the deceased and their achievements but also for acknowledging those who are referred to as "the in-laws across the wider clan". When somebody passes away in the Torres Straits, the Kala Lagaw Ya custom is for in-laws to step in and provide financial, spiritual and emotional support. Come tombstone unveiling time, there is general acknowledgement of their role. Once the tombstone is 'dressed', then the in-laws are called in and thanked for their support during the family's grief and loss period. You need to be in country at such times.

To highlight further complexities of Indigenous funerals, Williams explained how he has an Aboriginal partner from a Queensland clan. This inevitably brings into play cultural differences and they are likely to be grieving someone across these extended family networks most of the time. This is an ongoing and consistent reality for an Indigenous family which has to deal with expectations of "deaths after deaths after deaths". As a Torres Strait Islander man living remotely in Western Australia, members of his wider family are passing away, in a distant place, every few weeks as are members of his partner's family. What right does he have to seek some workplace acknowledgement of these frequent losses?

Attending to 'sorry business' entails consistent personal sacrifices: having to hold off your children's birthdays, late payment of bills, going without day-to-day necessities or family holidays. Most organisations will not allow you to take extensive leave for cultural obligations and so unpaid leave comes into play and that significantly impacts upon dealing with day-to-day necessities. In modern society, an Indigenous person suffers financial consequences of having cultural responsibilities. One might have certain understandings and arrangements with his or her manager but some workplace conditions cannot readily be changed and the whole of society needs to consider more seriously what could be changed in a manner which is respectful and more supportive.

Williams then offered the forum suggestions for organisational responses to increase understanding, and assist workplaces to be more supportive, of Indigenous cultures:

- offer workshops to raise awareness of:
    - the impact of cultural and legal adoption. There are still far too many children being removed from their families;
    - teenage pregnancy. Children are having children in Aboriginal communities and there is a need to heighten awareness and education around this issue;
    - domestic violence. This remains a grave scourge in Aboriginal communities and increased awareness and response are required;

- establishment of funeral funds. Consideration could be given to how organisations might play a part in assisting staff to secure funds from their workplace;
- strengthening collaboration with Aboriginal-controlled organisations in the development of culturally appropriate outreach programs. It has been proven that outreach camps in the bush, in an informal setting, when properly resourced and supported, work very effectively;
- assisting Indigenous carers with meaningful links and pathways to family support networks. This developmental need has its origins in the 'Stolen Generations' and being 'given away'. Nannas, grandparents, aunties and uncles all too often become the carers in place of dysfunctional or absent parents;
- achieving a balanced approach to "technology [which] owes ecology an apology". All too commonly in communities, technology has impacted on age-old cultural rituals and practices. Aboriginal peoples were once known for hunting and bush-tracking abilities but now one sees these people out with phones looking for a signal. Children are taken out into the bush hoping they will learn about their culture, but they all bring their phones with them.

Williams concluded with the imagery of "surfacing from the deep". Aboriginal and Torres Strait Islander peoples need to be allowed to surface from the deep and to "take a deep breath" so that they can move forward amidst the tensions of culture and modernity. They need platforms, pathways and collaboration to move beyond mere survival to flourishing in a true spirit of *makarrata*.

The Stolen Generation and Intergenerational Trauma

The second Indigenous 'voice' was that of Christensen. She began her presentation by building on Williams' comments on funerals and highlighting the difference between the grieving customs of people in the Torres Strait and on the Tiwi Islands. The Tiwi people have the Pukamani season. Families have poles made to honour the deceased, but the family does not pay for these. That has to be done by someone from a different skin group. The Pukamani season lasts for a year and then there is a smoking of the house where the person lived. Christensen commented that this custom was a good example of how Aboriginal spirituality can walk side by side with more traditional Catholic spirituality and practices. She stressed that the two spiritualities are not competing to lead or dominate but can find a way forward together. She summed it up as "to inter-marry".

Christensen's story is embedded in the Stolen Generation tragedy and its heart-rending trauma. Her father was a member of the Stolen Generation. She mentioned that, although he is now deceased, she talks about him because she witnessed his journey and she is a living example of the intergenerational trauma associated with the removal of children.

Christensen's father was removed as a child to a place in Alice Springs called The Bungalow where young Aboriginal children taken from their families were placed. The following is an extract from a 1929 letter to the then Commonwealth Minister for Housing and Territories, outlining conditions at The Bungalow:

> The accommodation provided for them exhausts my power to paint adequately. A rough floor of burnt lime and sand to make a form of cement has been laid down. A very rough framework of wood was put up, and some dilapidated sheets of corrugated iron roughly thrown over it. There are no doors or windows. A more draughty, ugly, dilapidated place one could hardly imagine. I think the children would be less liable to colds in the open than in the disgraceful accommodation provided for them. And that is not the worst. Boys and girls of all ages from one

> year old to sixteen are herded in this so-called room whose dimensions are about 24 feet by 50 feet. At present there are 48 children in the institution. The girls and boys are mixed indiscriminately. The children are issued with two blankets and lie on the floor. One small stove has to cook bread for over fifty people. They apparently have never had fruit or vegetables. The ration scale has been deplorable ... the scale is meagre in the extreme. The only lighting is two hurricane lamps. The children have no games or amusements of any description. Cooking utensils are practically nil. There are six bowls and twenty towels to serve everybody.[3]

Christensen presented this graphic description to highlight the image of her father, one minute being with his mother and then the next removed and living in squalor and neglect for no other reason than the colour of his skin. Christensen and her ten siblings were not brought up with the culture or language of her father's people. While Christensen's mother had also been removed, she did not lose her identity. The Tiwi Islands to this day are very strong in relation to preserving their culture and language and that has been a blessing for Christensen's mother and her siblings through the years. She remembers arguments between her parents because her mother was trying to teach the children her language. Christensen has no doubt that these tensions sprung from her parents' fear that the children would be removed. In fact, her four older siblings were removed in the early 1960s and she grew up wondering where they were. Only about five years ago she discovered that the official explanation for their removal was that the authorities deemed that her parents had not provided adequate housing for the family.

Christensen thinks often of her father, whose trauma manifested

---

3 The Bungalow operated in the period 1914-1942; see www.findandconnect.gov.au/ref/nt/biogs/YE00019b.htm.

itself within their family through alcoholism and violence. He did not know his own family and went through life thinking that the two girls being raised with him were his biological sisters.

She bears in mind the impact of colonisation on Aboriginal culture and, in particular, of the introduction of alcohol and all its associated vices. Christensen understands that her family experienced domestic violence as the result of her father's struggles to bury the confusion and pain of removal from his family as a young child. She commented that even today she is unnerved when people raise their voices as this recalls her experiences. She realises that her father did not have any appropriate male role models in his formative years and this is such an important teaching element of any culture and society. This was manifest in her father not being able to have a relationship with her three brothers and it was only after two of her brothers passed away that he was able to say sorry and that he loved them. He had never known how to express himself because he had never been shown or taught.

Despite the dislocation and distress experienced by Christensen and her family, she has a strong and enduring love for her father. She knows that the drinking and the violence were not part of their Indigenous culture. Importantly, he knew that, through education, it could be different for his children and, through holding down three jobs, he resourced their education. Christensen finds his commitment inspirational in her own educational career working with Koori students, which is her passion. Importantly, from her own experience, she has learnt not to judge anyone. The way forward is paved with empathy, unity and mutual support.

Closing the Gap Refresh

At this point the forum shifted emphasis from the personal to the political with the presentation by Kennedy.

Kennedy, a proud descendant of the Trawlwoolway and Plairmairrener clans from North East Tasmania, is married to an Aboriginal man who is one of seventeen children. Although Kennedy does not have biological sisters, she has numerous sisters and sisters-in-law within this family network and counts this as a great blessing. In mentioning her extended family, Kennedy was harkening back to Williams' reference to cultural connections and responsibilities within the extended family networks of Aboriginal and Torres Strait Islander peoples. Kennedy also acknowledged the previous two speakers with respect and admiration for the sharing of their often-painful lived experiences. She thanked them for conveying to all gathered a strong sense of the direct impact of trans-generational trauma caused by colonisation. She also commented that, in moving from the personal to the political, it is important to realise that the two are always intertwined, especially for Aboriginal and Torres Strait Islander peoples, for whom advocating for equality and human rights is a part of daily life.

In introducing the Closing the Gap campaign,[4] Kennedy placed it within an international context, including the global human rights movement. We were taken back to the beginning of the new millennium and to the vision of Kofi Annan, then Secretary-General of the United Nations. Kennedy highlighted his leading role in landmark global negotiations resulting in the United Nations Millennium Goals, the first international agreement of its kind. The goals represented very specific human rights and quality-of-life indicators that all nations globally should strive to achieve for all people. The eight goals were as follows:

- eradicate extreme poverty and hunger,
- achieve universal primary education,

---

4 For backgtound on Closing the Gap, see John Gardiner-Garden, n.d. "Closing the Gap". Canberra: Parliamentary Library; accessed at www.aph.gov.au/About_Parliament/Parliamentary_Departments/Parliamentary_Library/pubs/BriefingBook44p/ClosingGap.

- promote gender equality and empower women,
- reduce child mortality,
- improve maternal health,
- combat HIV/AIDS, malaria and other diseases,
- ensure environmental sustainability,
- develop a global partnership for development.[5]

In the early days, the focus of the Millennium Development Goals was very much geared towards under-developed and developing countries. In those years Australia, as a developed nation, understood itself as a funder of international development. That was how Australia perceived its place in the world. But what was to emerge in this country was another narrative. While Australia was seeking to play a leadership role in international aid, a stark and hidden story started to emerge. The media campaign that exposed the national reality was initiated by a group of Aboriginal and non-Aboriginal leaders who exposed the appalling living and health conditions of many Aboriginal and Torres Strait Islander peoples as well as human rights violations in this country. The Closing the Gap campaign emerged as a people's movement that built upon the momentum of the Millennium Development Goals. The phrase 'Closing the Gap' was coined to describe the life expectancy gap of seventeen years between non-Aboriginal and Aboriginal Australians.

In 2008 the Coalition of Australian Governments (COAG) came together to sign the Closing the Gap Agreement.[6] At last there was

---

5 For more details of the Millennium Development Goals, see www.undp.org/content/undp/en/home/sdgoverview/mdg_goals.html.

6 Australian Government, February 2009. *Closing the Gap on Indigenous Disadvantage: The Challenge for Australia*. Canberra: Commonwealth of Australia: accessed at www.dss.gov.au/sites/default/files/documents/05_2012/closing_the_gap.pdf.

a bright light shining on what was really happening in Australia in regard to Aboriginal and Torres Strait Islander communities living under developing world conditions. The advancement of the rights of our First Nations peoples was agreed as a national priority for the first time in the history of this country.

Kennedy asked the question: "So, where are we now in 2020?" There have been some gains. Areas of improvement include child mortality rates, life expectancy and rates of childhood immunisations. Kindergarten and Year 12 enrolments are increasing. Many of these developments are in line with global trends and show the impact of concerted efforts both in Australia and abroad. Although only two of the seven targets of the Closing the Gap strategy are currently on track, the progress that has been made is significant.[7]

Many are pondering why we have not seen as much progress as expected over the twelve-year period. In exploring this question Kennedy spoke at length on the idea of self-determination which she sees as a critical factor for improving outcomes across the board. When we think about self-determination, we think of sovereignty and self-governance, Kennedy said. Australia has referred to evidence around this issue from the Harvard University Project on American Indian Economic Development in order to examine the critical success factors of tribal nations.[8]

The Harvard Project reviews success factors such as health, family, personal income, business development, government funding and proximity to natural resources. The act of proclaiming

---

[7] Australian Government, 2019. *Closing the Gap Report 2019*. Canberra: Commonwealth of Australia; accessed at https://closingthegap.niaa.gov.au/reports-1.
[8] For further information on the Harvard Project on American Indian Economic Development, see www.hpaied.org/about.

and enacting self-determination was found to be the key difference between the outcomes for different tribal nations. Those enabled to practice self-determination had built structures of governance into their own communities, ensuring that development was claimed by their tribe and that people were accountable for its success and legitimacy. The Harvard Project has been influential in shaping Aboriginal and Torres Strait Islander affairs in recent years because it provides a strong evidence base for policy moving towards the advancement of their self-determination. It demonstrates that there is no one-size-fits-all formula when it comes to realising community development and self-determination. What is critical is that the solutions are owned, designed and upheld by the particular community.

Kennedy praised Victoria for its current reformist and progressive work in seeking treaty negotiations to be enshrined in legislation. In late 2019, forty-five Aboriginal people were elected to negotiate such a process.[9] Kennedy said that these are exciting times and encouraged ongoing awareness-raising and education in relation to issues associated with self-determination. She referenced another promising development of recent times when the Victorian Parliament legislated to transfer the guardianship of Aboriginal children in out-of-home care from the State Government to Aboriginal organisations.[10] When this idea was floated ten years ago people were very sceptical as to whether it could be successful but, in fact, the outcomes have been extraordinary.

---

9 For details of the Victorian Treaty process, see www.victreatyadvancement.org.au/. This process is also a focus of "Towards Treaties with Australia's First Nations Peoples" by Andrew Gardiner and John Lochowiak with Denis Fitzgerald in this volume.

10 Department of Health and Human Services, April 2018. *Wungurilwil Gap-gapduir: Aboriginal Children and Families Agreement*. Melbourne: State of Victoria; accessed at www.dhhs.vic.gov.au/publications/wungurilwil-gap-gapduir-aboriginal-children-and-families-agreement.

A further example of the Victorian Government doing business in a different way was the launch of the Aboriginal Housing and Homelessness Strategy[11] on the morning of Kennedy's presentation at the Catholic Social Services conference. The Aboriginal Housing Board of Victoria challenged the State Government to fund it for a process of consultation and engagement to develop the strategy. What it has developed is a framework and a strategy, owned by the Victorian Aboriginal community, that tells the story of where Aboriginal people want to be.

Kennedy spoke of the devastating impacts of racism and systemic discrimination. She sees it as the most insidious disease in Australia as it continues to infect the national psyche and work against a truly united Australian response to Closing the Gap. She referred to, and encouraged viewing of, the recent documentary, "The Australian Dream", which recounts the powerful narrative of the discrimination experienced by high-profile Aboriginal sportsman Adam Goodes.[12] A 2011 Victorian study indicated that 97 per cent of Aboriginal Victorians reported having experienced racism in the previous twelve months.[13] Further, there is a very strong correlation between racism and psychological distress. Kennedy reported that in her professional capacity she is aware that 33 per cent of Aboriginal

---

11 Minister for Housing, February 2020. *Tackling Aboriginal Housing Challenges Head On*. Melbourne: Victorian Government; accessed at www.premier.vic.gov.au/tackling-aboriginal-housing-challenges-head-on/.
12 The documentary can be accessed at https://iview.abc.net.au/show/australian-dream.
13 VicHealth, Lowitja Institute of the University of Melbourne and Beyond Blue, 2012. *Mental health impacts of racial discrimination in Victorian Aboriginal Communities*. Melbourne: Victorian Government; accessed at www.vichealth.vic.gov.au/media-and-resources/media-releases/vast-majority-of-aboriginal-victorians-are-targets-of-racism-shows-new-survey.

Australians experience psychological distress and are at risk of serious mental health issues.[14]

Australia has a new, refreshed Closing the Gap strategy, which was launched in July 2020. It is an opportunity to change the ways we work together to build our nation. Instead of governments determining targets for Aboriginal and Torres Strait Islander peoples, a coalition of First Peoples' groups and leaders has been working to produce their own roadmap for reform of action and accountability. Its focus will be on targeted partnerships rather than a series of goals.

Kennedy's challenge to conference delegates was to think about where Catholic agencies are based and how they might creatively and practically support the Closing the Gap campaign. She reminded us: "Think globally, act locally". Her key message, she stressed, was to play a part in addressing and redressing the entrenched disadvantage of Aboriginal people that is not their fault. She reinforced the strong message from all speakers at the forum that long-term disadvantage is a legacy of colonisation and the systemic disruption of families.

Kennedy concluded by recounting a professional experience of twenty years previously which, she said, indicated a mentality still somewhat evident in the Australian community. It challenges us all to move from blaming and disengagement to being willing to be part of the solution. She was in Griffith in New South Wales involved in a touring community leadership program and at lunch with the local mayor. She inquired of him about the relationship of the local community with the large Aboriginal mission on the

---

14 Department of Health and Human Services, October 2017. *Balit Murup: The Aboriginal Social Emotional Wellbeing Plan*. Melbourne: Victorian Government; accessed at www2.health.vic.gov.au/about/publications/policiesandguidelines/balit-murrup-aboriginal-social-emotional-wellbeing-framework-2017-2027.

outskirts of the town. She reported that, in a shocked and perplexed way, he responded: "Sorry, I don't know what you are talking about. We don't need to have a relationship with them. They have their own funding and their own resources".

Conclusion

As the forum drew to a close, some questions were offered to conference delegates as a stimulus for reflection and driving change:

- What can your organisations do to better understand and implement self-determination as a defining factor in your programs?
- How can you provide culturally safe, accessible services that stamp out institutional racism?
- How can you ensure that there is Aboriginal leadership driving and influencing your work?
- How can you contribute to closing the gap in life expectancy?

Throughout the forum, delegates engaged with the presenters with empathy and respect and greatly appreciated the reflectiveness and openness of the speakers. The forum was a significant and motivational experience for those present and set the scene for respectful listening and reflective participation throughout the remainder of the conference. Many of the issues presented were considered further in other conference presentations and workshops. The Aboriginal experience of trauma was explored in a workshop as were challenges of treaty across the country. Issues of housing and homelessness, domestic violence and the safety of children and vulnerable adults were also themes addressed in the following days.

The Journey Towards the Plenary Council

Gabrielle McMullen with Trudy Dantis, Denis Fitzgerald, Cath Garner and Lana Turvey-Collins

At the time of the 2020 Catholic Social Services conference, the Australian Catholic Church was eight months away from its first Plenary Council in 83 years.[1] A breakfast session at the conference focused on the "Journey Towards Plenary Council 2020". The occasion provided a timely opportunity to update delegates on the journey towards the Council and on how they could continue to contribute to the discernment process that would inform it.

Participants were briefed about groundwork for the Plenary Council by four presenters prior to participating in an open forum. This chapter captures the presentations and discussion on the occasion. The presenters were:

- Dr Trudy Dantis, Director of the Australian Catholic Bishops Conference (ACBC) National Centre for Pastoral Research,
- Lana Turvey-Collins, Plenary Council Facilitator, Australian Catholic Bishops Conference,
- Cath Garner, Group Director Mission and Cabrini Outreach, Cabrini Australia,
- Denis Fitzgerald, former Executive Director of Catholic Social Services Victoria.

---

1 Subsequently, due to the COVID-19 pandemic, the first assembly of the Plenary Council was postponed by twelve months.

Introduction

A Plenary Council is "the highest form of gathering of all local churches in a country" and has legislative and governance authority.[2] It encompasses "a formal meeting of the bishops and other representatives of all the dioceses and eparchies of the Catholic Church", in this case, of Australia:

> Its purpose is to discern what God is asking of us in Australia at this present time. While the church should be asking that question continually, a Plenary Council is a particularly graced instrument for seeking the Holy Spirit's guidance. And it has the authority to make church laws on the results of its discernment.[3]

The Plenary Council journey has four phases:

- Phase I: Listening and Dialogue – during 2018-2019, Church communities around Australia listened to and spoke with one another with a particular focus on the question: What do you think God is asking of us in Australia at this time? More than 220,000 people, either in groups or individually, contributed to the over 17,000 submissions received, revealing their concerns for the Australian Church and considerations for its renewal.

- Phase II: Listening and Discernment – in this 2019-2020 stage, Catholics from all over Australia continued to listen and discerned around six themes identified from the earlier submissions. As fruits of their experience of communal discernment, people could again submit responses either at a local or national level. National discernment responses

---

[2] Plenary Council 2020 website; see https://plenarycouncil.catholic.org.au/frequently-asked-questions/.

[3] Plenary Council 2020 website; see https://plenarycouncil.catholic.org.au/pages/about-us/theology/.

were published online[4] and shared with six Discernment and Writing Groups established to draft thematic papers to inform the main working document for the Plenary Council, the *Instrumentum Laboris*,[5] and ultimately the agenda for the Plenary Council Assemblies.[6]

- Plenary Council Assembly 1 – this was scheduled to be held in Adelaide during October 2020, bringing together some 270 delegates representing 'local churches', as determined by both Canon Law requirements and diocesan nomination processes. Due to the COVID-19 pandemic, the May 2020 ACBC Plenary Meeting postponed Assembly 1 until October 2021.
- Plenary Council Assembly 2 – originally planned for May 2021 and then rescheduled to July 2022, this convocation in Sydney will build on Assembly 1 to arrive at decisions that, following appropriate consultation with the Holy See, "become binding for the Catholic Church in Australia".[7]

Phase I: Listening and Dialogue

The focus of Dantis' presentation was on Phase I of the Plenary Council journey, Listening and Dialogue. The primary aim of this

---

4 Plenary Council 2020 website; see https://plenarycouncil.catholic.org.au/listening-and-discernment/discernment-submissions/.

5 The *Instrumentum Laboris* (Latin for 'working instrument') is an official Church document, representing another significant step in the national discernment process. It will build upon the input from the preparatory dialogue and discernment phases of the Plenary Council, provide a foundation for the development of its agenda, and guide discernment during the Plenary Council assemblies.

6 Following the conclusion of the Discernment and Writing Group process and as a result of the impact of COVID-19, discernment input via the Plenary Council website was extended.

7 Plenary Council website, see https://plenarycouncil.catholic.org.au/.

phase was "to listen to the voice of God speaking through the voices of the people, in order to gain a 'sense of the faith (*sensus fidei*)'.[8] For this reason, the diverse perspectives of many people were sought to contribute to the conversation".[9]

The Listening and Dialogue phase offered an opportunity from May 2018 to March 2019 for both groups and individuals to make submissions in relation to the following:

- What do you think God is asking of us in Australia at this time?
- What questions do you have about the future of the Church in Australia that you would like the Plenary Council to consider?
- You are invited to share a story about your experience of faith or an experience of the Church in Australia that has shaped you.

The ACBC National Centre for Pastoral Research (NCPR), of which Dantis is Director, was commissioned to design the submission process and to analyse the material received.

Dantis advised that NCPR staff utilised qualitative and quantitative methodologies to analyse "the over 17,000 submissions that represented some 222,000 people who participated in this process". The NCPR then compiled a 300-page report entitled *Listen to What the Spirit is Saying: Final Report for the Plenary Council Phase 1* to give a broad overview of the input received

---

8 In *Evangelii Gaudium*, Pope Francis reminded the Church of traditional teaching on this concept: "As part of his mysterious love for humanity, God furnishes the totality of the faithful with an instinct of faith – *sensus fidei* – which helps them to discern what is truly of God". Pope Francis, 2013. *Evangelii Gaudium – On the Proclamation of the Gospel in Today's World*, Section 119; accessed at w2.vatican.va/.

9 NCPR, 2019. *Listen to What the Spirit is Saying: Final Report for the Plenary Council Phase 1*, p. viii; accessed at https://plenarycouncil.catholic.org.au/resources/reports/.

and the demographics of participants in the Listening and Dialogue process.[10]

In the report thirteen chapters address major emphases from the submissions such as the Mass, Sacraments, Outreach, Evangelisation, Ministry and Young People. Dantis advised that the first chapter is on "Love God, Love Neighbour", which "emerged from the submissions as the top priority". Across these 13 broad fields, the NCPR identified 120 themes from its analysis of the data. The report summarises submissions under these themes. Dantis took, as an example, the theme of "Care for Neighbour". She said:

> When people spoke about Care for Neighbour, they described things like loving people, being kind to people, helping others, being non-judgemental, being tolerant, accompanying people, doing good, bringing hope, talking to one another, and having passion, concern and respect.

The 120 themes were taken to a gathering of the various bodies involved in guiding that stage of the Plenary Council's development: members of the Bishops Commission for the Plenary Council, Plenary Council Executive Committee, Plenary Council Facilitation Team and NCPR.[11] This group collaboratively arrived at six National Themes for Discernment in the Plenary Council journey. In Phase II, Catholics across Australia were invited to address these six themes; to reflect, to pray and to consider how God is calling us to be a Christ-centred Church in Australia that is:

- missionary and evangelising,
- inclusive, participatory and synodal,

---

10 The report can be accessed at https://plenarycouncil.catholic.org.au/resources/reports/.
11 For membership of these bodies, see https://plenarycouncil.catholic.org.au/staff/.

- prayerful and eucharistic,
- humble, healing and merciful,
- a joyful, hope-filled and servant community,
- open to conversion, renewal and reform.[12]

Subsequently, the NCPR prepared a report for each Australian diocese based on Phase I submissions received from people and organisations within the diocese and a 'snapshot' report for each of the six National Themes for Discernment.[13] The diocesan reports included the content of reponses and stories submitted from the respective diocese by those who had consented to having their de-identified submission shared publicly and with their diocese. For all submissions that included or were made in the form of attached documents, such as text, image or video files, these attachments were sent electronically to the relevant diocese.

At the time of the conference the NCPR was in the process of preparing, at the request of the Plenary Council Discernment and Working Groups (see below), a range of special reports on the Phase I input from particular demographic groups, for example on submissions from 17-35-year-olds, Aboriginal and Torres Strait Islander Australians, 'lapsed' Catholics, and priests.

Phase II: Listening and Discernment

Turvey-Collins introduced the second phase of preparing for the Plenary Council, Listening and Discernment. She highlighted the connection with Phase I and the emphasis there on dialogue:

> The first phase of Listening and Dialogue was about getting everyone listening to each other, talking to each

---

12 Plenary Council website; see https://plenarycouncil.catholic.org.au/themes/about-the-themes/.

13 The diocesan and 'snapshot' reports are available at https://plenarycouncil.catholic.org.au/resources/reports/.

other. By creating time and space to tell our stories, we aimed to connect with one another and to build bridges across difference.

Emphasising the importance of continuing the connection between Phases I and II, and moving toward discernment, Turvey-Collins remarked:

> I don't think we're excellent at this yet. When we begin to talk to each other we're often angry and full of emotion. That's a good thing to share but we also need to keep going, to ask: 'And what else do you hope for? And what else drives you?' If we do this, we can connect more deeply with one another ... I sense that this habit of listening to one another, of using the methodology of contemplative dialogue, will bear fruit for many years to come.

The Listening and Discernment phase is underpinned by the six themes, which emerged from the dialogue submissions noted above by Dantis, and discerning as to "what God is asking of us; how God is calling us to be a Christ-centred Church". Turvey-Collins noted two key strategies for Phase II, namely commissioned Discernment and Writing Groups and small group discernment in faith communities around Australia. Both focused on communal rather than individual discernment. The other important Phase II undertaking was the process of 'calling' delegates to the Plenary Council.

Discernment and Writing Groups

A major component of Phase II was Discernment and Writing Groups (Discernment Groups), one to address each of the six National Themes for Discernment. Following a call in July 2019 to participate in a Discernment Group, more than 400 applications were received. A 15-person team from around the country, implemented a robust HR selection process, including interview panels, to put together the six 10-15 member Discernment Groups. Their membership encompassed representatives from episcopal leadership, other clerical participants, religious and consecrated women, and laymen and laywomen of varying ages and backgrounds. Turvey-Collins described them as "little microcosms of the perspectives that exist in our Church".

In the period September 2019 to April 2020, each Discernment Group met regularly, undertook research, considered submissions received in relation to its theme, reflected on Scripture, and also considered Church teaching and contemporary pastoral practice as part of the communal discernment. Each then drafted a paper which would continue the national discernment process by informing the *Instrumentum Laboris* and ultimately the agenda for the Plenary Council Assemblies. The six Discernment papers were published at Pentecost 2020.[14]

Turvey-Collins highlighted that, through their reflections, the Discernment Groups sought to "name the pastoral reality in relation to their respective theme, and to prioritise – through their discernment – what the Plenary Council and the Church in Australia could address". The papers were to articulate the challenges facing the Australian Church and "means of moving forward".

Small Group Discernment

For Phase II, the Plenary Facilitation Team developed resources so that small groups could "gather anywhere and everywhere to enter into shared, communal discernment" on the six themes.[15] Turvey-Collins said:

> That was always going to be a challenge because discernment is an act of faith. You have to trust that God will lead

---

14 The papers can be accessed at https://plenarycouncil.catholic.org.au/continuing-the-journey-of-discernment/.

15 For examples of the resources, see https://plenarycouncil.catholic.org.au/resources/tools/.

the group. You have to let go of your own ego and trust that the group will also rely on God to guide you forward. From personal experience, this is very difficult ... We're using the resources to invite people to try ... Those resources are guides on how to begin learning, how to prayerfully make decisions with one another and with God, guided by the Holy Spirit.

Thus, faith communities across Australia were invited to gather in groups and to engage in a process of prayer, contemplation, sharing with one another and seeking God's direction. Following discernment on one of the six National Themes, the groups had the opportunity in the period August 2019 to April 2020 to have their responses sent to the relevant Discernment Group.

Plenary Council Delegates

Turvey-Collins advised that the delegates to the Plenary Council would be announced in March 2020. Canon Law specifies those who must be called as delegates to a plenary council, including bishops, vicars general, episcopal vicars, heads of seminaries and theological institutions, and leaders of religious congregations. For the contemporary Australian Church, these totalled approximately 180 delegates. At the same time, Canon Law allows for delegates who may be called as "others of Christ's faithful", the total of which cannot exceed half of the 'mandated' delegates.

Under this rubric, Turvey-Collins said, each diocese or other local Church entity[16] had been able to nominate one to four delegates depending on the local Catholic population. Each had put in place a process to call for expressions of interest and to select delegates. A month after the Catholic Social Services conference, 78 delegates were announced, together with the advice that a small

---

16 The term 'local church' encompasses dioceses, eparchies, ordinariates and a personal prelature; see www.catholic.org.au/about-us/the-catholic-church-in-australia.

number from national organisations representing education, social services, health and aged care, and Aboriginal and Torres Strait Islander Catholics would be advised subsequently. Anticipating the announcement of the delegates, Turvey-Collins reflected on the nominations received and delegates selected: "By the Grace of God, the spread was pretty good", including young delegates, some from "schools, hospitals, parishes and social services", and delegates with Indigenous backgrounds and from different cultural communities within the Church.

Between the announcement of the delegates and the first Assembly, a process of formation had been planned to prepare delegates for their role in the Plenary Council. Turvey-Collins concluded: "The Plenary Council delegates will take discernment through the final stages towards decision". It was intended that this decision-making process take ten months, the period bridging the two Plenary Council Assemblies. She said: "I know that, as Aussies, we just want to get on with it and do things and avoid having a 'talk fest'" but, as in Phases I and II, "dialogue and listening and discernment as ways of making decisions" remain critical in going forward.

Inside the Discernment and Writing Groups

The Plenary Council briefing then moved to two speakers who were Discernment Group members. The group of which Garner was a member had explored the "Inclusive, Participatory and Synodal" theme and Fitzgerald's addressed "A Joyful, Hope-filled and Servant Community". They shared with conference attendees why they sought to join one of the groups and what their experience had been.

Inclusive, Participatory and Synodal

"Why did I put my hand up for this group?", Garner asked and then advised that her motivation had been multifaceted. She indicated: "I believe that change is needed, and that this Plenary Council process may be able to deliver that change ... I'm keen to do what I can to support this process". It is "about taking personal responsibility and trying to be at the decision-making table if you believe that change is needed", she continued. From her background in Catholic healthcare, Garner said:

> ... organisations like ours have something to offer from our experience. We're 'in' the interface between the Church and the world; we're inclusive and outward-facing, and the services that we are part of are not always delivered by Catholics. I think we have an important contribution to make because this isn't about a Catholic Church with a group of signed-up members. There are a lot of other stakeholders involved with us.

In relation to her Discernment Group, Garner said:

> I'm optimistic about my experience in this process, although it hasn't been easy ... I've found that having a single issue in mind is not what discernment is about. The variety of people asking for the Church to be inclusive is so wide and people are asking for such different things. I now have a better sense of the enormity of the task and the risks involved. In our group, we really focused on the notion of a Christ-centred Church. That's the key to the way forward. It's been a very iterative experience and an opportunity for me personally to sit around the table with some great people and try to work out how to shape the Church going forward.

A Joyful, Hope-filled and Servant Community

Fitzgerald commenced by highlighting the importance of the Catholic social services sector being represented in Discernment Groups. He stated: "The Church is a complex entity ... the Sacrament of God's love in the world. We are all called to respond to God's love for us through love of God and love of neighbour, which are inextricably connected". In Catholic social services, "we're all people of God trying to bring Christ's love to the world". Fitzgerald continued:

> The world needs the balm and joy of the Gospel but the 'vehicle' we have for delivering this is not in great shape. It has probably never been in great shape ... The Church is a human construct as well as a sacrament of God's grace. That construct is sadly flawed. We're all aware of our own frailties and of the difficulties and challenges within our own organisations, the challenges of the structures in which we try to work and cooperate with each other. If the Plenary Council is to help guide the Church to be a better conduit of God's love in Australia, it needs perspectives from across the various parts of the Church – from Catholic healthcare, social services, parishes, theologians, people from all points of the compass, so I put my name forward.

His 11-member group, Fitzgerald advised, had two bishops, a deacon, a religious brother and seven lay members "from all around Australia, from all points of the theological spectrum – male, female, young, old" and with diverse experiences. In relation to their paper, he stated:

> I'm very pleased to have been involved with the paper ... which looked at renewal of parishes and at greater integration and recognition of services in the Church. The Church is here to be a conduit of God's grace, to be of service to the world and to bring the balm and joy of the Gospel to everyone.

Fitzgerald concluded by encouraging those present to "step up if you're able". His entreaty continued:

> If you're privileged to be able to contribute, then you have a duty to play your part. If you're part of the Church, if

you've benefited yourself or if you've seen the benefits that others have gained from the Church, then why not step forward? Why not try to rebuild our broken Church? Aiming to make it better is a task that we're all called to during this Plenary Council process and beyond.

Contributing to Listening, Dialogue and Discernment

Following the presentations, wide-ranging and lively discussion ensued. The occasion offered those present and, in particular, the Catholic social services sector an opportunity to be part of Plenary Council listening, dialogue and discernment.

A recurring theme was the critical importance of the Catholic social services sector having "a voice throughout the Plenary Council process", given its "care of the most vulnerable" which is integral to the "way of Jesus" and the very nature of the Church. Turvey-Collins drew attention to the focus of Plenary Council documents and processes on "a Christ-centred Church" which implicitly seeks to capture the breadth of what is Church, "all of our institutions, organisations and agencies, all of us". She advised that attention would be given to ensuring that the language of the Discernment Group papers reflected this breadth.

Fitzgerald added that his Discernment Group:

> was specifically about the Church being at the service of the people, which involves engaging positively with society and taking the vision of Vatican II seriously rather than being wary of the world and focusing on the negative side of developments there. To do that we have to be transparent and accountable. We have to build trust with our own people after the debacle of sexual abuse and cover-up. The question of how to be of service to the community needs to be addressed by the Plenary Council as a whole as well as in each part of the Church.

In relation to the Phase I survey data, a matter raised was the study's findings concerning women in Church leadership roles. Dantis responded: "A very significant theme of the Phase I report's leadership chapter is the participation of women, which came out strongly in responses from all over the country. It was talked about at the parish and other levels and the topic of women deacons and priests was also very strong". She indicated that women's leadership was raised a couple of 'orders of magnitude' more than many other issues recorded in the report. Garner was able to advise that women's leadership in the Church had been a focus of her Discernment Group and was addressed in its paper.

The suggestion was made that wider governance issues, including accountability and transparency in relation to Church processes, could perhaps have given rise to a seventh national theme based on the survey's findings. This led to the question: "How do you achieve more participatory governance within the Church, the sort of accountability that people are crying out for, the transparency?" How do you move from "the current pinnacle of authorised decision makers" with a "radical change to accountability, transparency and participatory governance"? Garner told those present that her Discernment Group had wrestled with these issues and its report would reflect thinking on being more a "synodal[17] and participatory" Church. Turvey-Collins advised that the six themes deliberately encompass participation and collaborative processes, not just in decision-making but also in the co-creation of ideas:

---

17 In his address on the occasion commemorating the 50th anniversary of the institution of the Synod of Bishops, Pope Francis encouraged the development of a synodal Church "journeying together". He said: "A synodal Church is a Church which listens, which realizes that listening 'is more than simply hearing'. It is a mutual listening in which everyone has something to learn" (17 October 2015); accessed at www.vatican.va/. In March 2018 Pope Francis formally consented to the Australian Church conducting its Fifth Plenary Council.

> There were many stories of people working really hard on an idea or a strategy, only for it to be shut down by a bishop or a priest or another figure of authority. We're in the habit of episcopal leadership giving a rubber stamp to ideas that they may not have had any involvement in developing. Taking a different approach, the process of dialogue, listening and discernment has been a practical example of what participation and synodality can look like. That is, addressing the importance of having informal, semi-formal and formal structures whereby ideas are co-created and decisions are made together. A significant change in culture and mind-set is still needed to achieve true synodality and collaborative leadership throughout our Church.

In relation to accountability and transparency, Fitzgerald noted concrete recommendations made through the Phase I survey. "One is that there be a pastoral council in each parish", he said, and that dioceses have pastoral assemblies and publish their financial statements; that "parish priests are required to work with others collaboratively". Primarily, parish priests' focus should be "spiritual leadership rather than total administrative authority". Fitzgerald continued:

> Many of the religious institutes have led the way on this. For example, if you go onto the website of the ACNC [Australian Charities and Not-for-profits Commission] and look up the Christian Brothers, you can see their accounts for the past few years, and the items there that relate to responding to abuse. You can see how much they've spent and how much they've set aside for this year and for the future. This contrasts with some key dioceses, which have no financial information in their ACNC records because they're exempted as a 'basic religious community'.

As the forum concluded, there was a focus on being well-informed about the preparations for and the processes of the Plenary

Council. Turvey-Collins alerted attendees to the e-newsletter, *PlenaryPost*.[18] She also noted that, even after the current thematic papers are published, there will still be continuing opportunities for people in general to be engaged and involved in preparing for the Council, both during the months when the agenda will be shaped for the Plenary Council and between the first and second sessions of the Council: "So, keep asking, we need to try and get it right".

Conclusion

The Plenary Council and the processes associated with it are critical undertakings for the Catholic Church in Australia. The first two years of the journey, informed by listening, dialogue and discernment, have commenced a hope-filled period of renewal and reform for the Church. With a particular focus on the question, What do you think God is asking of us in Australia at this time?, we have 'taken the temperature' of the Australian Church in an historic way. There can be no turning back. We must journey forward to the new era of an inclusive and participatory Church.

We have contributed to a process of "scrutinizing the signs of the times and of interpreting them in the light of the Gospel", of discerning "the joys and the hopes, the griefs and the anxieties ... of the followers of Christ".[19] Now our Plenary Council journey has been disrupted by the COVID-19 pandemic. With the fullness of time, we might look back and realise that the consequent extended period of discernment and preparation has better 'equipped' the Australian Church to "put out into the deep" (*Luke* 5:4).

---

18 Issues of *PlenaryPost* are accessible at https://plenarycouncil.catholic.org.au/plenary-post/.

19 Second Vatican Council, 1965. *Gaudium et Spes: Pastoral Constitution on the Church in the Modern World*, Sections 4 and 1 respectively; accessed at www.vatican.va/.

Building a Strong Future for Catholic Social Services

Patrice Scales and Joshua Lourensz with Claire Victory and Belinda Clarke

The "Building a Strong Future for Catholic Social Services" forum at the Catholic Social Services conference brought together a discussion panel of younger generation leaders. Their brief was to provide their insights into future challenges and opportunities for Catholic social service organisations.

Claire Victory, National President of the St Vincent de Paul Society,[1] Belinda Clarke, Executive Manager Social Impact at CatholicCare Tasmania,[2] and Joshua Lourensz, Executive Director of Catholic Social Services Victoria, formed the panel. Tiffany Davis, Communications Manager for the Catholic Archdiocese of Melbourne, chaired the panel. This chapter summarises the experiences recounted by the panel and their broad-ranging discussion, and highlights three initiatives that lead the way in the development of strong programs for the future.

While diverse views and a range of opinions were expressed during the free-flowing panel discussion, there was agreement on a fundamental message: the current conditions of our society dictate that there is much work to be done by social services generally,

---

[1] For information on the St Vincent de Paul Society, see www.vinnies.org.au.
[2] Information on CatholicCare Tasmania can be accessed at https://catholic-caretas.org.au/.

and that Catholic social services have a unique role to play in the flourishing of our society.

A number of important elements emerged as foundational for the future. Firstly, Catholic social teaching principles and especially recognising the dignity of each person, understanding the complexity of each person's needs, and providing services based on relationships, will continue to be a critical feature of our services. But it was noted that the resources and staff formation needed to provide this response are unlikely to be adequately funded by government.

Secondly, while some specialist services will continue to be provided by particular specialist organisations, collaboration between organisations will be more critical in the future. Multiple Catholic social service organisations, working together as a synergistic whole, will be key to keeping the dignity and needs of each person as our primary focus.

Thirdly, critical thinking, strong partnerships, and creative programs and ways of working will be essential to keep Catholic social services at the forefront of the response to unaddressed and emerging needs. These domains provide a solid basis for the crucial role that social services play in advocating for positive systemic and societal change.

The Challenges of our Times

Many Catholic social service organisations work with great dedication to make a positive impact in measurable ways. But, along with other community service providers, they are facing growing challenges of widening and deepening inequality and disadvantage throughout Australian society. Agencies are increasingly required to respond to community needs at multiple levels. There are both entrenched areas of disadvantage with which agencies are all too familiar, and now also emerging cohorts who are in need. For example, people who in the past were typically in work and able to meet their family's primary needs are becoming more reliant on social service support to supplement the family budget.

Homelessness across Australia has increased by 13.7 per cent in five years according to the latest census data.[3] In Tasmania 25 per cent of the homeless population are young people.[4] Young people can be particularly affected by insecure or precarious work environments, including the 'gig' economy and lack of secure work opportunities. In addition to lack of income, young people are reporting on the isolation that they feel – the sense that they are alone, and not able to play a part in the civic and social life around them. So, rather than feeling part of a society, a set of systems and structures that are supportive, they sense they are judged on whether they will 'make it' or not.

Current levels of workforce casualisation and under-employment are markedly high,[5] and this impacts negatively on many who have not traditionally needed to turn to social services. This safety net is thus being extended well beyond the many who remain entrenched in disadvantage.

Another aspect of the current reality is that there is a perception that Australians are all for a 'fair go', and we strive as a community for a level playing field, but in reality, this is far from universal. Many do not understand or appreciate that there are forces outside of an individual's control that impact on their lives.

The reality for people experiencing disadvantage and those who now find themselves in stressful situations is that community

---

3 These data can be accessed at www.homelessnessaustralia.org.au/about/homelessness-statistics.
4 For the Tasmanian data, see https://sheltertas.org.au/housing-in-tasmania/homelessness/some-facts/.
5 For details, see Independent Inquiry into Insecure Work in Australia, 2012. *Lives on Hold: Unlocking the Potential of the Australia's Workforce*; accessed at www.actu.org.au/media/349417/lives_on_hold.pdf.

attitudes can be judgmental and harsh. The prevailing narrative from some quarters is that there must be 'something fundamentally wrong' with those who seek social support, or that they have brought it upon themselves to be in this situation. Some government rhetoric, and often its policies, appear to 'demonise' the disadvantaged in our community who require help.

This is an extremely challenging environment in which to be providing services, let alone to bring about social change. Not only are Catholic social service agencies under stress to meet the emerging and increasing levels of need but, more than ever, agencies are placed in a position where they have to challenge attitudes implicit in societal narratives, and attitudes about how we see each other.

Historically, Catholic social service agencies have been established in direct response to the needs that have emerged in Australia over time. But today's social, political and economic environment is changing rapidly and, as noted later in this chapter, provides exceptional challenges to our organisations. Catholic social service agencies are having to adapt constantly to these changing demands in order to assist and serve people who are struggling effectively, as well as play their part in seeking to address the attitudes that underpin the negative narratives.

How Do Catholic Social Service Organisations Create Positive Change?

In Catholic social services organisations, any change that will affect people, and also be of benefit to society, should seek to encompass the principles of Catholic social teaching. Moreover, change starts with people, however challenging this is.

In this context, Victory spoke about her experience of the St Vincent de Paul Society (SVDP), well-known for its long history of responding to local need. The SVDP is a member-based organisation, and people and Catholic social teaching are implicit in its mode of operation. All the broader work of the SVDP emerges from the lived reality of its members – predominantly community member-volunteers – as they respond to the needs of their local communities.

Using local experience to direct the strategic objectives of the whole organisation can be both a strength and a limitation. A limiting factor is that, if the SVDP, as an organisation, endeavours to meet every identified local need, it risks spreading its resources too thinly and being incapable of being effective in any area. The SVDP fundamentally works from the basis of listening to members at the local level, and then identifying how the strengths of the organisation can be harnessed to work effectively together with other organisations, including other arms of the SVDP, to enable positive change to occur.

Seen in this light, the organisational limitations, in fact, are a strength. They come coupled with the power of having members who are actually connecting in a very personalised, authentic way with real people who are encountering disadvantage in their lives.

More generally, the panel noted that, for any organisation wishing to create effective positive change, there is a need to come back constantly to fundamental questions:

- What is our mission?
- What are the needs?
- What are our skills?

CatholicCare Tasmania knows well how challenging it is to implement positive change across a broad domain. As Clarke explained, CatholicCare Tasmania seeks to meet a diverse set of needs and, consequently, provides diverse services. Its services encompass housing and various care and place-based support programs, including school-based work. Its method of driving positive change starts with people – workers who connect with the lived experience and realities of their communities and listen to those whom they are supporting.

In order to bring about social change, CatholicCare Tasmania has found it critical to identify momentum within the broader society. For example, if there is pressure in the community to address an issue like homelessness, then relevant social service organisations need to be agile enough to harness their experience and move into the area of need, drawing on their expertise and mission-informed practice. It is necessary to consider not just the established areas of an organisation's work, but also continually to look outside pre-determined silos to 'see' new possibilities to address the need and thus build impetus to create change for people and communities most in need.

The challenge for Catholic social services is to make a concerted effort to find the 'levers' that exist around us to encourage and implement change. Often government chooses not to work in a certain area, but social services can fill that particular gap and meet the community's needs. In order to be an effective part of such work, agencies need to garner people and communities to work together. Often we need to look no further than to some of the staff in our own organisations who are an incredible source of knowledge and experience and can recognise opportunities and imagine new ways of addressing disadvantage.

Importantly and in line with mission-based strategic priorities, we need to identify which communities we can serve with available resources and expertise. Priorities need to be established through a process of discernment. Catholic social service agencies will be most effective when they continually come back to their core values to inform their work, and maintain their focus on disadvantaged communities where they can be a transformative presence. If Catholic social service agencies are genuinely at the margins, they will be uniquely placed to play a role in agenda setting for a better future.

Catholic social service agencies do not operate in a vacuum, but rather are surrounded by, and engaged with, a much broader community of works, institutions and knowledge. We are also a fundamental part of the Church. Through this vibrant set of connections and common ground, Catholic parishes, schools, hospitals and other organisations can be connected to a particular issue or problem, and work together to lift government sights above the politics of the election cycle to focus on community needs.

Building Prophetic and Responsive Catholic Social Services

In recent times, particularly related to the Church's sexual abuse record, the Catholic 'brand' has suffered, and it seems that often Catholic organisations and the institutional Church have been 'treading' too carefully because of this. The abuses of power by members of Catholic institutions are deeply sobering and require continual soul-searching and change. This remains an ongoing and humbling challenge for Catholic agencies, including social service organisations.

As we move into the future with a commitment to improved processes of governance and administration, we also need to ensure that we remain Christ-centered organisations. We stand on the shoulders of spoken and unspoken heroes of faith. Catholic social service organisations should not let the injustice and abuse, to which the Church was party, stand in the way of their calling out injustice and inequality. Our foundational driver is love of neighbour and love of God. This must compel us to move forward in a positive and radical way.

Our future modes of operating must both embody the humility that should come from our failings, and be in line with our fundamental principles. Catholic social service organisations need to get back to place-based responses. There is a renewal of energy in this space in both research and organisational approaches.

The future workplace in our sector will continue to be challenging. The majority of workers within Catholic social services are not Catholic or necessarily of faith. Further, funding models in the sector and the current economic environment do not necessarily allow the establishment of a settled workforce that can be formed in ethos and mission, as is the case in, for example, the Catholic education and, to a lesser extent, health sectors. Catholic social services will remain dependent on significant numbers of casual and contract employees. An ongoing challenge for our organisations will be to provide resources and make time for formation opportunities so that these staff understand our core mission and driving force, and find value in a way of working that is in keeping with the Catholic tradition. For a strong future, these are all issues that Catholic social services must address.

In past years, Catholic social services relied on religious congregations and clergy to enable and keep organisations grounded in the fundamental values and principles of the Catholic tradition. The concept of a vocation, as opposed to waged employment, with the former always evident in religious life and action, is no longer the norm. Many congregations are in the process of implementing new structures and ways of partnering with lay people, so their works can continue in the future as ministries of the Church. How this plays out over the coming decade will have a profound influence on the future of Catholic social services.

Working Beyond the Bounds of Funding

Increasingly in Australia, Catholic social services and other Church ministries have become dependent on government funding. The increasing disparity between the ways the Government perceives people and the reality of social investment needs necessitates that Catholic social services think of other ways to fund the salaries of workers to be the 'dot connectors' and community builders. In the current environment, this work will not be funded by Government.

Further, in some instances, there are conditions attached to Government funding which limit the capacity of our agencies to serve disadvantaged communities urgently needing support. How do Catholic social service agencies ensure that they have the resources for prophetic and principled work which results in strong communities?

Ensuring a strong and principled future for Catholic social services means that we will need to maintain and grow in commercial acumen, to raise the revenue that allows us to deliver our services and mission. It stands as a fact that we live in a market-driven country. This is not evil, in and of itself, and business, in and of itself, is not evil. Using market forces is not the antithesis of mission. Under the current conditions and circumstances, understanding market imperatives is vital to the ongoing work of social services. The core work of Catholic social service organisations is spending time with the people whom we seek to serve, and we need staff who are highly skilled and trained to meet their complex needs. That is predicated upon the ongoing financial viability for our organisations.

For the SVDP, this means employing staff who are able to support community members and volunteers so that their time spent with the people the Society serves complements the services provided by professional staff. If the SVDP had to recruit staff to fulfil every dimension of its face-to-face work or interaction, this would be a diversion from the fundamental community principles that enable a flourishing society. There needs to be an appreciation that volunteers, ministering in different ways and assisted by highly trained professional staff, are required to enable the mission. For the SVDP that means it requires staff support in order to facilitate membership-based work, not staff to take on all the roles.

At the present time, we need strong business expertise to ensure that we can provide services that address the needs of our communities. Simultaneously, the underlying conditions on which markets rest need to be constantly examined by Catholic social services, in order to determine which elements are useful and which are negative. Catholic social teaching should be an ongoing 'tool' to confront the logic of the market, which is profit-driven and in many ways negatively affecting the people whom we wish to serve and see flourish. At the same time, Catholic social service organisations will need to rely on their broader connections to community, other sectors and the Church to be part of a more fundamental shift in society towards a focus on the common good.

Finding and Developing the Leaders of Tomorrow

The members of the conference panel were of the view that current leaders in Catholic social services might do well in their search for future leaders to start by looking no further than those in their organisations. Some of tomorrow's leaders will be amongst staff who do the important 'hands-on' work, consistently and effectively, day in and day out, but do not seek accolades. These people are true heroes of social services work. As one panel member suggested, we should, "Look for those who unpack the dishwasher"!

In terms of improving governance and processes, it was suggested that younger colleagues can often play a key role, as they observe what we do with fresh eyes and can question established, and perhaps outdated, practices. Including younger people in working parties and on committees, rather than just the most experienced, is also a valid way of growing young leaders. A mix of formal and informal opportunities for developing leadership potential was encouraged.

It was also urged to pay attention to those who are open about their vulnerabilities and lack of experience and wanting to learn. The most authentic leaders are the ones who are open to exploring new options to make a difference in their communities. They will work towards continuous improvement and be open to trialing new ideas. Good leaders will also have the courage of their convictions and be able to "speak truth to power". This may challenge their colleagues, but this can be a spark that will build up into a flame with appropriate direction. Identifying individuals in organisations who are passionate and 'full of fire' about their work and the organisation's mission, and guiding and mentoring them, will often form a leader who can take the ministry into the future.

Conclusion

The vibrant "Building a Strong Future for Catholic Social Services" panel discussion was clear in its message: faith-based social service organisations are in a prime position to continue to meet the ever-widening needs gap in our community. There are, however, headwinds. Changing political, economic and social conditions, including the uncertainty and limited application of government funding, challenging staffing requirements, more complexity in client needs, negative perceptions of the Catholic Church in the community, and the changing religious connection to staff, will challenge Catholic social service agencies as they seek to meet their mission of Christ-inspired works.

Catholic social service agencies cannot be daunted by these challenges but, as in the past, must show themselves to be agile, responsive and committed to mission, if they are to survive and flourish. The younger generation of Catholic social service leaders, when consulted, developed, given opportunities, and allowed to flourish themselves will be more than capable of continuing a strong future for Catholic social services.

The following three examples of Catholic social service programs show ways that we can establish a strong future for the sector: namely, by developing young leaders, working in partnership with other organisations, and creating strong partnerships in advocacy.

Emerging Young Leaders Program

In 2017 the National Council of the St Vincent de Paul Society (SVDP) established a program to uplift young leaders' governance capability. The outcome was the Emerging Young Leaders (EYL) program which was piloted in 2018-2019. This program has achieved progress towards a more genuinely diverse group of leaders equipped to honour the Society's mission and history as it works to become a contemporary, innovative and sustainable movement.

Ten young Vincentians from around the country were accepted to participate in the EYL pilot, which commenced in July 2018 and ran until December 2019. The program provided governance training, but also took a holistic approach to leadership development. It included experience in reflective leadership practice, change management, program design and business case development, as well as some elements particular to the Society. The latter encompassed Vincentian values-based leadership, mentoring and a grounding in the challenges facing the Society in our region and around the world.

The participants undertook extensive pre-work, and participated in training from the Australian Institute of Company Directors and the Australian Institute of Management. This training was then grounded in the context of the Society in Australia through an open forum with current SVDP leaders. The participants were enabled to reflect on their individual objectives for their Vincentian journeys and matched with senior Vincentian mentors, selected on the basis of participants' EYL objectives. Throughout the program participants were brought into contact with the international elements of the SVDP and they grew in their understanding of the social services mission as a whole.

CatholicCare Tasmania Housing Projects

CatholicCare Tasmania, through its housing arm, Centacare Evolve Housing, has approximately 2,000 properties under management and provides a home for over 6,500 Tasmanians. Importantly, it realises that disadvantage cannot be addressed just with housing, and so has created partnerships with other Catholic agencies and parishes, Government and local communities to build housing and, at the same time, provide 'wrap-around' and 'integrated' support and connections that can create positive change for a community. CatholicCare has developed a social impact approach to work across seven holistic domains: housing, health, economics, education, safety, spirituality and community engagement. Its aim is not only to build bricks and mortar housing stock but, more importantly, to provide homes for particularly vulnerable cohorts. The focus is to work with other partners to improve individual, family and community wellbeing. Addressing the housing crisis in Tasmania has meant working across both transitional and more permanent accommodation options.

Social impact initiatives require dedication and time if they are to be successful. In particular, in place-based responses to need, there is a requirement to understand local issues and amplify the strengths that exist in communities. This has underpinned CatholicCare Tasmania's successful housing projects. With their 'wrap-around' and 'integrated' support and connection to parishes, they have opened up life-changing accommodation to many in Tasmania. It is important for people who are involved in such initiatives to participate actively in the community, shop at the local supermarket, walk around the local community and be a part of the conversations the community is having in order to gain trust, identify need and respond adequately. CatholicCare Tasmania's housing projects are a logical culmination of utilising its expertise, in partnership with others, to give practical life to the mission of Jesus.

The Catholic Alliance for People Seeking Asylum (CAPSA)

In 2014 Cabrini Health and Jesuit Social Services formed a partnership that would establish a mode of advocacy for people seeking asylum. It was envisaged that the initiative would be able to draw on the wider Catholic community in Australia for support. Thus, CAPSA was formed, brought together twelve national Catholic bodies as an advisory group, and gained financial support from many more organisations, especially religious congregations.

CAPSA has worked to build a movement of awareness, grass roots advocacy and institutional pressure on government for a more humane approach towards people seeking asylum. The alliance has established a national platform to connect and grow a movement of thousands within the Catholic community who advocate for people seeking asylum, and have organised multiple petitions, events and national weeks of prayer and action across Australian Catholic schools, hospitals, parishes and other organisations.

In 2019 CAPSA arranged for a group of Australian Catholic leaders from across the country to visit Papua New Guinea as an expression of solidarity with people there who are seeking asylum, to support the local Papua New Guinea Church and to inform continued advocacy. In Australia, CAPSA has organised many meetings with Members of Parliament and continues to provide a strong and united Catholic voice to further public campaigns regarding the rights of people seeking asylum and of refugees.

SECTION 2

Courage and Compassion in Action

Putting Courage and Compassion into Action

Jocelyn Bignold, Vincent Long Van Nguyen OFM Conv and John McCarthy with Patrice Scales

Introduction

While the values of courage and compassion underpin much of the work of Catholic social service organisations, the "Putting Courage and Compassion into Action" panel at the Catholic Social Services conference highlighted specific cases of these attributes at work in our organisations and the Church.

The panel chair, Joshua Lourensz, Executive Director of Catholic Social Services Victoria, introduced the three speakers, Bishop Vincent Long Van Nguyen OFM Conv of Parramatta in Western Sydney, Chair of the Australian Bishops Commission for Social Justice, Mission and Service; Jocelyn Bignold OAM, CEO of McAuley Community Services for Women; and John McCarthy QC, Chair of the Anti-Slavery Taskforce in the Archdiocese of Sydney.

In his introduction to the session, Lourensz noted that, with a CEO, a chairperson and a bishop on this panel, participants would hear about courage and compassion through three frames of Catholic social service work. And, he highlighted, all who serve in our organisations "stand on the shoulders of others who have gone before us", and this session was another link in the chain as we collectively build on traditions established and lessons learned.

Jocelyn Bignold: McAuley Works

Lourensz introduced Jocelyn Bignold and warmly congratulated her on the recent announcement of her well-deserved Order of Australia medal. McAuley Community Services for Women[1] supports women and their children who seek safety from family violence by providing 24/7 crisis support and temporary accommodation. McAuley also provides accommodation and support for women who are homeless, many of whom have experienced family violence. Lourensz invited Bignold to address the conference on McAuley's employment program called McAuley Works.

If you were experiencing family violence, if you were living in fear of your life, if your actions were being controlled, would you be out looking for a job? If you were not being paid fully for the work that you were doing, would you still do it?

This project is primarily about courage, but compassion features strongly too. I want to address one aspect of the work of McAuley Community Services, our women's employment program called McAuley Works.[2] McAuley Works is currently funded through Jobs Victoria and has one of about 50 such Victorian Government-funded contracts. The Victorian Government has a responsibility to vulnerable Victorians and they were not getting the service that they needed from the national system, Jobactive. Our agency is a family violence and homelessness response organisation. It is very unusual for a family violence support or-

---

[1] Details of McAuley Community Services for Women can be accessed at www.mcauleycsw.org.au/.

[2] For further information on McAuley Works, see www.mcauleycsw.org.au/our-work/employment-support/.

ganisation to have an employment program. We have not seen a similar approach elsewhere in Australia in terms of an employment program matched with a family violence response.

Our contract specifies two payable outcomes, and we get paid on milestones. The first payable outcome is the number of women we have placed in jobs, and the second is the number of women who achieve 26 weeks of paid employment for no less than 15 hours a week. We are not paid unless we can prove these outcomes.

We have 350 participants currently signed up across Victoria. This number represents the number of women who want to work and have sought the assistance of McAuley Works. We get five referrals every week. We do not advertise. We currently have 101 women placed in employment. Thirty-three of these women are placed in employment for which we do not get paid, so they are unclaimable. There have been 39 payable outcomes to date which means we are way behind our contract requirements to have 100 employed and meeting the Government's criteria by now.

Over 90 per cent of the women with whom we work have experienced, or are experiencing, family violence. That is not to mention the fact that they might have a disability or a mental illness, speak English as a second language, live in a rural area, have no access to a car or some or all of these factors combined. None of those things are taken into consideration in the program funding. We are behind on our outcomes and we are under constant pressure to achieve the goals that we said we would achieve. And this is where our courage waivers. Under the pressure of that contract, we thought we might need to say "no" to some women whom we thought were just never going to get a job. So, we undertook an analysis which is summarised in Table 1.

Table 1: Analysis of Participants in the McAuley Works Program

Severity of Family Violence	Employability Readiness					Total people
	Poor 5	Challenged 4	OK 3	Good 2	Excellent 1	
Minimal	2	3	2	0	0	7
Minor	1	3	1	0	0	5
Moderate	6	12	6	3	1	28
Major	6	2	5	0	0	13
Critical	3	6	5	0	0	14
Total people	18	26	19	3	1	67

The matrix in Table 1 analyses characteristics of participants in the program. It shows, along the top row, an employability rating. A 'poor' rating means a client is unskilled, unqualified with no specific experience, has not held a position in more than 18 months, and/or is not fluent in English. Women in this group may also have a diagnosed mental illness and a learning disability, as well as not being located in proximity to employment, and having limited opportunities to access public transport. The rating at the opposite end of this scale is 'excellent'.

Down the left-hand side, we have a family violence rating ranging from 'minimal' – where a family violence incident has not occurred in the last 12 months, to 'critical' – where the participant requires immediate protection. We then plotted outcomes for all the women whom we had placed in employment under this program.

At that time there were 67 in employment and we rated them against the two scales of employability and susceptibility to family violence as presented in Table 1. Then we thought, "So now, who do we focus on, who do we exclude?"

We found to our astonishment that most of the women who were placed in employment were in the darkly shaded zone; that is they were rated moderate to critical on the family violence scale, and poor to average on the employability scale. These were the women who were getting jobs!

At that time, 46 women were placed in jobs in that extreme zone, and 15 more were in the lightly shaded zone, with an average employability rating. Importantly, this matrix does not take into account all the other factors that might be going on for women in their lives. Thus, the analysis showed us that we were working with the right group of people: the women who wanted to get jobs.

Out of this, we figured that the x-factor – the factor that was not reflected in our matrix – was their determination, their courage to get a job. So, we had to keep going, while not being very well paid to do so, I have to say.

We could see there are difficulties in the target group. One is the time that it takes to place them in employment; then they have to keep the position for the requisite period. For example, women whose location is discovered by a violent partner have had to abandon their job to go to a refuge, and are not able to complete the 26 weeks continuous employment. In other instances, women have chosen not to give us evidence they have got a job because they say, "Great, thanks McAuley. Got my job. I'm out of here. I don't want to see you ever again". That is what we want but, in fact, we have been penalised for it. We have been told that our program is empowering women to get their own job because we do it differently as we are not a placement service. We work behind them; we help them get their own jobs. When they are off to their interview, we are sitting in the car waiting for them to finish, and have a cup of coffee with them afterwards. "Okay", we say to them, "if you didn't get that job, let's go for the next one". In effect, we are penalised because we are empowering women.

To sum up, we know that this work does pay for itself from an economic point of view. We engaged Deloitte Access Economics to analyse 30 case studies, because we knew that what we were doing was right. The Deloitte estimates were conservative. Its analysis indicated that over 85 per cent of the 30 case studies demonstrated a positive or equal return on investment. It said that this was – and I am going to quote this comment because I like it: "an astonishing result for clients as vulnerable as those included in the study. Some of the most vulnerable in Victoria with high and complex needs starting their journey with McAuley with no income, no job, mental health concerns, trauma and escaping family violence".[3]

---

[3] For details of the findings, see www.mcauleycsw.org.au/value-of-mcauleys-work-confirmed-by-deloitte/.

To finish, when we talk about courage and compassion: the women have it in spades. It is service providers who are the ones that sometimes 'wobble at the knees'!

John McCarthy: Anti-Slavery Taskforce

In introducing John McCarthy, Chair of the Anti-Slavery Taskforce, Lourensz noted that the Anti-Slavery Taskforce arose out of the Archdiocese of Sydney's commitment to participate in the Catholic Church's response to end modern slavery. Lourensz pointed out that the fact that Australia has a robust sector dedicated to the eradication of human trafficking and modern slavery, and has legislation in effect to combat modern slavery[4] is due to countless hours of work by the Taskforce and many other organisations. He mentioned in particular ACRATH, Australian Catholic Religious Against Trafficking in Humans,[5] which since 2013 has mobilised members of religious orders in Australia around this cause; some ACRATH members also participated in the conference.

I am pleased to address you on a subject about which I am most passionate, modern slavery and human trafficking. This is a great cause where the Catholic Church in Australia is on the front foot, and a cause in which I believe that you will see victory in your lifetime.

The continuing existence of slavery in its modern forms requires a critical 'health check' on our globalised world. Human trafficking, slavery and slavery-like practices involve the exploitation of people, and use violence, threats, false promises, manipulation,

---

4 *Modern Slavery Act 2018* (Cth).
5 For information on ACRATH and its "People are NOT for sale" message, see https://acrath.org.au/.

abusive power and other forms of coercion for the profit or gain of someone else. Put simply, it is about taking someone's freedom.

Eradication of modern slavery is about overcoming a cruel injustice. Supposedly, modern slavery is illegal everywhere, but tens of millions of people are trapped in factories, fields, fisheries, mines, on construction sites, on ships, in private homes and in many other workplaces. It is estimated there are around 40.3 million people in the world in some form of modern slavery: in forced labour, in forced marriage, and in production of ordinary goods and services in the economy. According to the Global Slavery Index, 15,000 of these victims are estimated to be in Australia.[6]

Some slaves are held in physical captivity; many are kept in 'prisons without walls'. All of them are producing and providing goods and services for those who wield power and control, or satisfying the constant supply and demand of a culture that is driving our global economy. They are the living embodiment of the chilling observation: cheap goods, cheap labour, and cheap sex.

What about ourselves? The truth is that slavery touches the lives of most of us every day through the supply chains of the goods and services we purchase. Do you own a telephone or a computer, clothing, shoes? Do you drink coffee or tea? Do you wear jewellery or make-up? Do you buy seafood, pet food, meat, fruit, vegetables, or eat fast food?

I am afraid you and I cannot deny that we benefit from the exploitation of other human beings, in a large part because they are invisible to us. Today the risk that a product or service is tainted with slave labour somewhere in the supply chain occurs in almost all industries. From electronics and high-tech industries, to automotive, steel, mining, agriculture, coffee, seafood products. The list is almost

---

6 Information on the Global Slavery Index 2018 and Australian statistics can be accessed at www.globalslaveryindex.org/2018/findings/country-studies/australia/.

limitless. All countries are affected. So, too are the supply chains of the Catholic Church and its institutions and agencies in Australia. Modern issues, such as welfare, immigration, defence and tax, divide public opinion across the world. But, in the case of modern slavery, agreement is total. All 193 United Nations member states have committed to eradicating child slavery by 2025, and all modern slavery and forced labour by 2030. That is our Government's policy; that is our Church's policy. That is what we want – eradication of modern slavery. We, as citizens and taxpayers, must all start demanding that of our governments and keep reminding them about it constantly.

There is a mandate in Catholic social teaching in relation to the eradication of modern slavery and human trafficking, and an urgent need for all Catholics, and indeed for all Catholic institutions, to take steps to bring freedom to those enslaved.

The election of Pope Francis to the Chair of Saint Peter in March 2013 has proved to be momentous for the anti-slavery movement in the contemporary world. He is perhaps the greatest anti-slavery advocate in our world today. From Rome, over the past seven years, the Church and the world have heard a constant flow of statements and exhortations from the Holy Father in respect of the eradication of modern slavery and human trafficking.

In 2013 Pope Francis declared human trafficking to be an open wound on contemporary society, a scourge on the Body of Christ, and a crime against humanity. In 2014 he pledged, with other global religious leaders, to work collectively to bring each faith community together to rid the world of the affront to human dignity and defilement that is human trafficking and modern slavery. In 2015 the Holy Father was more than the inspiration in the adoption of Goal 8.7 of the Sustainable Development Goals,[7] which demands

---

[7] United Nations, October 2015. "Transforming our World: The 2030 Agenda for Sustainable Development"; accessed at https://sustainabledevelopment.un.org/sdgs.

immediate and effective action to eradicate forced labour and human trafficking by 2030.

Pope Francis is firm and consistent in his strong conviction that we will be victorious over modern slavery and human trafficking. He exhorts the contemporary world and the contemporary Church to provide the collective will and organisation to defeat modern slavery in all its manifestations in this generation. That is us: you and me. Without a doubt this is one of the great and most inspiring visions of freedom in our world.

How has Australia responded to this challenge? In March 2017 Archbishop Anthony Fisher OP of Sydney went before the Parliament of New South Wales and pledged that there would be a program directed towards the eradication of modern slavery in the supply chains and life of the Archdiocese. And he, in that way, demonstrated that he believed that what Pope Francis wanted was clear. In proposing action in his own Archdiocese, Archbishop Fisher stated:

> It is not enough for groups such as churches to lecture or exhort the rest of the community in such matters [as modern slavery and human trafficking]. We must demonstrate our own willingness to act where we can. The Vatican has already committed itself to slavery proofing all its procurement practices and supply chains. It is no small task to ensure everything we use has been obtained ethically, that everything we obtained has been produced and supplied ethically and sustainably, and that those upon whom we rely and with whom we are affiliated are like-minded. It is no small task, but we must try.[8]

---

8 Archbishop Anthony Fisher OP, 2017 in Catholic Archdiocese of Sydney website, n.d. "Modern Slavery"; accessed at www.sydneycatholic.org/solidarity-and-justice/anti-slavery/modern-slavery/.

Pope Francis has pointed out that buying goods is not just a commercial matter. It has moral dimensions. To drive change, Archbishop Fisher established a taskforce of which I have the honour to be the Chair. The Taskforce produced a report for him on the risk of exposure to modern slavery and human trafficking in the supply chains of the Archdiocese of Sydney. The report also proposed a supply chain anti-slavery strategy, an ethical purchasing strategy, an anti-slavery education and external engagement strategy, anti-slavery welfare services, and an ethical investment policy. This represents a significant Catholic anti-slavery response to the Australian Parliament's *Modern Slavery Act 2018* (Cth) (the Act), which requires large Australian entities in all sectors, including religious organisations, to prepare Modern Slavery Statements reporting their actions against the risk of modern slavery in their supply chains and operations.

In another major Catholic response to the Act, in 2019 the Sydney Anti-Slavery Taskforce convened a national conference of representatives of dioceses, community services, healthcare agencies and school commissions. ACAN, the Australian Catholic Anti-Slavery Network,[9] was formed in response to the recommendations of this conference and 36 participating Catholic agencies have now pledged to report on their anti-slavery activities.

For everyone in the anti-slavery cause, it is well to remember that St Josephine Bakhita, the patron saint of modern slavery victims (who was canonised by St John Paul II in 2000), was herself a slave. On St Bakhita's Day 2020 (8 February), Archbishop Fisher received a letter from the Hon Jason Wood MP, the Australian Government Minister administering the Modern Slavery Act, commending the Archdiocese of Sydney and the Anti-Slavery Taskforce in relation to the work that the Catholic

---

9 Information on the Australian Catholic Anti-Slavery Network can be accessed at www.acan.org.au.

Church is doing against modern slavery, both in Australia and internationally.

To date, in the Archdiocese of Sydney, there is an ethical purchasing scheme, Shop for Good, which is taking root in parishes, to enable the purchase of ethically sourced products by parishes and parishioners.[10] Further, Sydney Catholic Schools is sponsoring anti-slavery programs in Archdiocesan Catholic schools.

Let me conclude with the following. I am a grandfather. In April last year our youngest and third daughter had her third daughter who was born on Easter Saturday. Our daughter and her family live in Connecticut. That little girl will never be a slave, and all the work that we contribute may result in achieving the situation that other little girls and boys born on the same day will also avoid slavery. What we are talking about, and what the Pope wants, is that our generation works to eradicate modern slavery now and for all time to come. We must not have another generation in which the misery of slavery continues to exist.

The most famous quote in the whole of the anti-slavery cause is that of William Wilberforce in a speech to the British parliament in 1792 when he outlined much of what was wrong and dreadful and appalling about slavery. He turned to everyone in the House of Commons, as I turn to you, and said:

> You may not do anything about it, but never again can you say you did not know.

Bishop Vincent Long Van Nguyen OFM Conv: Refugees and Asylum Seekers

The final speaker on the Courage and Compassion panel was Vincent Long, Bishop of Parramatta in Western

---

10 Shop for Good Resources can be accessed at www.sydneycatholic.org/solidarity-and-justice/anti-slavery/shop-for-good/.

PUTTING COURAGE AND OMPASSION INTO ACTION

Sydney and chairperson of the Bishops Commission for Social Justice, Mission and Service. Lourensz introduced Bishop Vincent by commenting on his work on behalf of refugees and asylum seekers, and in supporting the work of many social service organisations including the Brigidine Asylum Seekers Project, the Jesuit Refugee Service and the Catholic Alliance for People Seeking Asylum.

I am very privileged to be at this national conference of Catholic Social Services whose mission I am particularly close to by virtue of my personal interest, as well as my being chair of the Bishops Commission for Social Justice, Mission and Service. As you know, I am also a former boat person and the issue of people seeking refuge and asylum becomes rather personal for me. I consider it my vocation to tell people that the vulnerable wanting to have a dignified life, wanting to have a better future for themselves and their children, should not be simply seen as a burden or a liability to our society. Rather, if they are welcomed here, they can and they do indeed become great contributors to and builders of our nation.

The public discourse in this country on asylum seeking is still very toxic, characterised by demonisation and the fear of the other, the outsider. And I think it pertains to us to change that discourse, to change the political narrative into something more positive, a narrative about the courage and the determination and the drive for a better future.

The experience of the Vietnamese refugees is clear evidence that even the most traumatised group of people can be integrated into our multicultural society and can make a positive contribution. The fear that our social cohesion might be undermined or that our very future might be compromised has largely been proven unfounded. Today, Asian Australians have joined mainstream Australia in every aspect of our society. Our nation has evolved to become a much more dynamic, diverse and prosperous nation. To be sure, each group presents its own challenge to Australia, and yet we have consistently risen to the challenge and become more enriched, more diverse as a result.

I contend that Australia fails to live up to our best tradition as a generous, compassionate society and we demean ourselves when we adopt harsh policies towards refugees and asylum seekers. It pains me to witness the dismantling of our country's long-held tradition of welcoming migrants and refugees. That tradition has been enshrined, even in our national anthem: "For those who've come across the seas we've boundless plains to share".

Pope Francis is not afraid of calling out systems that drive oppression and exploitation. And unless the systems are recognised, exposed, confronted and dismantled, fundamental change will not occur. The change we need goes beyond national interests. And Francis pointed out, the system, or the systemic and structural change we need, is what he called the globalisation of hope. The globalisation of hope is the hope that springs from people and takes root among the poor and must replace the globalisation of exclusion and indifference.

As we know, Pope Francis does not only talk the talk, he also walks the walk. He puts courage and compassion into action doing very unpopular things. For example, he went to Lampedusa, an island that is Italy's equivalent of our Christmas Island, at a time when the socio-political climate in Europe had turned against migrants, especially Muslim African migrants. The Pope's action provoked strong and fierce criticism, even from his own flock. It almost amounted to a kind of existential risk. This risk, associated with the fights in favour of God's justice for the poor, places one in a liminal place, a place where the Christian leader bears prophetic witness as he speaks words of hope.

I endeavour to follow Pope Francis' lead in advocating for asylum seekers and refugees. I have been privileged to take part in many public events for asylum seekers and refugees, Palm Sunday rallies, public demonstrations, forums and face-to-face meetings. Last November I went with a delegation of Catholic leaders, including our conference convenor, Joshua Lourensz, to meet some of the asylum seekers who had been transferred from Manus Island to Port Moresby. We wanted to show our solidarity and support to these, our fellow human beings. And there was an incident which I thought highlighted the kind of demonisation and fear that is so embedded in our anti-refugee, anti-asylum seeker culture.

We gathered in front of a so-called immigration facility built by the Australian Government and located in Bomana, which is just a few miles from the capital Port Moresby. We formed a circle and we linked hands and prayed outside the prison where some of the asylum seekers were kept in a deplorable environment. Ten minutes or so into the course of our action, an Anglo-Celtic person emerged out of the facility and gave orders to the local staff to ask us to leave, even though we were simply praying in front of the facility, an area which was devoid of people and in quite an isolated location.

This is the kind of response that is driven by fear. And yet I believe that it is for the sake of the vulnerable, the oppressed, that we, as Christian people and Christian leaders in particular, must be involved for the long game. It is not simply about the end of a policy in a certain area. But it demands that we witness to the gospel of life and dignity as we continue to be advocates for a world, a society, that is in accordance with the Gospel.

Conclusion

The Courage and Compassion panel showed three elements of Catholic social service at work in the contemporary Church.

Each of the presenters highlighted problems and issues facing our community that we, as Catholics and providers of social services, cannot ignore. They each spoke about the steps that their organisations, the Catholic Church itself and ordinary Catholic Australians are taking, to give dignity and power back to the most disadvantaged, vulnerable and enslaved of our brothers and sisters.

Through the presentations of the panel, conference participants heard about the compassion that motivates organisations and individuals to strive for fairness and equality for those whom we serve. Compassion to provide work opportunities for vulnerable women; compassion to strive to eradicate modern day slavery; and compassion to join in solidarity and prayer with incarcerated asylum seekers. And it is courage – the courage to find a job in the most difficult circumstances; the courage to speak up for a Modern Slavery Act and eradication of contemporary slavery; and the courage to be a visible presence for incarcerated asylum seekers – together with compassion that brings the greatest hope in the work of Catholic social services.

The Centrality and Challenge of Child Safety

Maria Harries and Robyn Miller[1]

Introduction

> If in ten years' time, you have every policy and procedure in place, and you meet every mandatory standard, but you do not have a genuine culture of safety then you will fail. What we have seen over the decades is that bad culture breeds bad conduct. (Robert Fitzgerald,[2] 21 March 2018)

Building communities and cultures that are safe for children! This is unarguably what all adults should do, and all public policy and practice should support and sustain such a critical imperative. On the other hand, it is evident we adults have failed, and continue to fail, in this very human requirement in multiple ways. Despite the centrality of the requirement, there remain numerous challenges.

Keeping children safe from the inevitable environmental hazards in our natural and built-up worlds has been a concern of families, communities and public policy initiatives over generations. However, keeping children safe from intentional harm caused by adults who should be caring for them has only become an increasing preoccupation in recent years – particularly since the 1960s when Kempe raised the alarm about the 'battered child syndrome' that he had observed and researched in a hospital

---

1 This chapter is based on a workshop presented by Professor Maria Harries AM, Chair of Catholic Social Services Australia, and Dr Robyn Miller, CEO of MacKillop Family Services, at the 2020 Catholic Social Services conference.
2 Robert Fitzgerald AM served as one of the Commissioners of the Royal Commission into Institutional Responses to Child Sexual Abuse.

setting. What Kempe highlighted[3] was that children were being harmed by those who were meant to care for them – family and friends as well as 'strangers' entrusted with their care. Central to this chapter is the knowledge of the complicity of clergy and laity in our Catholic institutions entrusted with the care of children who abused that trust, and the imperative we now share to ensure child safety and assist in the healing of victims.

Since the 1960s, reports on the abuse of children throughout the world have escalated exponentially. Most of these reports relate to children who have been unintentionally impacted by the adversities facing their families and communities. Poverty, mental illness, family dislocation, domestic violence, racial discrimination loom large as vectors herein. In addition, there are the intentional harms – terrible things done purposively to children. Of the intentional harms, few are more repugnant and traumatic than sexual abuse of children. The immediate and long-term impacts of child sexual abuse are myriad, toxic and debilitating and lead to incalculable morbidity as well as mortality and untold mental health consequences in later life.[4]

Child sexual abuse includes all forms of sexual activity of an adult with a child who is below the age of consent or non-consensual activity between minors or any sexual activity between a child under 18 years old and a person in a position of power or authority (e.g. parent or teacher). While the incidence (occurrence) of child sexual abuse internationally is apparent and significant, its prevalence (amount in the population) in Australia

---

3 C.H. Kempe, F.N. Silverman, B.F. Steele, W. Droegemueller and H.K. Silver, 1962."The battered-child syndrome", *Journal of the American Medical Association*, 181, 17-24.

4 P.E. Mullen and J. Fleming, 1998. "Long-term effects of child sexual abuse" (Issues in Child Abuse Prevention No. 9). Melbourne: Australian Institute of Family Studies; accessed at www.aifs.gov.au/nch/pubs/issues/issues9/issues9.html.

and worldwide is not known and is hard to determine. It remains evident that most of such abuse is perpetrated by family members or people in communities who are known to children or families. Whatever the amount of abuse or the nature of its perpetrators, it is a destructive blight that we must all fight to eradicate. Those in service organisations have a particular responsibility to ensure our organisations are places of safety and that we are alert to the insidiousness of this crime and the devious artfulness of perpetrators within our institutions and within the communities in which we and our children live.

The Royal Commission into Institutional Responses to Child Sexual Abuse[5] has had a pivotal role in Australia in 'wrenching open' the sordid history of hidden historical sexual abuse within institutional settings; enabling survivors to testify to their experiences and the consequences of this abuse; forcing individuals and systems to face their responsibilities and abuses of power; and creating opportunities and requirements for institutions to ensure as much as is possible that safety from sexual abuse is a paramount legal and institutional obligation.

The authors of this chapter have worked in child and family welfare services and child protection services for over eighty years collectively and were involved in various ways with the Royal Commission. We reflect on the significance of the Royal Commission findings and how these and other learnings might assist us in building a community that is safe for children, in the community at large and within Church institutions. Included in the chapter are comments made and issues raised by participants at the 2020 Catholic Social Services conference workshop.

We commence with a brief background to the Royal Commission

---

5 The Royal Commission into Institutional Responses to Child Sexual Abuse ran from 2013-2017; see www.childabuseroyalcommission.gov.au/.

and its processes and include in this the contribution of the Catholic Church in particular. We then provide some of the findings of the Royal Commission which are relevant, albeit familiar to most of us. Central to these findings is the culpability within our own Church for the sexual abuse of children and vulnerable adults. We highlight some of the recommendations made by the Royal Commission and describe the response of the Church so far in terms of healing, redress and ensuring safety in our services. Finally, we reflect on the responsibilities we have as church agencies for prevention as well as intervention within our institutions and in the broader communities within which we work.

The Royal Commission

In November 2012, Prime Minister Julia Gillard announced the creation of a national royal commission into institutional responses to instances of child sexual abuse. She said the commission would look at "all religious organisations, state care providers, not-for-profit bodies as well as the responses of child service agencies and the police".[6] The Royal Commission into Institutional Responses to Child Sexual Abuse commenced in January 2013. The Truth Justice and Healing Council (TJHC) was established by the leadership of the Catholic Church to co-ordinate the Church's response to the Commission, to help develop the Church's reform agenda and to act as the public voice of the Church during the life of the Commission.

The daily revelations during the Commission continuously alerted a shocked public to the pain and suffering of far too many children – now adults – and the culpability of institutions in the ongoing denial of the sexual abuse of children over generations. Our Catholic Church was unremittingly present as an institution

---

6 The Prime Minister's speech is accessible at www.abc.net.au/news/2012-11-12/gillard-launches-royal-commission-into-child-abuse/4367364.

whose leaders had been complicit in much abuse and, tragically, in managing reputational risk, had placed the interests of the Church ahead of the interests of children and vulnerable adults. The Commission delivered its *Final Report* in December 2017.[7] Fifty-seven public hearings and over 8,000 private sessions were held. Four hundred and nine recommendations were made – all aimed at making institutions safer for children. All the recommendations of the Royal Commission were examined by the TJHC and advice provided to the Church leadership.

The findings of the Commission are too numerous to list. Apart from providing overwhelming evidence of the failure of our Church and other institutions to protect children and the courage as well as the continuing suffering of victims, there were important consistencies in the data:

- The proportion of allegations that were estimated to relate to an institutional context were similar across all jurisdictions.
- From the data gathered, it remains impossible to estimate definitively the incidence of child sexual abuse in Australia:

  However, these estimates are at this stage very tentative, due to the vast discrepancies in reporting rates for child sexual abuse in different jurisdictions, the exclusion of key institutional categories and the likelihood that reports to police under-estimate the actual incidence of abuse.[8]

- While the reports of sexual abuse within an institutional context were overwhelming, it accounted for only a small percentage in the incidence of child sexual abuse. The best available

---

7 For the Royal Commission's *Final Report*, see www.childabuseroyal-commission.gov.au/final-report.
8 L. Bromfield, C. Hirte, O. Octoman and I. Katz, 2017. *Child Sexual Abuse in Australian Institutional Contexts 2008–13: Findings from Administrative Data.* Sydney: Royal Commission into Institutional Responses to Child Sexual Abuse, p. 14.

indicators for institutional abuse produced national estimates of somewhere in the order of 5 per cent of all cases of recently reported allegations of child sexual abuse. This would provide an estimated annual overall total of around 400 to 600 allegations of recent child sexual abuse in an institutional context.[9]

Denial, Trauma and the Response to the Royal Commission

One of the saddest aspects of the Churches response to the brave children and adults who came forward and tried to disclose sexual abuse was the denial, minimisation and scapegoating of the victims. It is also true, and documented in the Royal Commission records, that many good people in the Church have given just, sensitive and inclusive support and validation. However the Commission found that the dominant culture was one that further wounded survivors and their families by excluding them by a cold rejection and misguided loyalty to the institution – where the reputation of the Church and the protection of clerics was the priority, not the protection of children or the prevention of further harm.

The hypocrisy and shameful denial of Gospel values has alienated many from the Church. Judith Herman, a renowned expert on sexual abuse and other trauma, writes that in the aftermath of traumatic events the care and comfort of significant others and the community is the basis of recovery:

> Trauma isolates; the group recreates a sense of belonging. Trauma shames and stigmatises; the group bears witness and affirms. Trauma degrades the victim; the group exalts. Trauma dehumanises the victim; the group restores her humanity.[10]

---

9 Ibid.
10 J.L. Herman, 1992. *Trauma and Recovery: The Aftermath of Violence.* New York: Basic Books, p. 214.

The importance of cultural and familial connections is widely documented in the trauma, attachment and family therapy literature. Miller and Dwyer[11] have written about their work with families following intra-familial sexual abuse and documented the importance of engaging the non-offending parent/s in a believing and supportive response as a critical component to the young person's recovery.

The theme of social connection, belonging and attachment mediating the adverse effects of trauma is pervasive in the research and clinical literature, and intuitively makes sense to us as human beings. Bessel van der Kolk,[12] a renowned researcher and clinician in the trauma field, has stressed we are mammals. We are biologically programmed to connect; our social services must be places of safe connection that value the rights of children to be treated with respect and, if they are harmed, respond with justice and compassion.

It is also worth noting that while the Commission was heavily critical of governance within the Catholic Church, favourable commentary was made about the governance and professional standards of the Catholic social service organisations which appeared before the Commission. Of this mention, our social services should indeed be proud. Importantly, we are now in a position to build on some solid foundations. How do we now combine our efforts to keep children safe?

Child Safe Institutions

What defines an institution that provides safety for children? Enormous efforts involving policy makers, survivors, researchers, pro-

---

11 R. Miller and J. Dwyer, December 1997. "Reclaiming the mother-daughter relationship after sexual abuse", *Australian and New Zealand Journal of Family Therapy*, 18(4), 194-202.
12 B.A. van der Kolk, 1999. "Trauma and memory: Psychobiological processes and therapeutic interventions". Workshop presentation in Melbourne.

fessionals, families and numerous other advisers have contributed to models now in place. These are loosely defined as institutions that create cultures, adopt strategies and take action to prevent harm to children, including child sexual abuse. A preoccupation with the requirement to define and establish child safe institutions has tracked alongside the work of the Royal Commission and continues unabated. We have adopted the definition of a child safe institution given by the Royal Commission, as one that:

- consciously and systematically creates conditions that reduce the likelihood of harm to children,
- creates conditions that increase the likelihood of identifying and reporting harm,
- responds appropriately to disclosures, allegations or suspicions of harm.[13]

Not the least of these organisations working to ensure our institutions are safe for children has, of course, been Catholic Professional Standards Ltd (CPSL). The significance of this initiative cannot be underestimated. The Church's official response to the Royal Commission recommendations[14] mentions CPSL on 164 occasions and notes that CPSL is responsible for the implementation of 60 actions which address recommendations of the Royal Commission. A continuing commitment by the Church and its services to an independent CPSL is foundational to the safety of children and the re-establishment of trust in the integrity of our Church. We return to describing the structure and work of

---

13 Royal Commission, 2017. *Final Report*, Vol. 6: *Making institutions child safe*, p. 12; accessed at www.childabuseroyalcommission.gov.au/.

14 Australian Catholic Bishops Conference and Catholic Religious Australia, August 2018. "Response to the Royal Commission into Institutional Responses to Child Sexual Abuse"; accessed at www.catholic.org.au/acbc-media/media-centre/media-releases-new/2139-acbc-and-cra-response-to-the-royal-commission/file.

this entity when we discuss the response of our Church leadership to the Royal Commission findings.

Child Safety and Learnings from the Royal Commission

One of the many key findings of the Royal Commission was that poor institutional culture both enabled the perpetration of abuse and prevented abuse from being disclosed:

- Children who complained were punished, disbelieved or accused of lying, with no further action taken.
- There was failure to enforce and educate staff on existing child protection policies.
- There were systemic failures to protect children in the institution through recruitment and staff training.
- Leaders actively denied responsibility for the abuse that occurred and worked to insulate the institution from outside threats.[15]

Some key learnings for all of us in relation to the above are apparent and important if we are to ensure the safety of children in the times we are in and the times ahead.

The agency culture and leadership at every level is key to creating a safe environment for children. The integrity of the adults whom we recruit and trust to care for our community's most vulnerable children forms the basis of our human services. Our most important leaders are those who are closest to the children and families and there must be a culture of brave conversations if there are concerns at any level.

Leaders must be present and energetically engaged and motivated to have the rights of children as the basis of all practice. How do we walk our talk? Strong presence, leading by example

---

15 Royal Commission, op. cit. n.13, pp. 148-149.

and a commitment to competence and best practice are so critically important. Equally, professional humility and a culture of critical reflection that evaluates outcomes, is in our view a necessary basis so that we remain open to what we do not know. We need to embed a learning culture that strives for best practice, creativity and innovation despite the insufficient resources, overwhelming demand and 'wicked problems'. Therefore, holding the line on our values and on good practice has to be visible.

The evidence is in: relationship-based practice is key to healing from trauma and abuse. It is the quality of the relationship which the professional forms with the child and family that is the single greatest determinant of a good outcome. We need to recruit very carefully and understand that sexual predators can be as skilled at grooming selection panels as they are at grooming children. We cannot be naïve and think that a Working with Children's Check and a diploma/degree makes everyone suitable. Sex offenders will be attracted to working wherever they have easy access to vulnerable children. They usually have very good 'relationship skills' and are expert groomers, winning the trust of children, their parents and the other team members. Any boundary violations need to be taken seriously as offenders will often test the strength of the agency's procedures and child safe standards by grooming those around them to ignore the bad behaviour or rule violations, "because he was such a nice guy". The Royal Commission's case study on the YMCA employee Jonathan Lord is a 'must read'.[16]

Listening to children and young people's disclosures and putting them first, before the reputation of the organisation, are critically important if we want genuinely to consider ourselves a

---

16 Royal Commission, 2014. *Report of Case Study No. 2: YMCA NSW's response to the conduct of Jonathan Lord*; accessed at www.childabuseroyalcommission.gov.au/.

competent and ethical service focused on safety as well as healing. If we truly adhere to Catholic social teaching and living out Gospel values in our services on the ground, every single day, it requires enormous commitment and the smartest systems. These systems of supervision, professional development, performance management, work health and safety, and regulatory oversight along with good governance across the back of house and all programs, are critical to ethical practice. We need agencies that are both warm and welcoming, strength-based and forensically astute.

The Response of the Church

Despite initial disbelief, struggle and indeed resistance on the part of so many clergy, church leaders and members of the faithful, our Church along with most others has now acknowledged their toxic failings in relation to the extent and the denial of child sexual abuse within their institutional jurisdictions. Two comments by Catholic leadership stand out and testify to both shame and promise. These are from Archbishop Mark Coleridge and Richard Lennan SJ, respectively:

> I think the Church has failed lamentably and therefore we have to cop whatever criticism comes our way, deal with it in a way that doesn't cause paralysis and paranoia but does prompt us to action.[17]

> The manifold losses that survivors have endured and the scandal brings into stark relief the need for a change in direction and the need for 'cultural conversion' – in all organisations … We are in a time of change in the Church.[18]

---

17 M. Bowling, 2020. "Archbishops head to Rome for high-level meetings", *The Catholic Leader*, Archdiocese of Brisbane; accessed at https://catholicleader.com.au.

18 R. Lennan, 2019. "Beyond Scandal and Shame? Ecclesiology and the Longing for a Transformed Church", *Theological Studies*, 80(3), 590-610.

In the context of this chapter, four important decisions were made by the Church post the Commission findings:

- acceptance of the recommendation of the TJHC to establish an independent standard setting and monitoring entity for the Catholic Church – instituted as Catholic Professional Standards Ltd (CPSL),
- endorsement, support and engagement with a national redress scheme which enabled survivors to seek redress that limited future trauma,
- establishment of the Independent Advisory Group (IAG) – an advisory body to influence and monitor the Church's response to the Royal Commission and its recommendations,
- a review of governance and management of dioceses and parishes. This review committee was commenced in May 2019 under the chairmanship of Chief Justice Neville Owen, the former TJHC chair. The Governance Project Team had six panel members (including three women) and delivered its report to the Australian Catholic Bishops Conference (ACBC) and Catholic Religious Australia (CRA) in mid-2020.

The endorsement of the redress scheme and the establishment of the other three entities provide a pivotal axis for coordinating a new and trustworthy future for a Church, its services and its people. Explicit in this quartet is the understanding that we have learned and will continue to learn from the appalling nature of past failings, help redress some of the pain and suffering, assist survivors in healing, and commit to new standards of child safety and governance The importance of the latter governance review is highlighted in the comments of Sr Monica Cavanagh RSJ, then President of CRA:

> The Royal Commission uncovered some practices that could have exacerbated the abuse of children and hampered

the response to that tragic reality. The establishment of this panel is another step in our serious response to the Royal Commission and will help establish a way forward for the Church into the future.[19]

Child Safety and Catholic Professional Standards

The continued pursuit of all the objectives within the four responses of the Church named above are vital for the future of our services, their value, authenticity, integrity and efficacy. Of the four, the one that is central to this chapter is, of course, that of the establishment of CPSL. The fact that it was pivotal to the implementation of 60 actions addressing recommendations of the Royal Commission, makes it central to the response of the Church too.

CPSL was established in 2016 by the ACBC and CRA as an entity that is independent of the Church to:

- set safeguarding standards to ensure the safety of children and vulnerable adults who engage with the Church at any level anywhere in Australia;
- provide training and support to enable Church authorities, entities, organisations, ministries and anyone involved in the Church to create a culture of safety for everyone;
- support the Church to build a culture of safeguarding;
- audit the compliance of Catholic entities, organisations, and ministries in accordance with the standards; and
- publicly report the results of those audits.[20]

---

19 Catholic Religious Australia, 1 May 2019. "Respected leaders named to conduct Church governance review in response to the Royal Commission", media release; accessed at www.catholicreligious.org.au/.
20 CPSL, n.d. "About CPSL"; accessed at www.cpsltd.org.au/media/1473/cpsl-brochure-general-information.pdf.

The chart (Figure 1) below captures the objectives and complex work of CPSL.

Figure 1: CPSL Service Model (2019, reproduced with the kind permission of CPSL)

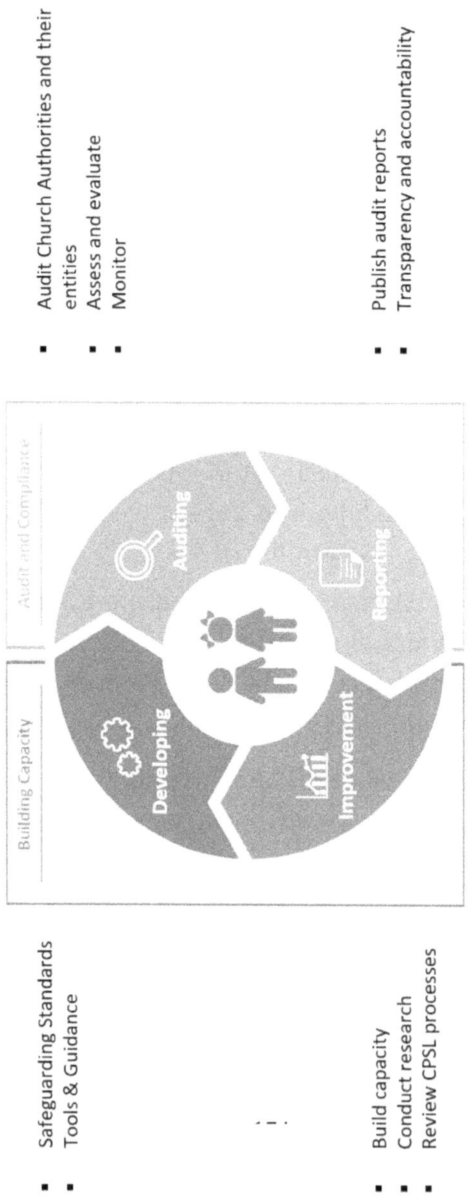
Audit Church Authorities and their entities
Assess and evaluate
Monitor
Publish audit reports
Transparency and accountability
Audit and Compliance
Auditing
Reporting
Building Capacity
Developing
Improvement
Safeguarding Standards
Tools & Guidance
Build capacity
Conduct research
Review CPSL processes

Following a comprehensive process of consultation, the National Catholic Safeguarding Standards were developed and finalised by CPSL and adopted and published in May 2019.

These standards apply to everyone involved in any capacity within the Catholic Church – bishops, leaders of religious institutes and other Church authorities and to the services and ministries they oversee, including parishes, schools, social services, health and aged care services, and all other Church agencies.

Governance Reform and Child Safety Standards

It is patently evident from the findings of the Royal Commission and their analysis, that complex transformations are required within the Church and our community if we are to reform our systems and our ways of thinking and working in order to ensure the safety of children and all vulnerable people. It should not have taken a Royal Commission to show us the truth about the systemic failures in recent and contemporary workplaces that have claimed to be dedicated to care and safety, but it did. As already noted, the Royal Commission found that poor governance practices contributed strongly to the failure to protect children and respond to concerns of abuse.

Good governance involves ensuring all arrangements, structures, policies and mechanisms within institutions are accountable and that, at every level, their people are held to account. Most Catholic social services have been refining their governance structures in recent years. We now know reform leadership is critical at every level of service and governance – even for those organisations that figured they have 'nailed it'.

The reforms in Victorian child and family services in the past 15 years created a rich context for identifying key elements of organisational leadership, resulting in the development of the

Seven C's of Reform Leadership.[21] The Seven C's include: commitment, collaborative leadership, critical reflection, congruence, coherence, champions and community (Figure 2). These elements of the Seven C's are interconnected, making a contribution individually and collectively to organisational change. Importantly, cultural reform requires multiple and concurrent actions to achieve change that will improve and sustain the safety of our children within our institutions and prevent sexual abuse and exploitation.

The Seven C's of Reform Leadership

Commitment

Reforming children's services and our Church culture requires an intentional and enduring commitment to change. As Connolly and Smith[22] note, leaders need to appreciate that embedding change takes time – five to seven years according to some writers.[23] Building partnerships in the change process, where communication and trust develops over time, is important. Reserves of energy are often required to work through issues when there is conflict and/or criticism; here leadership involves perseverance and commitment to remaining positive over the long haul. This includes balancing the day-to-day demands of busy services with inadequate funding, with the ongoing embedding and sustaining of the reform effort.

Commitment is also required to the integration of research into practice, and the development of knowledge-based practice

---

21 R. Miller, 2014. *Promoting cultural reform in Victorian child protection and family services through the Best Interests Case Practice Model*, PhD thesis. Melbourne: La Trobe University.
22 M. Connolly and R. Smith, 2010. "Reforming child welfare: An integrated approach", *Child Welfare*, 89(3), 13.
23 B. Lonne, N. Parton, J. Thomson and M. Harries, 2009. *Reforming child protection*. London: Routledge.

Figure 2: The seven C's of reform leadership

frameworks, including ethical approaches "that can help workers navigate their way through the murky relational dimension of practice".[24] Knowledge frameworks also need to demonstrate a commitment to the rights of children and families, and to models of continuous improvement where the views of service users are both sought and considered in the development of services.

Collaborative Leadership

According to Head and Alford,[25] collaboration helps to address "wicked problems" when "there are multiple parties with differential knowledge, interests, or values". This is certainly the context within which child protection operates, and collaborative leadership has the potential to inspire and authorise reform. It supports the sharing of information and power, and builds collaboration into

---

24 M. Connolly and K. Morris, 2012. *Understanding child and family welfare: Statutory responses to children at risk.* London: Palgrave MacMillan.

25 B.W. Head and J. Alford, 2015. "Wicked problems: Implications for public policy and management", *Administration & Society*, 47(6) 711-739.

governance processes, advocating for resources, and collectively evaluating reform efforts. Collaborative leadership engages staff across the organisation creating a sense of 'one team' and fosters meaningful partnerships across the sector. Functional collaborations across sectors create a "collaborative advantage", that better understands the problems, promotes the possibility of finding 'provisional solutions', and creates a stronger context for good implementation through coordinated actions and shared contributions. As Agranoff notes, it is rare for one organisation to have the monopoly on solutions – collaboration provides a richer solutions context when collaborative relationships are strong.[26]

Critical Reflection

The importance of critical reflection has been identified strongly in the child protection and social work literature now for some time[27] and supervision has been identified as a site for critical reflection.[28] Critically reflective leaders bring a further dimension to the role enabling a deeper understanding of the problems at both the practice and policy levels. Organisational policies and practices can have unexpected consequences that are not always helpful in providing good outcomes for children. Reflective leaders review the system's policies and responses to ensure that they are not creating or maintaining problems. Reviewing practice outcomes becomes

---

26 R. Agranoff, 2007. *Managing within networks: Adding value to public organizations.* Washington, DC: Georgetown University Press.

27 C. Morley, 2014. *Practising critical reflection to develop emancipatory change.* Surrey, UK: Ashgate; E. Munro, 2011. *The Munroe review of child protection: Final report – A Child-Centred System.* UK: The Stationary Office Limited, p. 17; M. Jones, 2004. "Supervision, learning and transformative practices" in N. Gould and M. Baldwin (eds), *Social work, critical reflection and the learning organization.* Aldershot: Ashgate Publishing.

28 R. Egan, J. Maidment and M. Connolly, 2016. "Supporting quality supervision: Insights for organizational practice", *International Social Work*, 61(3), 353–367.

part of a reflective learning process that is modelled throughout the system, providing a context of collaborative learning and knowledge sharing across sectors.

Congruence

The demands of a busy child and family service system can create many stressors for frontline workers. Child protection work is unpredictable, and uncertainty often permeates practice. Reform efforts that land on the frontline can seem disconnected – yet another demand that threatens to compromise their day-to-day work. An integrated reform package may not look that integrated to busy practitioners who are faced with implementing new ideas. Connecting the dots between reform strategies, creating a shared language about the reforms, and connecting the reforms to their underpinning evidence base creates a 'big picture' congruence that will make better sense to the workers on the ground. Seeing how the reform efforts fit together in ways that benefit children and families has the potential to engage and motivate the organisation to embrace and embed change.

Coherence

Connected to the notion of congruence, coherence is about being logical and consistent in the messaging relating to organisational vision, strategic direction and reform. A child safe organisation needs to have coherent strategies that make sense and provide consistent messaging and actions. Waves of reform effort can create reform fatigue, and workers will not expend their precious energy reserves on change that is transient. Multiple reform efforts – particularly when they lack coherence – can also undermine external confidence in the organisation. Promoting a coherent and consistent reform agenda will have benefits within and outside the organisation.

Champions

John Maxwell suggests that if you really want to build an organisation's potential, then you need to focus on growing leaders.[29] Identifying people who share a commitment to the promotion of cultural reform and have the capacity to lead is essential. Trying to control everything from the top fails to harness the rich contributions of people at all levels of the organisation. Champions who positively influence reform efforts, who resolve disputes and find creative local solutions, are critically important to successful change at the local level. It is the role of the transformational leader to inspire, enable and empower champions to influence local engagement in ways that create local dialogue and action.[30]

Community

Developing communities of practice – like-minded people who are inter-dependent in achieving good outcomes – can really support collaborative reform agendas in child protection. Communities of practice have become a means through which organisations and groups can improve their performance. In essence, "communities of practice are groups of people who share a concern or a passion for something they do and learn how to do it better as they interact regularly".[31] Within the child protection context, and guided by the broader vision, they can become multi-disciplinary and inclusive professional networks that support and inspire the effort required for reform. They can close the policy, research and practice gaps through intentional dialogue, shared understanding and mutual support that specifically target the achievement of change on the ground. Relationships across traditional research, policy and

---

29 J.C. Maxwell, 2013. *How successful people lead.* New York: Centre Street.
30 Head and Alford, op. cit. n. 25.
31 E. Wenger-Trayner and B. Wenger-Trayner, 2015. *Communities of practice: A brief introduction*; accessed at http://wenger-trayner.com/wp-content/uploads/2015/04/07-Brief-introduction-to-communities-of-practice.pdf.

practice silos create strong networks of support and energy for the change effort, potentially generating sustained buy-in at all levels of the organisation.

Although we have presented seven C's of reform leadership in this chapter, it could easily have been 8 C's – with the inclusion of Compassion. Managing change and developing responsive systems requires the kind of compassionate leadership that is attuned to the interests and needs across the system: the needs of vulnerable children and families, the needs of workers who strive to mobilise change in the face of significant pressures, and the needs of systems that are subjected to waves of criticism and challenge.

We need practitioners who will provide innovative responses to the needs of children and families, who will challenge oppressive systems, and who develop reflective practice skills. We need practice leaders and supervisors who will create the kind of environment within which innovative practice thrives.

The Challenge of Child Safety: Standards Are Not Enough

As Robert Fitzgerald stated so cogently, if you "have every policy and procedure in place, and you meet every mandatory standard, but you do not have a genuine culture of safety then you will fail". Almost all organisations facing inquiry within the context of the Royal Commission, claimed to have policies and standards in place. Most had them: however, most of their frameworks were also found to be insufficient, not contemporary and even dangerously outdated, un-utilised, un-audited, dismissible. In some instances, they were absent.

An appealing assumption is that establishing, following and auditing standards for compliance provides the complete answer to previous failures and guarantees child safety. Certainly, such standards are necessary, and they need to be continuously updated and compliance needs to be constantly checked. Standards are necessary but they are not sufficient in themselves. Policies and practices in our Church and its services and elsewhere have been found to have failed abundantly. The culture of child safety that needs to accompany a massive cultural shift in our thinking and practice, requires more than best practice, and monitored standards that undergo compliance testing. The menaces of predatory grooming, artfully concealed abuse and avoidance of reputational damage have emerged as toxic factors within our clerical Church culture but are undeniably not limited to the clergy.

Child sexual abuse within our community as well as our families and institutions is a scourge still to be adequately confronted. Among the many corrosive 'intruders' that subvert standards are individual pathology and malevolence, power, greed, privilege, fear and systemic biases associated with matters such as gender, race and class. These corrosive intruders are all easily concealed. What needs to change in addition to meeting standards is culture!

Organisational culture is variously described. Essentially, it comprises the values, behaviours, beliefs and shared vision, that inform the policies and relationships within any organisation or community, including families. As Edgar Schein sagely observed over thirty years ago, "it is what decides the way individuals interact with each other".[32] Much earlier, the British anthropologist Edward Tylor described culture more comprehensively as "that complex whole which includes knowledge, belief, art, morals, law, custom, and any other capabilities and habits acquired ... as a member of society".[33] Given that organisational culture involves a complex

---

32 E. Schein, 1985. *Organizational Culture and Leadership.* San Francisco, CA: Jossey-Bass.

33 E. Tylor, 1871. *Primitive Culture: Researches into the Development of Mythology, Philosophy, Religion, Art, and Custom*, Vol. 1. London: John Murray, p. 1.

web of relationships between individuals, it is evident that cultural change requires us to pay attention at multiple levels. Individuals enter organisational cultures with their own preconceptions, cognitive distortions, beliefs and customs. We are often not aware of our own internal processes, let alone those of the people within our work cultures.

It is easy to point the finger at others in our organisational past who have failed to report abuse they have witnessed or believed had occurred, or who have claimed not to have been aware of such abuse or breaches of codes of conduct, let alone standards of practice. Despite the best of standards and the best of intentions, there are multiple ways that each of us can avoid being aware of such organisational risks and misconduct. It is easy to conspire inadvertently with unhealthy cultures and not to allow ourselves to see what is wrong, let alone to decide not to report wrongdoing. We all know the price paid by whistleblowers. Human reasoning is often frail.

There are many ways of categorising errors in human reasoning that potentially get in the way of objectivity let alone discernment of abuses and misconduct. In his powerful recent treatise on judgment and decision-making, Kahneman observes "the mental work that produces impressions, intuitions, and many decisions goes on in silence in our minds".[34] Cognitive dissonance makes it hard to see what we cannot believe. It is easy to be seduced by a culture in which one plays safe and keeps one's job! Power imbalances are a feature of all organisational life and power plays are rife in human relationships – public and private. Group think is a feature of all community life, that is, our need for harmony and cohesion often leads to a tendency to agree with each other at all costs.

Referring specifically to errors in human reasoning that lead to

---

34 D. Kahneman, 2011. *Thinking Fast and Slow*. London: Allen Lane, p. 4.

the failure to detect and report child sexual abuse, Munro and Fish identify three major failings:

- *Confirmation bias*: Once we have formed an opinion, we are slow to revise it; we are more likely to notice evidence that supports it and overlook or interpret ambiguous evidence in a way that confirms rather than challenges our opinion.
- *Representativeness heuristic*: This entails assessing people or objects based on their similarity to the standard for that category. Most people working in children's services are caring and well-motivated in their actions towards children ... The default position is to think well of a new colleague.
- *Hindsight error*: Once we know what happened, we overestimate how obvious it was (or should have been) to those involved at the time.[35]

It is important to be reminded that these errors in reasoning are not simply historic ones attributable to past offenders and miscreants. Along with the others noted previously, these reasoning errors are potential features of all decision-making and operate 'in silence' amongst the stakeholders as organisations establish and monitor standards. To aspire to a "genuine culture of safety" we need to remain alert to the challenges that are present in leading real change; to generate a culture that invalidates gender biases; to create an alertness driven by the voices and wisdom of the children and young people themselves; to build trust alongside critical reflection; and to be prepared to be open to the scrutiny of others without defensiveness.

As noted earlier, the responsibilities for prevention as well as intervention within our institutions that we have as Church

---

35 E. Munro and S. Fish, 2015. *Hear no evil, see no evil: Understanding failure to identify and report child sexual abuse in institutional contexts.* Sydney: Royal Commission into Institutional Responses to Child Sexual Abuse, pp. 18-25.

agencies do not stop at the door of our agencies as we accept and conform to child safe standards. By far the greatest extent of child sexual abuse occurs within families and, increasingly, in the community. Our children are now particularly vulnerable to grooming via social media. Our responsibility to be vigilant in relation to abuse and responsive to the children, families and broader communities within which we work provides another set of challenges.

It will take all of us involved in Catholic human services to ensure the safety of children and other vulnerable adults in the years ahead. We are all called to discern for the change that heals and makes a real difference for the vulnerable. In his 2018 *Letter to the People of God*, Pope Francis said:

> It is impossible to think of a conversion of our activity as a Church that does not include the active participation of all the members of God's People. Indeed, whenever we have tried to replace, or silence, or ignore, or reduce the People of God to small elites, we end up creating communities, projects, theological approaches, spiritualities and structures without roots, without memory, without faces, without bodies and ultimately, without lives … This is common in many communities where sexual abuse and the abuse of power and conscience have occurred.[36]

How are we to avoid the risk of complacency, keep remembering where we have failed, remain vigilant, maximise the opportunity to adopt and follow state-of-the-art standards and keep central the challenge of child safety?

We must, of course, diligently monitor all standards. That is, however, not enough. Sr Nuala Kenny MD is a Canadian paediatri-

---

36 Pope Francis, 2018. *Letter to the People of God*; accessed at www.vatican.va/.

cian who was involved in the 1989 inquiry into the scandals of clerical sexual abuse in Newfoundland. She has worked with survivors and written evocatively about the crisis of child sexual abuse within the Church and of the need to work differently to avoid blindness to the past and passivity in the future. We finish with her words of advice on how to proceed. Eloquently, she suggests we need:

> A long and available memory
> A sense of pain and loss
> The active practice of hope
> An effective mode of discourse.[37]

---

[37] N. Kenny, 2012. *Healing the Church: Diagnosing and Treating the Clergy Sexual Abuse Crisis.* Toronto: Novalis.

Advancing Dignity and Equality within the Framework of the NDIS

Gabrielle McMullen with Helen Burt and Anne Kirwan

The National Disability Insurance Scheme (NDIS) is an Australia-wide policy reform introduced under the *National Disability Insurance Scheme Act 2013* (Cth) to enable people with disability to receive the care and supports that they need and to choose who will provide the services. The NDIS website states:

- National: The NDIS is being introduced progressively across all states and territories.
- Disability: The NDIS provides support to eligible people with intellectual, physical, sensory, cognitive and psychological disability. Early intervention supports can also be provided for eligible people with disability or children with developmental delay.
- Insurance: The NDIS gives all Australians peace of mind [that] if they, their child or loved one is born with or acquires a permanent and significant disability, they will get the support they need.
- Scheme: The NDIS is not a welfare system. The NDIS is designed to help people get the support they need so their skills and independence improve over time.[1]

---

1 NDIS, n.d. "What is the NDIS?"; accessed at www.ndis.gov.au/understanding/what-ndis.

This statement reflects the Government's vision for the NDIS. But what is the reality 'on the ground'? In particular, what role should Catholic agencies play in delivering the NDIS?

The 2020 Catholic Social Services conference addressed these questions in a workshop entitled "Advancing Dignity and Equality within the Framework of the NDIS". The first presenter was an NDIS provider; the second an NDIS client:

- Anne Kirwan, who has held the position of Chief Executive Officer of CatholicCare Canberra and Goulburn since 2014 and led her organisation's participation in the NDIS,
- Helen Burt, policy adviser, who worked for over 30 years in the community sector, mostly in faith-based organisations. Due to a progressive illness, she now uses NDIS services and, at times, undertakes advocacy around disability-related issues.

The workshop was chaired by Tony Hollamby, who has had over 20 years experience at the executive level in the health and disability sectors and, in his most recent role, led St John of God Accord through the transition to the NDIS. His background enabled Hollamby to inform the discussion following the two presentations.

Joining the NDIS

Under the leadership of Kirwan, CatholicCare Canberra Goulburn (CCCG) participated in the trial period for the NDIS and now has six years of experience in its delivery. In her presentation, Kirwan shared CCCG's learnings to assist other agencies with their programs. She noted that her presentation would be "organisation-centric" while that by Burt would be "consumer-focused".

Prior to the introduction of the NDIS, disability care had been a major component of CCCG's services, representing 50 per cent of its funding, and CCCG was considered a large provider in the

Australian Capital Territory (ACT). It had been estimated that there were 5,000 people in the ACT eligible to participate in the NDIS (it was later established actually to be 7,000). CCCG commenced significant planning and Kirwan stated: "We were just so excited, and we thought, finally, this is it. This is going to actually help people and be a more equitable system for people".

While some Catholic agencies withdrew from disability care due to the challenges posed by the NDIS, CCCG was of the view that the fundamental principles of the scheme[2] and the purpose of the National Disability Insurance Agency (NDIA),[3] the statutory body implementing the NDIS, "align with what we believe and what we wish to deliver". Kirwan stated:

> ... our agency values guide us and define who we are. Human dignity is central and, in fact, respect is one of our organisational values ... And my personal position is that the Catholic Church has taken a position around a commitment to families of people with disability. Therefore, I believe Catholic agencies need to remain in the market despite how difficult it is.

Implementing the NDIS

In relation to its introduction, in the trial phase, Kirwan spoke of "the NDIS tsunami". That terminology reflects the pace of change as well as its very different service and funding model. CCCG had an NDIS implementation plan, building on its 'brand' and predicated on its belief that "people would get the funding that they needed to have their needs met". Ultimately, it hoped to be able to expand its services to address unmet needs in the regional areas of the Archdiocese of Canberra and Goulburn, which extends hundreds of kilometers north-west from Canberra, and, in the

---

2 *National Disability Insurance Scheme Act 2013* (Cth), Section 4.
3 Ibid., Section 118.

opposite direction, to the New South Wales south coast and the Victorian border.

CCCG started to move its approach from services previously funded through program grants to individual NDIS packages and discovered that its fixed costs related to rostering, management, the 24 hour-on-call service, training, supervision and quality assurance were too expensive. The NDIS funding model allowed for only nine per cent of funding to be used for such infrastructure. Further, whereas under the earlier scheme, funding had been provided to the agency in advance, now funding is provided in arrears, once specified criteria have been met, creating a cashflow problem.

CCCG took the decision to utilise reserves to maintain necessary 'backroom' services but it still had to cut management positions by 25 per cent, corporate positions by 50 per cent and case management (as distinct from case worker direct service provision) positions by 80 per cent, which impacted severely on staff morale. Further, with skills shortages in the ACT, maintaining the 'right' staff, who were matched to the new system and CCCG values, was challenging. Human resources had to be up-skilled in change management and finance staff in client interaction, aligned with the CCCG mission and values. Kirwan said: "The constant message is staff have to do more with less". She highlighted an element of the contrast between the pre- and post-NDIS services as follows:

> ... families who called in three times a week to organise their six or 10 hours of care suddenly ring in and there isn't a case worker ... case worker loads used to be about eight families per full-time worker. Now the case loads are upwards of 30 families per worker. And that's because they're paid in case management hours and have to generate a certain number of hours per fortnight to cover their salary.

To reduce its exposure and underpin its overheads, CCCG sought to increase its other care services and reduce its disability services to 40 rather that 50 per cent of its operations. Kirwan advised: "But actually what happened was ... an increase in referrals and more and more business came CCCG's way ... it almost doubled in client numbers, but the income stayed the same. So, it gives you an indication of how things changed in that market". Other ACT agencies had to close down. CCCG had to stop rolling out services into regional areas, due to their additional travel costs. With the increased focus on resourcing disability care, Kirwan noted:

> What you hear from your staff is, 'all management cares about is money' ... But it's very frustrating because the real challenge is first of all, trying to protect your staff so that they aren't aware of the struggles that are happening back of house. They need to be in the homes providing great quality care to people.

Kirwan stressed that for the CEO the most important thing is "to get your board on board". Board directors need to share the mission-driven commitment to "stay in this market despite how difficult it is" and, at least in the transition phase, be willing to commit reserves and/or other resources to NDIS implementation. A good management team is also critical. CCCG estimates that it is going to take about ten years for the NDIS market to settle down. While it is a very difficult environment in which to operate, gaps in the ACT and other markets have emerged, which create some opportunities.

Mission versus Margin

A real challenge is 'mission versus margin'. CCCG seeks to prioritise person-centred services but must do so in challenging circumstances:

you will lose good staff and you will lose good families. People will get frustrated or they will decide they can't work in that environment and they will leave, and you have to understand that. We have lost some amazing families during this six-year transition and we need to learn from that.

... we had a discussion in our organisation around dignity. Every human being is worthy of time and respect. So, if you look at the fundamental purpose, nothing has changed in terms of how we're approaching people in our care. It's just all the back of house stuff that has changed ... in terms of dignity, clients and families have the right to say who comes into their home, when and what they will do while they are there ... We've seen in the NDIS over the last six years more and more clients and their families have a voice to say that they like this staff member or they don't want this person back. I think that's a fantastic outcome ... And dignity is about clients being able to spend time with their families as families, not as carers. And the ability to have control in decision-making, and the fact that commitment to the dignity of all has to come from all areas of the organisation, including CCCG's 'backroom' staff.

Significantly, CCCG's corporate services are also immersed in delivering the NDIS – for example, finance staff "have to contact, communicate and engage with clients. So, it's a big change". Kirwan advised that increased use of technology to enhance communication has been key in building relationships with clients and their families.

Daily work with clients has not changed. Staff still go out into the homes, and "deliver the best quality care that they can ... staff are responsive". Kirwan asked: "Has culture changed? ... I think if you asked the staff, they would say, 'for sure'. But is that a bad thing?"

Kirwan identified four key issues to be addressed by those entering provision of services under the NDIS. How do mission and margin interact in relation to:

- client choice and control, and is that actually being delivered,
- dignity for people with a disability,
- respect, and
- quality?

CCCG would say the Government has not yet got it right. It is still underfunding the NDIS and, as a result, people are cutting corners. Kirwan concluded that it is not yet being delivered as envisaged.

Kirwan stated that there is opportunity for growth and innovation; you need to be "nimble" and have "a mix of services" – for example CCCG has just opened its second art studio for artists with a disability, and also has a lifestyle hub delivering cooking classes and teaching living skills. CCCG offers independent living, which includes shared accommodation and individual one-on-one support, and provides accommodation for people with an acquired brain injury. Many clients have co-morbidity conditions, some of which are addressed through CCCG's other services, including those relating to drug and alcohol dependence, mental health, aged care, speech therapy, psychological assessment, and gardening and home maintenances.

Kirwan offered advice to agencies proposing to be an NDIS provider. The "ingredients to success", she said, are "get the right people in the right seats, get rid of underperforming and toxic staff ... Set expectations", empathise with and support staff and their professional development, and monitor progress and effectiveness of services in the context of changed internal and external environments. Further, she advised:

You've got to expect complaints to go up, not only

because people are empowered, but also because of all the changes that are happening ... but it's a good way to know what's actually happening on the ground. You need to be an organisation that's open to risk-taking, and prepared to invest, and see whether that will deliver a new and sustainable service.

Kirwan's concluding message was: "If you believe that the provision of quality services to people with a disability and their families is a calling of your organisation, something that you want to do ... you've got to hang in there and work your way through it".

Hopeful Vision for a Better NDIS[4]

Helen Burt

A vision of equality and dignity inspired the NDIS, which was introduced in Australia on 1 July 2013. Developed by the amazing work of people with disabilities, their families and supporters, moulded by the Productivity Commission, and finally embraced by the Australian community and Parliament, the NDIS is a major social reform that offers people with disabilities the chance to move forward, claim their rightful place in society and live out their human potential.

Community supports for people with disabilities evolved over many hundreds of years, reflecting attitudes to difference and the social systems for managing poverty. It was only in the 1970s that Australia saw large institutions that had developed in the early years of the colonies begin to close. For many people, life in an institution was replaced by life on the streets, or a regimen in group

---

4 This contribution by Helen Burt draws heavily on her article that was originally published on 10 February 2020 in *Eureka Street* and is reproduced with the kind permission of the magazine's editor; see www.eurekastreet.com.au/article/hopeful-vision-for-a-better-ndis. That article also formed the basis of Burt's presentation at the conference workshop.

homes, which replicated institutional life. It took many years for governments to realise that despite being housed in the community, people with disabilities were often not part of the community, or able to achieve their goals and potential.

An adequately resourced support system based on the individual needs and aspirations of Australia's people with disabilities, whether they be physical, intellectual or psycho-social, has taken nearly 50 years to establish and will probably take even more time to implement fully and consolidate.

Prior to the NDIS, formal supports for people with disabilities were fragmented, poorly funded, and an inequitable service system, based firmly on an outdated welfare model. The NDIS as proposed turned this on its head, promising a national, universal system allowing people with disabilities themselves choice and control over their services – what is needed, and how, when and where it is provided. This vision is clearly alive, even while the reality is very much a mixed bag.

My personal experience, during the first 18 months of involvement with the NDIS, was disappointing, frustrating and particularly deflating for someone who had written submissions and emailed politicians and understood the potential of the scheme. My only contact seemed to be with an immovable, impossible-to-navigate bureaucracy determined to stand in the way of me receiving any of the support that I was promised.

I am now in my second year as a part of the scheme, and the NDIS is beginning to offer me the sort of transformative support originally envisaged. 'Small things', such as access to the support services I need for a few days holiday (something that had not been possible since I have been in a wheelchair); and 'big things', which will change my life by giving me the opportunity to live in an apartment adapted for my needs.

Even while I celebrate these changes for my life, I am acutely aware that I am one of the lucky ones. Not everyone will enjoy such life changing opportunities. Benefitting from the scheme depends on who and where you are, and where you started from in the system. As an educated person living in an urban area, I am in pole position. Despite this, it was not until my second plan was done that I obtained significant benefits in my life. By this time, I had a supportive and knowledgeable team around me, knew what to ask for, and what would lead to tangible benefits.

Unfortunately, many people are unable to get access to the NDIS at all. The following picture also shows great inequality, even among those who become NDIS participants:

> There is an emerging and troubling picture that some people get good plans while others, particularly from marginalised groups or communities are left with poor quality plans, with limited access to supports and services that are included in their plans.[5]

There is much to criticise about the current operation of the NDIS. Most prominently, there is the failure of the scheme to live up to its potential as a universal, accessible and coherent service system able to decrease disadvantage among the lives of people with disabilities, particularly those whose disability intersects with broader social disadvantage.

I remain hopeful that a proactive focus on access and equity, along with a determination to rid the organisation of unnecessary

---

5 People with Disability Australia, November 2019. Submission to the Tune Review; accessed at https://pwd.org.au/submission-to-the-tune-review-of--the-ndis-act/. For the review report, David Tune, December 2019. *Review of the National Disability Insurance Scheme Act 2013: Removing Red Tape and Implementing the NDIS Participant Service Guarantee*, see www.dss.gov.au/sites/default/files/documents/01_2020/ndis-act-review-final-accessibility--and-prepared-publishing1.pdf.

regulations and bureaucracy will see the NDIS take its place among the great Australian social reforms.

Issues for the Sector

Following the two workshop presentations, the discussion was wide-ranging and informed by the experiences of the attendees, who were from a diverse range of agencies. Issues raised included the hourly rate that those working in this demanding sector are paid under the NDIS and the consequences thereof. A speaker said:

> ... the fact that our staff can earn more at [supermarket] Aldi than they can providing care in people's homes is a disgrace. There's no pathway there for people to progress, promotion, training, education, ... our constant position is they need to increase the hourly rate to ensure that we can guarantee quality services, that our staff are supervised, that they are trained in medication management, restrictive practice, all these obligations that we need to meet. Quality comes at a cost.

Another contribution focused on how different the new NDIS system is and the resulting challenges of attracting quality staff, when "they're underpaid, we're understaffed" and the number of funded hours does not equate with providing the level of care required. Then there is the further issue of properly training staff within the constraints of the nine per cent overheads provided:

> ... we can't get the quality of staff we really, really need. We cannot provide the training that we should. Everybody needs to be trained in any NDIS disability, any specialised task, they need to be trained in the specific needs of their clients ... it is really important that we have this forum to express our concerns.

A particular strength of the NDIS is enabling clients to choose services and customise care for themselves. However, it was highlighted that the model fails to recognise the complexity of realising this end and the associated costs. Those in the sector are advocating for an increase in the hourly rate of funding so that it realistically covers the costs of delivering services.

The workshop was advised that a key issue is recognising the 'value' of disability care workers. A comparison was made with allied health workers such as physiotherapists and occupational therapists, who are funded at a substantially higher level. Disability care workers are in people's homes every day, responsible for their clients' care; this is a very different commitment to someone who comes in to provide an occasional 'treatment'. Importantly, incorporating professional services, such as speech therapy, into an agency's services is a way to subsidise other services, because there is a higher margin that "props up day-to-day care and medication management or whatever".

Discussion ranged over waiting periods in being assessed for NDIS support, being given an inappropriate care plan, and delays in having supports approved and/or delivered. The example was given of children with a disability physically outgrowing requested equipment before it is delivered. Those with access to an advocate to accompany them on their NDIS journey are fortunate and more likely to access an appropriate plan in a timely manner. That is part of the back-of-house unfunded work of an agency like CCCG.

Given such challenges, some players have withdrawn from disability care. Kirwan stated: "We would not pull out because it's our mission". It would affect "hundreds of families and children". Kirwan said that a challenge for CCCG in seeking better funding is "I can't bluff the government because I wouldn't really be prepared to follow through, and they would know that". She also noted that for-profit providers in her region are not entering the 'market'. Kirwan likened the change of service delivery in moving from previous block funding to the NDIS to trying to turn around the Titanic with "icebergs everywhere".

Conclusion

The workshop closed with supportive comments in relation to the NDIS intent of supporting people with a disability to have quality of life and greater potential to enter the workforce. Significantly, attendees recounted instances of the still-frequent discrimination of people with disabilities in the workplace. This challenges us as Catholic agencies to work even more diligently towards change.

The workshop provided a forum for informed presentations and open discussions in relation to the roll-out of the NDIS. Such engagement can assist in moving from the current reality of the NDIS to the ideal envisaged for support of people with a disability. With their mission focus on the dignity of every person, Catholic agencies can play a key advocacy role in this journey.

Restorative Justice: Signs of Hope

Patrice Scales with Daniel Clements and Deanna Davis

The Restorative Justice workshop at the 2020 Catholic Social Services conference brought together an engaged group of people seeking to understand the practice of restorative justice and its role in the wider criminal and youth justice environment. The purpose of the workshop was predominantly to understand and reflect on the principles and practice of restorative justice. It also offered insights into the practice of youth justice group conferencing, and of group conferencing in other settings.

Most of the workshop participants were not directly involved in restorative practice in the criminal justice system; however, many participants worked in related areas, such as pastoral care of prisoners, health services to prisoners and Aboriginal health. They brought a fertile and intelligent range of insights, questions and responses to the workshop table.

The workshop was led by Daniel Clements, the General Manager - Justice Programs at Jesuit Social Services in Melbourne.[1] His background and experience have been in social sciences, in the homeless sector, and in the management of programs. Over the last ten years he has worked with Jesuit Social Services on programs for young people and adults who come into contact with the criminal justice system.

---

1 Clements stepped into the role of presenter in place of Genevieve Higgins of Jesuit Social Services and Clint Wardle of CatholicCare Sandhurst, both of whom were unavailable to present due to illness. Their preparation of content presented at the workshop and informing this chapter is acknowledged with gratitude.

Deanna Davis, General Manager, Family and Community Services, Centacare, Catholic Diocese of Ballarat (Centacare), who has a wealth of experience in restorative practice, chaired the workshop. Davis contributed invaluable insights throughout the workshop drawn from the work that Centacare does in youth justice conferencing, diversion and other community youth justice programs across the Diocese of Ballarat.

This chapter draws on the input by workshop participants about restorative practice and group conferencing programs, and elements of the more formal workshop presentation by Clements.

Figure 1: Young People Aged 10-17 in the Victorian Criminal Justice System 2015

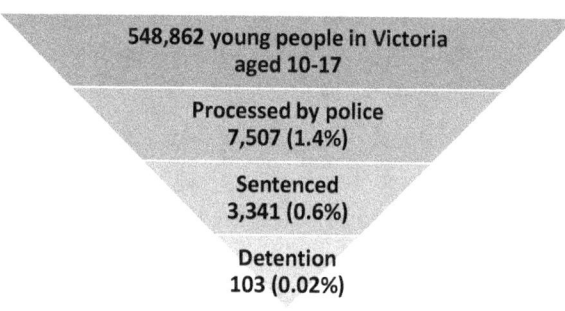

(Adapted from Sentencing Advisory Council, 2016[2])

The Victorian Youth Justice Setting

In introducing the restorative justice setting, Clements referred to Figure 1 to show the number of young people aged between ten and 17 years of age in the Victorian criminal justice system.[3] It shows that 103 young people were in detention in Victoria in 2015, representing 0.02 per cent of those aged between 10 and 17 in Victoria. In the same year, 3,341 young people, or 0.6 per cent

---

2 Sentencing Advisory Council, 2016. *Reoffending by Children and Young People in Victoria*, p. 2; accessed at www.sentencingcouncil.vic.gov.au/publications.
3 Sentencing Advisory Council, 2016, op. cit. n. 2.

Table 1: Young People aged 10-17 Characteristics of Children and Young People in Custody

The results of an annual survey of 166 males and 8 females detained on sentence and remand at Parkville and Malmsbury Youth Justice precincts on 31 December 2018 show:

- 64 per cent had never been subject to a child protection order
- 16 per cent had been subject to a previous child protection order and were subject to a current child protection order
- 18 per cent were previously subject to a child protection order but were not subject to a current child protection order
- 1 per cent were subject to a current child protection order with no previous history of a child protection order
- 67 per cent were victims of abuse, trauma or neglect
- 68 per cent had previously been suspended or expelled from school
- 48 per cent presented with mental health issues
- 27 per cent had a history of self-harm or suicidal ideation
- 38 per cent presented with cognitive difficulties that affect their daily functioning
- 12 per cent were linked with the Forensic Disability Service offered through DHHS
- 4 per cent were accessing NDIS funded disability supports or services
- 7 per cent had a history of alcohol misuse
- 22 per cent had a history of drug misuse
- 54 per cent had a history of both alcohol and drug misuse
- 10 per cent had offended while under the influence of alcohol but not drugs
- 26 per cent had offended while under the influence of drugs but not alcohol
- 43 per cent had offended while under the influence of alcohol, and also while under the influence of drugs
- 25 per cent spoke English as a second language

Further, following completion of the annual survey, it was possible to ascertain the accommodation outcomes of those young people who had participated in the survey and had then been released from custody. Of the young people who had been released from custody, 24 per cent were residing in accommodation other than living with family, relatives or kin, or a residential care or out of home care placement.

(Adapted from Youth Parole Board, 2019, op. cit., n. 3)

of the age cohort, were sentenced, and a total of 7,507, equal to 1.4 per cent of the age cohort, were processed by police, and thus were in formal contact with the justice system. Clements made the point that while these figures were from 2015, there would generally be only minor differences from year to year.

Clements noted that, informed by media headlines, there are often community perceptions of 'gangs on the loose'; 'thugs everywhere'; 'teenage rampage'. "But at the end of the day", said Clements, "about 7,500 young people come into the justice system and the majority of them only touch the system: the police have a conversation with them – and they have a range of options: caution, formal caution – and we never see them again".

A snapshot of the characteristics of those children and young people who are incarcerated is provided in the Youth Parole Board's annual report, and Table 1 shows the results as at 31 December 2018.[4] Some features stand out: 36 per cent were or had been subject to a child protection order; 67 per cent were victims of abuse, trauma or neglect; 68 per cent had been suspended or expelled from school; 38 per cent had cognitive difficulties that affect their daily functioning. This is clearly a very disadvantaged group of young people.

In relation to Indigenous children and young people, Clements noted that Aboriginal and Torres Strait Islander young people in Victoria are significantly over-represented in the youth justice system, at eleven times the representation of non-Indigenous young people – sadly, one of the lowest levels of over-representation in the country. This figure rises to 21 times as likely to be under

---

4 Youth Parole Board, 2019. "Characteristics of Young Offenders", *Youth Parole Board Annual Report 2018-19*, p. 29; accessed at www.justice.vic.gov.au/justice-system/youth-justice/youth-parole-board-annual-report-2018-19.

supervision in Western Australia.⁵ In relation to incarceration, the Victorian over-representation rate remained at eleven times that of non-Indigenous young people, but in Western Australia this soars to an astounding 45 times the rate of non-Indigenous young people.⁶

Victoria, Clements commented, has a reasonably good tradition of keeping children out of the criminal justice system through State-wide diversion programs, and, at two per 10,000, has one of the lowest rates of incarceration of young people within Australia.⁷ But the fact remains that many of those who are incarcerated are from non-English speaking backgrounds – in 2017, 19 per cent of those incarcerated were from an African background.⁸ Most of them are males and many have unique circumstances around settlement and trauma.

Clements added a further introductory reflection. During 2018-2019 there were 34 children aged from 11 to 13 detained in Victoria, around five per cent of the total who were detained. Across Australia, the proportion was twelve per cent.⁹ "We don't believe primary aged children should be locked up. We certainly do not see many of them, but there are some 10-year-old children in our services that we do see. We do know that the younger they touch the criminal justice system, the more likely they are to re-offend later on".

---

5 Australian Institute of Health and Welfare, 2020. "Youth Justice in Australia 2018-19", p. 9; accessed at www.aihw.gov.au/reports-data/health-welfare-services/youth-justice/overview.

6 Ibid.

7 Ibid.

8 Youth Parole Board, 2018. "Characteristics of Young Offenders", *Youth Parole Board Annual Report 2017-18*, p. 21; accessed at www.justice.vic.gov.au/justice-system/youth-justice/youth-parole-board-annual-report-2017-18.

9 Australian Institute of Health and Welfare, 2020. Table S74b "Young people in detention during the year by age, states and territories, 2018–19", *Data Tables: Youth Justice in Australia 2018-19 Supplementary Tables – Detention: S74 to S127s*; accessed at www.aihw.gov.au/reports-data/health-welfare-services/youth-justice/data.

What is Restorative Justice?

> A process whereby all parties with a stake in a particular offence come together to resolve collectively how to deal with the aftermath of the offence and its implications for the future.[10]

> Restorative justice is an approach to justice that focuses on repairing the harm caused by crime while holding the offender responsible for his or her actions, by providing an opportunity for the parties directly affected by a crime – victims, offender, and community – to identify and address their needs in the aftermath of a crime and seek a resolution that affords healing, reparation, and reintegration, and prevents future harm.[11]

As these two definitions indicate, restorative justice asks: what happened, how did it affect you, and what can we do to make things better? It is an approach that takes justice outside the court room. "Restorative justice is a way of doing justice that thinks differently about what justice is", Clements said. "It doesn't shy away from holding people accountable, but it means, in the context of group conferencing, that we have a shared responsibility".

As Davis commented, so many times the young person has no insight into the impact on someone's life or family of something that was intended to be 'a lark'. "The exact purpose of group conferencing is to have that combined discussion around responsibility which seeks to make a difference for both parties".

Restorative justice is a particular form of restorative practice, highlighting the importance of giving all parties a voice in the process and of the acknowledgement by the offender of the

---

10 Tony F. Marshall, 1996. "The Evolution of Restorative Justice in Britain", *European Journal on Criminal Policy and Research*, 4(4), 21-43.

11 Robert Cormier, 2002. *Restorative Justice: Directions and Principles – Developments in Canada*. Ottawa: Public Safety Canada; quotation accessed at www.ncjrs.gov/App/Publications/abstract.aspx?ID=232488.

charges and the damage inflicted. Restorative practice is neither offender-centric nor victim-centric; it is people-centric and this is an important difference.

There is a defined set of principles around restorative practice, whether used in the youth justice system, family conflict, community or school or work settings. These principles[12] are:

- do no further harm
  - facilitate a process that is safe for all participants, meeting the individual needs of young people, families, persons affected by harm, and communities;
- work with, rather than doing things to or for, someone
  - get the right people in the room to help us understand what happened and how people have been affected;
- restore or re-set right relations
  - reduce conflict within people, between people and between groups.

The process is designed to:

- expand the network of people who can provide insight, support and oversight and engage families and carers;
- involve that network of people in truth-telling and problem-solving;
- through truth-telling, transform conflict into cooperation;
- harness that cooperation for problem-solving and then for developing a pragmatic plan to:
  - respond with authority to harm,
  - prevent further harm,
  - promote wellbeing;
- set relations right, restore relationships;

---

12 Australian Association for Restorative Justice, n.d. "Restorative Justice"; accessed at https://restorativejusticeaustralia.org.au/restorative-justice/.

- coordinate resources to provide ongoing support and oversight with a documented plan for moving forward.

Restorative practice has its origins in the practices of First Peoples and fits intuitively within the communities of those people. Restorative practice therefore can be tailored for different cultural groups. Clements further commented that there are many opportunities for using restorative justice, but structures around the justice system and judiciary are a barrier to working restoratively. One participant from Western Australia observed that some Indigenous families have issues around 'shame' and are reluctant to have young people go through a restorative process because of that shame.

Youth Justice Group Conferencing

The *Children Youth and Families Act 2005* (Vic), at s415 (4) and (5), sets out the objective of group conferencing under that Act:

> (4) The purpose of a group conference is to facilitate a meeting between the child and other persons which has the following objectives:
>
> - to increase the child's understanding of the effect of their offending on the victim and the community;
> - to reduce the likelihood of the child reoffending;
> - to negotiate an outcome plan that is agreed to by the child.
>
> (5) An outcome plan is a plan designed to assist the child to take responsibility and make reparation for his or her actions and to reduce the likelihood of the child re-offending.

Those eligible for participation in youth justice group conferencing are young people who have appeared in the Criminal Division of the Children's Court and who have:

- been found guilty of offences that do not include homicide, manslaughter or sexual offences;
- committed offences that warrant a sentence supervised by youth justice;
- consented to participate; and
- been assessed as suitable by youth justice.

Four mandated parties must be involved in a criminal justice group conferencing context: the young person, police, lawyers and a convenor. Clements added that "the process seeks to expand that group to involve anyone who can get to the truth, to help illuminate or shine a light on what is or was happening for that young person, and for the person or family who was harmed to have a voice".

"There is nothing more powerful than having a victim, or a family member of the victim, in the room", said Clements:

> I remember a conference where the victim did not come, but his mother did. She explained that her son's jaw was so badly broken that he had to drink out of a straw for three months. He was too nervous to catch a train by himself and missed months of school. The offender was a big strong guy who had been 'off his face' when he seriously assaulted the young person and had no memory of it. He was in tears at hearing what he had done. So, the victim experience or statement brings the human story and the emotion into the room.

In Davis' experience, it is sometimes difficult and traumatic for the victim to participate in a group conference: "Sometimes they will send a representative to speak for them, or there could be a victim impact statement read by the convenor".

It was also commented that it can be challenging for some members of the police force who have an attitude of 'just lock them up' to be involved in what they might see as a 'soft option' for young offenders. However, Clements noted that, overwhelmingly, once they have been part of group conferencing, they understand the purpose of the process and invariably say: "Yes, I get it now". In regional areas Davis noted that community police can be more engaged and have the capacity to be involved in the process. Once it is understood that the program is actually supporting the victim to have a greater voice and participation, group conferencing makes more sense.

The group conference itself, which may entail quite a large group of people over and above the four mandated parties, is the final step in a process, following a long preparation for everyone involved, particularly the young offender and the victim. At times, the convenor may consider it not appropriate to continue because, for example, the young person does not have an acceptable level of insight into their part in the group conference; or lacks understanding of the crime they have committed, or of the reparation they may be able to make to the victim. In some cases, the process may also be discontinued at the request of the young offender.

Clements reinforced that group conferencing is an extension of the Children's Court; it is not separate to the Court:

> It is a mandated process of the Children's Court and we report back to the Court, to the magistrate, on the nature of the conference, including whether it went ahead or not.

He also drew attention to some of the stark dividing lines within the justice system, and their impact on future wellbeing:

> From my perspective, prisons are dangerous institutions; once a person goes into the prison system, it is as bad as it gets. More than half will go back. So, our view is to do everything we can to keep young people out of the adult justice system.

Group Conferencing in Other Settings

Restorative practice and group conferencing have proven valuable in many other situations including in schools, with families, on pre-release, in the adult jurisdiction, in the community, and in Koori and other culturally specific settings. As in the youth justice system, in these settings restorative practice facilitates a process that creates an opportunity for dialogue between people, groups and a community affected by conflict. It takes a problem-solving approach to the presenting situation and addresses the needs of all participants.

Clements spoke about two Jesuit Social Services' initiatives that use a restorative practice approach. The 'Engage' pilot is an initiative of Jesuit Social Services and the Department of Education and Training (DET) and uses restorative practices to work with students, school staff, peers and family or carers to address conflict in the school setting. It is in place with several schools to deliver safe and effective restorative interventions aligned with the daily operations of the school. The program delivers school-based group conferences with a focus on reducing suspensions and expulsions. Complementing existing DET policies, it works with school communities to promote wellbeing and fosters collaborative approaches to conflict resolution and school inclusion.

The Jesuit Social Services' 'Restore' program is an initiative with the Melbourne Children's Court that offers a restorative practice approach to working with young people who use violence in the home, and family members affected by that violence. Research shows there are many factors which contribute to adolescents using violence against family members,[13] including:

---

13 See, for example, Karey L. O'Hara, Jennifer E. Duchschere, Connie J. A. Beck and Erika Lawrence, 2017. "Adolescent-to-Parent Violence: Translating Research into Effective Practice", *Adolescent Res. Rev.*, 2, 181–198; accessed at https://doi.org/10.1007/s40894-016-0051-y.

- a young person who has a history of or is currently experiencing family violence;
- parenting styles and family dynamics;
- a range of other complex co-occurring problems such as substance abuse, mental health issues, disengagement from education, experiences of loss, neglect or abuse.

The program uses interventions that address more than the adolescent's instrumental use of violence to gain power and control. Therapeutic interventions address other characteristics of adolescent violence such as:

- difficulty in managing emotions like anger and shame;
- obscuring, minimising, distorting and disregarding the real consequences of their actions and displacing responsibility;
- dehumanising or degrading a family member;
- resorting to decision-making which is limited to aggressive solutions when they are in conflict with others, and with themselves.

Conclusion

This wide-ranging workshop provided practical and theoretical insights into restorative practice, restorative justice, youth group conferencing, and the various settings in which group conferencing can be held.

The principles of restorative practice, namely doing no harm; working with rather than to or for someone; and restoring or re-setting right relations, are fundamental to a process that does justice in a different way. As Clements said, restorative practice is not a 'magic bullet' that will solve all ills, but when combined with good case management and support and appropriate housing, it offers far better outcomes in the long-term and, importantly, a real prospect of keeping children and young people out of a life in the criminal justice system.

Towards Treaties with Australia's First Nations Peoples

Andrew Gardiner and John Lochowiak with Denis Fitzgerald

Introduction

The 2020 Catholic Social Services conference opened with a Welcome to Country, and a reflection on the "Uluru Statement from the Heart" and healing the wounds of the past.[1] A workshop at the conference, titled "Towards Treaties", built on that opening session. It extended the dialogue about the importance of formal treaty arrangements, and how everyone can contribute to those processes.

The two lead workshop speakers were Andrew Gardiner, a descendent of the Wurundjeri clans of the Woiwurrung people of the Kulin Nation and Chief Executive Officer at Dandenong and District Aborigines Co-operative Ltd, and John Lochowiak, Chairperson of the National Aboriginal and Torres Strait Islander Catholic Council, who has strong ties to many language groups including Pitjantjatjara, Kaurna, Ngarrindjeri and Arrernte. The workshop was chaired by Professor John Warhurst AO, Chair of Concerned Catholics Canberra Goulburn.

This chapter reports on the speakers' input and discussion at the workshop, which explored the process of treaty, its relationship to

---

1 Peter Hudson with Sherry Balcombe, Helen Christensen, Helen Kennedy and Henry Williams, 2020. *"Makarrata*: Healing the Wounds of the Past" in this volume.

dispossession and disadvantage, and the benefits that it offers. The role that all Australians, individuals and institutions, can play in support of the process, is then considered.

The Treaty Journey

The "Uluru Statement from the Heart" included a call for a Voice to Parliament, which has not yet been acted on at a national level. Parallel to this, commencing in 2016, the Victorian Government set in train a process towards Treaty, which involved the passage of the *Advancing the Treaty Process with Aboriginal Victorians Act 2018* and the subsequent election in December 2019 of the First Peoples' Assembly of Victoria, "the elected voice for Aboriginal people and communities in future Treaty discussions".[2]

Gardiner, an elected member of the Assembly, reflected on its inaugural meeting in the Legislative Council chamber in Parliament House, and his sense of the importance of the task before the Assembly. He drew on his address to that session in relating that his vision for Treaty was "to recognise traditional ownerships or custodianships and through that bring opportunity to communities across the State". His statement had highlighted the Assembly's role in addressing the past and looking forward:

> We are simultaneously tasked with honouring history and legacy to those that preceded us, meeting the expectations of those who have elected us, and imagining giving effect to the aspirations of those to come.

He told the workshop that he spoke at the Assembly of the "unfinished business that exists between the State of Victoria and the communities we each represent", and of "the obligations of our past, present and future generations". Gardiner highlighted the

---

2 First Peoples' Assembly of Victoria, n.d. "The Assembly"; accessed at www.firstpeoplesvic.org/about/the-assembly/.

advancement of the Treaty process in Victoria "while the nation struggled with the invitation given by the 'Uluru Statement from the Heart'", and called on Victoria to "continue to be courageous ... to be generous, ... to allow our process to take shape at a pace that is comfortable for our people ...". We must, he urged, "provide a system that is workable for us to progress to a better, transformative future".

At the same time, Assembly representatives have to ensure that they keep their communities well informed about the process and seek their comments and contributions to inform negotiations with Government. This will be no quick fix. At the workshop, Gardiner referenced the experience of British Columbia:

> I've just come from a meeting at the Aboriginal Advancement League this morning. When I left, they were having an audio conference with the traditional owners of British Columbia. It took them thirteen years to go through all the processes of negotiating a treaty with the British Columbia provincial government and the Canadian federal government.

But the process is neither open-ended nor bi-partisan. Gardiner saw an imperative to make progress before the next Victorian State election, in November 2022, as "then we'll be faced with the threat the opposition made at the last election, to derail and repeal the legislation that has been established".

Participants in the workshop were from across the country, but recent formal developments were focused on Victoria. Lochowiak noted that the process of working on a treaty in South Australia had not been easy, but was moving forward. He identified the strength of community as an important factor in achieving progress: "The mob from Murray Bridge, the Ngarrindjeri people, they're united and they're moving towards treaty". Gardiner briefly reviewed the situation in other states: the Northern Territory has indicated it is going to follow up on what Victoria has done, as has the Australian Capital Territory. Queensland, with the largest number of Aboriginal and Torres Strait Islander people, is "still talking about it". New South Wales and Western Australia, he assessed, "don't have the political will".

The issue of constitutional change arose in discussion. While speakers welcomed the 1967 referendum, Gardiner took a strong stand about the way forward: he characterised the Australian Constitution as a document that disadvantages Indigenous peoples, and argued that, in those circumstances, a preamble would make no sense. He continued:

> The Constitution for me is totally flawed. It was written by non-Indigenous people for their own interests. Let's be clear about that. The Constitution of each state and territory was written for the interests of each state and territory. It's no wonder that our people feel disengaged nationally.

Thus, Gardiner explained, "It's important for treaty to give us the power to stand up and talk within government". At present there is a sense of powerlessness in Indigenous communities, and "having a treaty is so important to get us where we need to be".

Nor should we imagine that this destination would be too overwhelming for Australian society. Both speakers referenced Prime Minister Kevin Rudd's 2008 "Apology to Australia's Indigenous Peoples".[3] They noted that it was restricted to the Stolen Generation but saw in it a precedent, and as offering some other learnings. Lochowiak stated:

> I often think of Kevin Rudd and the apology. They talked

---

3 K. Rudd, 13 February 2008. "Apology to Australia's Indigenous Peoples"; accessed at www.aph.gov.au/hansard.

about it for years and years, and no Prime Minister had the guts to do it. But when it happened it wasn't a big deal. I think that, by simply acknowledging something, you can fix it. That's the key.

Treaty and its Relationship to Dispossession and Disadvantage

The treaty process did not develop out of a vacuum. Gardner, Lochowiak and others spoke of the traumas of peoples who have been dispossessed in their own land, and of the pressing need for the way forward that treaty offers. A moving discussion touched on the massacres that were part of physical dispossession: Gardiner related that there are twenty-two registered massacre sites in Victoria, and that hundreds of his people were killed at those sites. Wider discussion ranged across the Stolen Generation, the loss of culture, economic exploitation through, for example, withheld or stolen wages, and the discrimination of people in different ways over the decades.

The lack of recognition of people who fought for Australia during the two World Wars of the 20th century was an injustice that resonated with both speakers. They spoke about relatives who enlisted, some in spite of official resistance, but who were not able to stay on in the military or be eligible for soldier settlement land after returning from war.

The recognition that Maori people have won in Aotearoa New Zealand and their strong cultural presence were referenced on a number of occasions. Lochowiak related a self-deprecating, poignant tale of culture, relating to his attendance some time ago at a conference in New Zealand:

> They rocked up at this conference and the Maori people did their welcome and sang in their language and danced. Then they said to my Auntie and these two Aboriginal blokes, 'Okay, you do your welcome now'. And the two

blokes whispered to my Auntie, 'We've got no welcome. What are we going to do?' And she said, 'Just stamp your feet and clap your hands', and she would sing a song in language. All the Maori people applauded them and said, 'That was a beautiful welcome', and the two blokes said to my Auntie, 'We didn't know you knew a welcome song'. She said, 'That's not a welcome song, that's Little Peter Rabbit!'

Importantly, the presenters summarised this area of discussion as follows: "These are the things that we need to share purposefully with you so you can go away and think, 'You know what, that isn't fair'".

Treaty and the Benefits that it Offers

In a free-ranging discussion, the forum touched on a number of ways in which the treaty process is expected to benefit Aboriginal communities. Acknowledgement of the importance of each person and each community was seen as important – simply listening to the stories of individuals and families would make quite a difference as to how we all react to them. The treaty would facilitate this acknowledgement.

Workshop participants raised aspects of educational curricula and their importance. Treaty is relevant here too, because of the empowerment it brings to individual students and families, and to the community, to enable active engagement with the education system. Such engagement should impact on the depiction of Aboriginal people in history. Lochowiak related his vivid memory from school days:

> I can still picture the book in my head, the pictures of Captain Cook getting off the boat. In the distance there were some trees, and on one side of the trees there were some kangaroos and emus, then there were some fellas

holding spears. That picture itself is significant, because at that time and for many years after, we came under the Flora and Fauna Act. It's not a nice thing to say, but if you treat people like animals, how are they going to start behaving?

A treaty should also impact positively on languages. Gardiner spoke about the teaching of Aboriginal languages and noted that Northcote Primary School in Melbourne is the first school in Victoria where his language, Woiwurrung, is being taught. "Hopefully", he shared, "those kids can share that knowledge with all their friends and colleagues down the track, when they go to university or whatever professional industry they get into".

Finding ways to say "Sorry" was identified as another positive feature of treaty. The apology statement made in 2008 by the then Prime Minister Kevin Rudd[4] was a good start, but it addressed only the Stolen Generation. It did not acknowledge the extent of everybody's disadvantage. Gardiner reflected that treaty provided great opportunities to reflect on and discuss how we as a country can make reparations and say sorry for the past; say sorry for, for example, the legal extinguishment of native title where that has occurred.

Treaty was seen by a number of workshop participants as a vehicle for overcoming discrimination and disadvantage. Gardiner thought it should bring support to communities and increase their capacity to assist in disengaging young people from criminal behaviour, "breaking them out of the cycle of going to jail just because they've been institutionalised to do so". He acknowledged that there are already relevant programs in place, but the inconsistency of their funding needs to be overcome – with short-term funding, half the time available may be spent starting up the program or finishing

---

4 Ibid.

it up. Treaty should establish a longer-term, better-resourced framework to achieve better outcomes and improve communities.

A Role for all Australians

Treaty was presented as involving all the community and, in that context, the workshop discussed the role that all of society, individuals and institutions, can play in support of the process. Gardiner sought the support of workshop participants:

> You can go out and talk to local members and other people in the community, create a groundswell of support for our cause ... If local members can be influenced, they can influence the Premier and the Cabinet and the [Victorian] Minister for Aboriginal Affairs. The aim is to have better outcomes when the negotiations are brought to bear.

Sherry Balcombe, an Olkola/Djabaguy woman from Far North Queensland and Coordinator of Aboriginal Catholic Ministry Victoria, stressed the importance of the whole community 'walking with' First Nations peoples. She spoke of the inspiration that she received from activists, such as her own father and the leaders of the workshop, and of her dream for a treaty "because it's the right thing to do. It's the just thing to do". She spoke of her pride in being part of the longest continuous culture on the planet:

> That's something for us all to be proud of but we can't do it alone. We need to have everybody walking with us.

There were questions about how this support could best be provided: "How do we walk alongside you in the most appropriate way?" A response that was echoed a number of times was about awareness across the community: "Educate yourself about the issues and educate your family and friends, your colleagues" as "the number of people who support us will determine the success of the treaty".

Some participants spoke about Reconciliation Action Plans as supporting Indigenous communities in many ways, such as employment, health awareness training and so forth. The question was asked as to whether such plans could support the treaty process.

Ensuring that such plans delivered what they promised, and holding an organisation accountable for that, was, for Gardiner, a central point here: "Lots of people have Reconciliation Action Plans but they never really perform against them". By way of counter-example, he spoke positively about steps taken at Monash Health. Cultural awareness training for all board members, establishment of an Aboriginal employment strategy with quantified targets, establishment of an executive role with responsibility for the plan, and responsibility for engagement and influence with the CEO and other executives; these are, he suggested, the sorts of steps that should bear fruit in terms of understanding, engagement and real benefits for communities.

Ensuring consultations with communities was presented as something in which social service organisations should be actively engaged. Lochowiak stated:

> It doesn't matter what colour you are, you can't go into a family with an issue and expect to fix it. But if you ask them how to fix it, they'll usually tell you ... Treaty is about offering communities the support to engage with ... the community's obligations to itself, so they can deliver them for themselves. It's in your interest as social service organisations to engage Aboriginal community members and help them to participate in treaty. At the end of the day, they will turn out and they will thank you in spades.

Conclusion

Participants in the workshop were party to a moving encounter, where personal and family experience was interwoven with current social and political imperatives. The Victorian treaty process was presented as an important element in building a society where the wrongs of the past can be addressed, at a personal and a political level, and where all Australians can contribute to a more just future for our country.

The workshop was hopeful about the future, but conscious that the path ahead cannot be taken for granted. Lochowiak summed up this realism:

> I quite often think about 1988, when Bob Hawke was pushing for treaty. He was sincere and he really wanted it but it was blocked by some of the states. I sometimes wonder where we'd be today if we had that treaty back then.

But, he concluded, "the positive story is that, thirty years ago, we wouldn't be here. This [workshop] wouldn't be possible. The positive story for me is that there are people like yourselves out there, wanting to know what you can do, how to deal with these issues".

It is now up to Catholic social services to play their part in building that positive future.

Responding to Homelessness: Building Houses or Creating a Community?

Netty Horton with Jack de Groot, Tony Nicholson and Sally-Anne Petrie

Introduction

Ask any social service provider about major needs within the community and there will be one consistent response: a lack of access to affordable housing. This is regardless of the nature of the service – homelessness, family and domestic violence, substance abuse, emergency relief, employment, disability, and the list goes on. Dig a little deeper, and discover that less than 0.5 per cent of all private rental housing in Victoria is affordable for people on an unemployment benefit[1] and that there was an 11 per cent increase in the number of people experiencing homelessness in Victoria, to just under 25,000, from the 2011 to the 2016 national census.[2]

With such poor access to the private rental market for those on benefits, and the growing numbers of people who are homeless, many look to social housing to provide a solution. There are many

---

1 Anglicare Victoria, 2020. *Rental Affordability Snapshot 2020 – Victorian Rental Market*, p. 3; accessed at https://anglicareras.files.wordpress.com/2020/04/victoria.pdf.
2 Australian Bureau of Statistics, 2018. *Census of Population and Housing: Estimating homelessness, 2016* in attached Table 1.3 "Number of homeless persons, by selected characteristics"; accessed at www.abs.gov.au/ausstats/abs@.nsf/mf/2049.0.

dependable and innovative providers in this sector, but regrettably there is just not enough stock available. The share of social housing in the national housing stock has declined over recent decades to four per cent from a high of seven per cent[3] and in Victoria it is a little below the national average. This represents a disappointing response to the growing numbers of people who find themselves excluded from safe, stable and affordable housing, and therefore from being a part of their local community.

These are issues that invite response from across Australian society. As part of that broad base, many within the Catholic community, believing that "a little bit of Christ dwells within each of us", ask how an effective response can best be articulated. How can resources, experience and mission be directed to deliver housing to the poor, the homeless, those without income, those without dignity and those without employment? And is providing housing enough, or can the Catholic response offer more meaningful inclusion and participation in a healthy community?

The 2020 Catholic Social Services conference included a workshop on "Responding to Homelessness", which considered such questions. The presenters brought a wealth of experience from their participation in relevant services:

- Jack de Groot, CEO, St Vincent de Paul Society NSW, spoke to a major housing initiative that his organisation is currently delivering,
- Sally-Anne Petrie, Pastoral Coordinator, CatholicCare Melbourne and Gippsland, outlined an initiative in Melbourne to partner with parishes to provide housing and other support to people seeking asylum,

---

3 RMIT ABC Fact Check 2019, 27 September 2019. "Have social housing levels fallen to historic lows?"; accessed at www.abc.net.au/news/2019-08-12/fact-check-social-housing-lowest-level/11403298.

- de Groot and Petrie joined leading social policy advocate Tony Nicholson in reflecting on current challenges in this area, and in envisioning a stronger future for Church-based responses to homelessness and housing.

Social Housing – An Ongoing Catholic Response Program

de Groot linked his account of a major current initiative to the long history and strong reputation for delivering services to homeless people of the St Vincent de Paul Society in New South Wales ('Vinnies'). Like many agencies involved in seeking to address homelessness, Vinnies was very aware of lack of access to social housing and to ongoing and much needed supports for most of the individuals and families seeking assistance. The creation of the Social and Affordable Housing Fund by the Baird Government in 2016 provided Vinnies with the opportunity to seek Government funds to provide 502 housing units over twelve sites across New South Wales.

The contract requirements included two phases: a three-year building component followed by a 25-year contract to provide tenancy and associated supports in partnership with the New South Wales State Government. Vinnies report a number of considerations to be taken into account and challenges to be addressed in entering into the contract. Most importantly, the Society was required to transform from a traditional role of providing support, often crisis-driven support, to one incorporating, and even driven by, property development. The Society's Board agreed to take on an initial loan of $190 million, financed by Catholic Development Funds (CDFs). This investment in itself represents a significant change and could be a precedent for future investment. The capacity of the CDFs across Australia is considerable and they could be encouraged to invest in social housing as part of a collaborative Catholic effort to respond to homelessness.

Described as "not a project for shrinking violets", Vinnies needed to obtain expert advice in the areas of financing, construction and tenancy management. It also had to address the issues of its own significant equity of $23 million, providing land for development, and committing to a 25-year agreement with Government.

There are still challenges, some yet to be faced, including a post-construction phase when the focus will return to the tenants and supporting them in living as part of the newly built communities. An opportunity has been identified in relation to building organisational capacity to respond to the new roles, especially in establishing support at each new site as construction is completed. Further, there is the critical role of the traditional Vinnies' conferences which reflect their local communities and can provide the bridge for the new developments to become part of that community. Welcoming people to the community enables a shedding of the stigma of isolation, poverty and unstable housing from the past, and provides the chance to participate fully in a neighbourhood, perhaps for the first time.

A Practical Parish-Based Response

Petrie explained that the CatholicCare Asylum Seeker Support Program in Melbourne aims to provide asylum seekers and refugees with the support required for a successful transition to the local community. Parishes partner with CatholicCare to provide housing, possibly owned by a parish or rented through parish resources. The program recognises the vulnerability of asylum seekers, who can arrive with little or no financial resources, no rental history, limited English language skills and perhaps a lack of understanding or experience of Australian culture and community structures. However, they generally have an incredible drive to contribute and succeed.

Parishes commit to supporting the family as required. Parish volunteers are encouraged to offer assistance and invite families to accept support, without expectation of acceptance. In addition to housing, support may include the provision of clothing, food and/or meals, help with shopping, and other material and financial assistance. Most importantly, parishes look to provide pathways to volunteer work, training, casual work and employment with an aim to increase capacity for independence.

Whilst the individuals and families are supported through the parishes, the CatholicCare coordinator supports the parishes. This may include the provision of basic orientation to asylum seekers' experiences, needs and vulnerabilities. It also involves selecting families who will be receptive to parish support, and perhaps coordinating professional services and other community supports such as the involvement of schools, local businesses and philanthropic and community resources.

The benefits of the collective efforts of this program are highlighted by two case studies described briefly below.

Case Study 1

An asylum seeker family was referred to the program from crisis accommodation. At the time, the mother was pregnant, and neither partner had work rights. The family was offered accommodation rented by the parish and volunteers supported them for two years as the family expanded to three small children. The parish linked the father to a 'Men's Shed' and made sure the mother was connected to maternal health services. Although English skills were limited, with the assistance of the parish, the family was soon able to access mainstream services. The father was very motivated and was able to move from volunteer to casual to full-time work. Eventually, the parish was able to transfer the lease to the family who were then able to remain permanently within this supportive community.

Case Study 2

A vulnerable family was referred to the program after several months of couch surfing within Australia. They were without income or work rights and included an eighteen-month-old child with significant special needs. A parish property was provided for about eighteen months, during which time parish volunteers offered the family a range of supports. The father was able to become an Uber driver and the mother was able to improve her English and complete aged care training, resulting in employment within the industry. Most significantly, the parish had a connection with a service providing specialist education support which was available for the little girl for up to 30 hours each week, resulting in huge improvement in her ability to connect with her family. Thanks to their determination and the constant support and encouragement from the parish community, this family was able to secure independent rental accommodation, having achieved income security and other attributes over the course of parish involvement.

These case studies depict both the range of supports required and what it is possible to achieve when financial, material, personal and community resources are coordinated and offered in a supportive environment.

Questions and Challenges in Providing Community within the Context of Social Housing

Catholic Land Assets and the Need for Different Governance Arrangements

Provision of appropriate properties is a critical factor in developing new social housing. There is a strong perception, from both internal and external stakeholders, of extensive land assets held by the Catholic Church. Although Catholic institutions undeniably hold significant assets, their availability for repurposing can be a complex issue and, across the Church, the appetite for the development of social housing varies.

Many parcels of land are not suitable or viable for social housing or alternative development. In other cases, there is a financial imperative driving parishes or other Catholic institutions to seek commercial returns which will mostly preclude the use of land for social housing. Examples of land being made available for social housing generally feature mission as the key driver. On the other hand, there are examples in the aged care space of successful partnership arrangements leading to the development of communities that are successful in both mission and financial terms.

Providing land for social housing is often challenging for organisations, particularly when the assets have served another ministry for many decades and were gained through parish or local community efforts. Long-term leases or transferred ownership is generally required if a project seeks to attract government funding and such arrangements can be challenging for faith-based organisations. Some Church agencies have established particular governance arrangements, such as separate companies or other special purpose 'vehicles', to enable land to be utilised for a government-funded development, providing a degree of comfort and security to all stakeholders. However, experience shows the need for the development of trust for these organisations to deliver successful projects reflecting ethos and mission.

Opportunity for Community Involvement

If the ambition is to build vibrant communities, rather than just developing housing, there are opportunities to draw on community resources to assist people to build a 'good life'. These include the following:

- Parish Involvement: The engagement of parishes is usually predicated on the willingness and leadership of the parish priest, but also other parish leaders and the parish council.

Experience indicates the necessity, in parish-enabled housing developments, to have written agreements with a parish, particularly about the nature, responsibilities and roles of each of the partners. This has become even more important as awareness of the need for child-safe practices and the protection of vulnerable people has evolved.

- Volunteer Support: Training, support and supervision of volunteers have become critical elements in ensuring the most effective use of volunteer supports, and the strongest engagement of the entire community.
- Tenancy Support: In the provision of social housing, as in the provision of any housing, matters will arise regarding maintenance, behaviour, payment of rent, and other tenancy issues. The provision of support to tenants to assist in managing rental payments and addressing legal, mental health and other issues can make a major difference in the tenants' ability to maintain housing over the long term.

Opposition from the Community

As much as local parishes or particular stakeholders may wish to build community, the opposition from existing neighbourhoods to social housing is a feature of many development processes. There are strong learnings from successful initiatives of the need to invest in community development before, during and post-construction and on a continuing basis. There are countless examples of gradual acceptance of new communities by established communities but, almost always, this is dependent upon skilled relationship and communication management.

Prioritisation of Need and Focus on Long-Term Outcomes

Given the requirement for housing extends to almost all who can be described as 'in need', it is difficult to prioritise the relative needs of various sections of the community: of the elderly, youth, singles, families, over those escaping domestic violence, those with substance abuse issues, etc. The workshop discussion highlighted that, regardless of the particular need being addressed, the critical issue is to ensure that appropriate supports are provided and tailored to particular needs, in order to provide the best chance of sustaining housing as part of a healthy community.

The argument was also developed that the welfare framework currently operated by many community service agencies does not always encourage aspirations for either mainstream employment or retention of viable housing, and yet these can be essential for successful housing outcomes. Further, social housing is necessarily focused on provision of long-term housing, but traditionally the Australian housing response to homelessness has been based on crisis and transitional housing – there is a gap to be bridged.

Significantly, the recent Victorian State Government strategy to address rough sleeping[4] found that many of those affected had:

- been evicted from social housing,
- lived on the streets during the daytime and went to social housing at night, and
- were in receipt of unemployment benefits and were expected to be work ready.

Clearly, we need to adopt a long-term focus, and address causes of homelessness, to achieve lasting outcomes.

Looking to the Future

There is much to be done, and there are many springs of hope which can inform further initiatives in the various states.

---

4 Department of Health and Human Services, 2018. *Victoria's Homelessness and Rough Sleeping Action Plan*; accessed at www.dhhs.vic.gov.au/sites/default/files/documents/201802/Rough%20Sleeping%20Action%20Plan_20180207.pdf.

Whilst the provision of social housing can legitimately be considered a solution to homelessness in its own right, the workshop asserted the importance of a broader response from the Catholic community. Wider support, employment and, most of all, inclusion in a welcoming community are also major factors in ensuring the ongoing wellbeing and community participation of individuals and families. These can all be provided through a collaborative response.

Within Victoria there are two Catholic registered housing providers which are eligible to apply for Government funds for social housing management or developments. The four-diocesan structure of the Catholic Church in Victoria has traditionally impeded State-wide initiatives. However, the Province of Victoria, as it is known, has supported a feasibility study to examine the possibility of establishing a Victorian Catholic social housing provider. Whilst there are many challenges and opportunities to be addressed, if it is established, a Catholic Housing Victoria initiative would have the potential to combine the resources, skills, experience and shared mission of the four Dioceses to develop positive communities which enable their members to be supported to "live life to the full". What a transforming development this would be!

As this chapter indicates, the "Responding to Homelessness" workshop was informed by the wide-ranging and long-standing experiences of its speakers. In the open forum which followed their presentations, participants engaged in lively discussion, exploring the challenges of establishing community-embedded social housing while encouraged by visionary initiatives like the St Vincent de Paul Society's major undertaking in New South Wales. Catholic social services are called to be the presence of Christ in the contemporary world:

I was homeless, and you gave me shelter (*Matthew* 25:35).

Domestic Violence: Awareness, Prevention and Progress

Janene Evans, Cabrini Makasiale, Felicity Rorke and Michael Tonks

Domestic and family violence is a significant social issue that impacts the direct victim survivors and those who experience it without being the intended primary victim. It is pervasive and ongoing, and the impacts can be devastating on the health and social, emotional and economic wellbeing of those affected. It is a whole of community responsibility to prevent it occurring and to deal with those impacted. Against this background the 2020 Catholic Social Services conference included a workshop on domestic violence.

Chaired by Felicity Rorke, Executive Director of the Good Samaritan Inn, the first part of the workshop focused on the family violence reforms being implemented in the State of Victoria and was presented by Janene Evans, General Manager, Safety and Resilience, Good Shepherd Australia New Zealand. The second part looked at two initiatives implemented by New Zealand Catholic Social Services as described by Sr Cabrini Makasiale from Catholic Social Services Otara, Hamish Mephram, a social worker from Catholic Social Services Dunedin, and Michael Tonks, Director of Catholic Social Services Dunedin.

Family Violence Protection Act 2008

The Victorian *Family Violence Protection Act 2008* defines family violence as behaviour that is physically, sexually, emotionally, psychologically or economically abusive; is threatening or coercive; "controls or dominates the family member and causes that family member to feel fear for the safety or wellbeing of that family member or another person"; or "causes a child to hear or witness, or otherwise be exposed to the effects of, any behaviour referred to" above.[1]

Domestic violence occurs in domestic settings between two people who are, or were, in an intimate relationship. It includes physical, sexual, emotional, psychological and financial abuse.

Family violence is a broader term than domestic violence. It refers not only to violence between intimate partners, but also includes violence between family members, for example elder abuse and adolescent violence against parents. It also includes violence within extended families and between people living in share housing.

Children are victim survivors of domestic and family violence whether they are direct targets of the violence or not, and whether they have actually witnessed the violence or not. They are living it along with the primary victim survivor.

The following describe the typical types of domestic and family violence:

- *Controlling behaviour* is how an abusive person gains and maintains power over someone else. Controlling behaviour usually starts slowly and is not always obvious. The abuser may try to justify their actions by saying they are just concerned for the victim or care about them too much. Controlling

---

[1] The *Family Violence Protection Act 2008* (Vic) can be accessed at www5.austlii.edu.au/au/legis/vic/consol_act/fvpa2008283/s24.html.

behaviour tends to become more overt and aggressive over time.
- *Financial abuse*, also known as economic abuse, is when one person uses money or finances as a means to gain power over and control someone else, or unreasonably impacts their financial autonomy.
- *Sexual abuse* is any forced or coerced sexual activity by one person to exert power and control over another. An individual act of sexual abuse is called a sexual assault. Perpetrators of sexual assaults are not just strangers; in fact, sexual assaults most commonly happen between people who know each other.
- *Physical abuse* is the intentional unwanted use of physical force to cause fear or harm. Sometimes physically abusive behaviour does not cause injury or pain, but it is still abusive.
- *Emotional abuse* is any act intended to undermine someone's self-esteem, intimidate them, or isolate them.
- *Psychological abuse,* in the context of family violence, is when someone makes another person question their sanity or recollection of reality through manipulation and lying. Psychological abuse and emotional abuse often occur in tandem, and emotional abuse can have psychological impacts (like causing depression and anxiety) but psychological abuse is slightly different to emotional abuse.
- *Spiritual abuse* is the denial or use of spiritual or religious beliefs and practices to control and dominate a person. Spiritual abuse can impact on a someone's self-esteem and confidence, make them feel guilty, damage their spiritual experiences, and isolate them.

In Australia we know that one woman is murdered every week

by her current or former partner. We also know that over 30 per cent of women/girls have experienced physical violence since the age of 15 years.[2]

According to *Destroy the Joint*,[3] 62 women lost their lives in 2019 and, so far, eleven women have died in 2020 (current at 22 April 2020). Around the world, an average of 137 women are killed by a partner or family member every single day, according to data released by the United Nations Office on Drugs and Crime, making the home the most likely place for a woman to be killed.

Background of Victorian Reforms

The Victorian Royal Commission into Family Violence[4] was established in 2015 after a number of family violence-related deaths in Victoria, most notably the death of eleven-year-old Luke Batty in 2014. Luke was killed by his father who had spent years harassing and coercively attempting to control Luke's mother, Rosie Batty.

In 2013 there were 44 family violence-related deaths in Victoria and in the year 2013-2014 there were 65,154 family violence incidents reported to Victoria Police, an increase of 83 per cent in the period 2009-2010 to 2013-2104.[5] The estimated annual cost of family violence to the Victorian economy in 2009 was $3.4 billion.[6]

The three key aims of the Royal Commission were to make recommendations in relation to:

---

2 Data are available at OurWatch.org.au as well as in Appendix 1 to this chapter, which presents family violence statistics.
3 *Destroy the Joint* is a web-based platform that promotes gender equality and civil discourse in Australia. Its name came from 2GB broadcaster Alan Jones' on-air comment on 31 August 2012 that "women are destroying the joint".
4 This was Australia's first Royal Commission into family violence; see www.vic.gov.au/about-royal-commission-family-violence.
5 These are Victoria Police data presented to the Royal Commission into Family Violence.
6 Ibid.

- preventing family violence,
- improving support for victim survivors,
- holding perpetrators to account.

The Royal Commission made 227 recommendations and the Victorian Government has committed to implementing all of them. Some of the key recommendations include the following:

- setting up an independent Family Violence agency – Family Safety Victoria,
- the development of Support and Safety Hubs, also called The Orange Door,
- law reforms including information sharing and the Multi-Agency Risk Assessment and Management Framework (MARAM),
- increased perpetrator accountability,
- more focus on children and young people,
- addressing the needs of Aboriginal communities with the establishment of a State-wide culturally appropriate response within five years.

Family Safety Victoria was created on 1 July 2017 to deliver family violence reform and drive action to end family violence. Its main roles were to implement key recommendations from the Royal Commission into Family Violence through:

- establishing and operationalising seventeen Support and Safety Hubs across Victoria,
- establishing a Central Information Point, which will allow police, courts and government to share critical information to support women and children to remain safe,
- services to track perpetrators and keep victims safe, and

- establishing and housing the new Centre for Workforce Excellence in order to build workforce capacity and capability in partnership with the family violence sector.

Support and Safety Hubs

The Orange Door[7] is a new way for women, children and young people experiencing family violence or families requiring assistance with the care and wellbeing of children to access the services they need, in a timely and efficient way, in order to be safe and supported. The Orange Door is being rolled out across Victoria and currently operates in five areas: Frankston, Inner Gippsland (Morwell), North East (Heidelberg), Mallee (Mildura) and Barwon (Geelong). These service hubs provide a 'visible' contact point so that people know where to go for assistance. They offer specialist support and tailored advice for victim survivors, families and children with a strong focus on perpetrator accountability. The advice is based on the best available information and risk assessment tools and a coordinated and integrated service response where practitioners draw on specialist expertise as well as a connection to a wide range of supports across the spectrum of prevention, early intervention and response. Over the next few years, the remaining twelve Orange Doors will be commissioned and this service will then operate in all seventeen Department of Health and Human Services areas across Victoria.

Law Reform

The Royal Commission report has nine recommendations relating to family violence and the law and 27 relating to courts but the most critical of these concern information sharing laws and MARAM

---

7 For further background on The Orange Door, see Orangedoor.vic.gov.au/find-a-service-near-you.

(Multi-Agency Risk Assessment and Management Framework).[8] In June 2017, legislation was passed to establish MARAM and create a specific family violence information sharing regime with the intent to ensure a person's safety will 'trump' a perpetrator's right to privacy.[9] Key agencies and workers can access and share up-to-date information to protect victim survivors better and keep perpetrators in view. The implementation of MARAM is inextricably linked with the implementation of the information sharing schemes in four inter-related ways:

- Both require similar changes to practice, processes and culture by the same people in the same organisations.
- Contributing to information sharing is a stated responsibility within the MARAM framework.
- A solid understanding of family violence risk, which is being brought about through the application of MARAM, is an essential part of the process of information sharing.
- Without strong risk assessment processes in place, some organisations and professionals can be hesitant to participate in some forms of information sharing, which in turn inhibits good quality risk assessments from occurring when required.

MARAM is a suite of policies, practice tools, training, legislation, regulation and formal reviews that aims to change both the practice and culture around how professionals and organisations respond to family violence. The legislation establishing MARAM outlines ten principles underpinning the framework. The principles support four 'pillars', against which prescribed organisations are required to align. The pillars consist of the following:

---

8 For details of the MARAM initiative, see www.vic.gov.au/maram-practice-guides-and-resources.
9 See Part 11 of the *Family Violence Protection Act 2008* (Vic), op. cit. n. 1.

- Pillar 1: *Shared understanding of family violence*, to provide information on what constitutes family violence, underlying drivers, prevalence and impact;
- Pillar 2: *Consistent and collaborative practice*, to ensure prescribed organisations assess risk through structured professional judgement, use assessment approaches that are consistent with evidence-based risk factors, and understand the continuum of risk management responses, including strengthening formal and informal collaborative arrangements;
- Pillar 3: *Responsibilities for risk assessment and management*, to describe the range and increasing level of responsibilities of prescribed organisations in risk assessment and management practice across the system. This pillar guides organisations to determine their roles in the system, and the family violence responsibilities they are expected to enact in practice;
- Pillar 4: *Systems, outcomes and continuous improvement*, to outline how prescribed organisations can contribute to continuous improvement through data collection, monitoring and evaluation of tools, processes and implementation of the framework.[10]

MARAM builds on a review of contemporary international evidence, recognising a wider range of risk indicators, including for children, diverse communities and at-risk age groups, across identities and family and relationship types, and will be supported by comprehensive practice guidance. Implementing MARAM is a large, multi-layered and complex task. It will ultimately bring into play more than 355,000 staff in over 5,800 organisations.[11]

---

10 Ibid.
11 For further information, see Family Safety Victoria at www.vic.gov.au/family-safety-victoria.

Perpetrator Accountability

An increased focus on those who perpetuate family and domestic violence includes:

- increased dedicated funding for perpetrator programs,
- research trial to evaluate interventions for perpetrators,
- an improved process for monitoring attendance at Behaviour Change Programs,
- establishment of a Central Information Point (CIP) to keep perpetrators in view.

The 2019-2020 State Budget provided $1.6 million in ongoing funding to support the delivery of future perpetrator programs which include ten perpetrator intervention programs being trialled targeting diverse cohorts, with 250 people receiving a tailored intervention under the trials. Approximately 900 perpetrators received case management support and approximately 5,400 men participated in a Men's Behaviour Change Program.[12]

Central Information Point (CIP)

Family Safety Victoria, Victoria Police, the Magistrates' Court of Victoria, Corrections Victoria and the Department of Health and Human Services are now working side by side to provide information about perpetrators or alleged perpetrators of family violence into a consolidated report (CIP report) for family violence risk assessment and management. These reports are used by practitioners at The Orange Door to support risk assessment and safety planning for adults and children affected by family violence. Information from the CIP is also used to help keep perpetrators accountable. Since the initiative commenced in April 2018, more than 3,500 CIP reports have been produced and ongoing positive feedback has

---

12 Ibid.

been received from The Orange Door. Work is underway to create a CIP operating model that is scalable and sustainable to meet future demand and allow its expansion to other services working across Victoria to keep adults and children affected by family violence safe.[13]

Children and Young People

The *Family Violence Protection Act 2008* (Vic) was amended to establish a rebuttable presumption that, if an applicant for a Family Violence Intervention Order has a child who has experienced family violence, that child should be included in the applicant's order or protected by their own order. Other initiatives that focus on children and young people, under the Victorian Government reforms, include capacity building for staff in refuges, funding for family violence therapeutic interventions and funding for Flexible Support Packages[14] to meet the needs of children and young people.

The *Child Information Sharing Scheme*, another reform, was developed in response to many independent reviews and inquiries over the past decade. These recommended streamlining Victoria's information sharing arrangements to improve outcomes for children; this will be realised by promoting shared responsibility for their wellbeing and safety and increasing collaboration across the service system.[15]

MARAM requires that children be recognised as victim survivors of family violence in their own right, with specific risks and needs. It identifies evidence-based risk factors specific to

---

13 Ibid.
14 *Flexible Support Packages* are brokerage funds available to those meeting certain criteria who have experienced family violence; see https://providers.dhhs.vic.gov.au/program-requirements-delivery-family-violence-flexible-support-packages.
15 Resources for information sharing are available at www.vic.gov.au/guides-templates-tools-for-information-sharing.

children that are caused by perpetrator behaviours. The *MARAM Practice Guide* provides assistance in identifying and screening for family violence risk with children and young people, including deciding when to talk to a child directly and prompt questions to ask them. A *Child Victim Survivor Assessment Tool* has been developed and published as a part of the MARAM Practice Guide. A risk management tool specifically for older children and young people has been developed and the risk management tool for adults can include safety planning for children. A screening tool to assess family violence risk with children directly is also in development.[16]

Aboriginal Communities

The reforms require services to conduct cultural safety reviews and to work in partnership with Aboriginal communities to develop action plans and, in particular, a strategic response to improve the safety of Aboriginal children and young people and provide support to Aboriginal parents. In October 2018, Family Services Victoria launched *Dhelk Dja: Safe Our Way – Strong Culture, Strong Peoples, Strong Families,* the new Aboriginal 10-Year Family Violence Agreement, an initiative led by key Aboriginal stakeholders.[17]

The *Korin Balit-Djak: Aboriginal Health, Wellbeing and Safety Strategic Plan 2017-2027* and the *Wungurilwil Gapgapduir: Aboriginal Children and Families Agreement Strategic Action Plan* seek to ensure cultural competency; the requirements of which will be assessed by Aboriginal people and/or Aboriginal organisations. Approximately $17.8 million has been allocated to build and upskill the Aboriginal workforce, to support Aboriginal service providers

---

16 The MARAM Practice Guide can be accessed at www.vic.gov.au/maram-practice-guides-and-resources.
17 *Dhelk Dja* can be accessed at www.vic.gov.au/dhelk-dja-partnership-aboriginal-communities-address-family-violence.

to undertake workforce planning and development to meet the demands of current reforms, and to improve access to appropriate cultural supports and specialised training to reduce the impacts of vicarious trauma and support worker health and wellbeing.[18]

Faith Communities

Three specific Royal Commission recommendations focused on faith communities, highlighting the important role faith-based communities and organisations can play in the lives of Victorians impacted by family and domestic violence. The Royal Commission report notes that faith leaders and communities should examine how they respond to family violence, develop training packages for faith leaders and communities, and remove any capacity for family violence accommodation and service providers to discriminate against a particular group within the Victorian community.

A *Multifaith Advisory Group (MAG) Family Violence Working Group*, established in August 2016, is working with relevant organisations to develop strategies to progress these initiatives. The working group agreed to support a Participatory Action Research model at its meeting in December 2017. The group has met regularly and includes representation from peak faith bodies, inTouch Multicultural Centre Against Family Violence and Our Watch. The working group engages with faith communities and leaders in order to:

- identify current practices that may operate as deterrents to reporting of, or recovery from, family violence, and may be used by perpetrators to excuse or condone abusive behaviour;
- identify existing resources across faith communities that provide family violence awareness and referral information; and

---

18 *Korin Korin Balit-Djak* can be accessed at www.dhhs.vic.gov.au/publications/korin-korin-balit-djak and *Wungurilwil Gapgapduir* at www.dhhs.vic.gov.au/publications/wungurilwil-gapgapduir-aboriginal-children-and-families-agreement.

- co-design targeted projects with government, expert family violence practitioners and other relevant stakeholders for faith communities and leaders in order to build the capacity of faith communities to prevent family violence, facilitate reporting and support community members to recover from experiences of family violence.

The University of Melbourne and the Multicultural Centre for Women's Health are working in partnership with the MAG to build an evidence base of what works in faith communities to prevent and respond to family violence, and to support selected faith community organisations to develop tailored projects.

New Zealand Responses to Family and Domestic Violence

The Catholic Social Services conference workshop on family violence included two presentations from New Zealand, namely the "Pacific Living without Violence" program from Auckland and "Game On: A Parenting Course for Dads" from Dunedin.

The *Pacific Living without Violence Programme* was initiated in response to a request from Pacific church ministers and community leaders for assistance in addressing family violence within their congregations and communities. What the church ministers had experienced is supported by statistical data. The New Zealand Family Violence Clearinghouse states that family violence remains a very significant problem in Aotearoa New Zealand and that comprehensive strategies and investment are required to address it effectively. In terms of family violence and ethnicity, the Clearing House states that domestic violence affects every ethnicity in New Zealand, but some groups are at higher risk than others. A survey of New Zealand women found that lifetime prevalence of physical and/or sexual intimate partner violence (IPV) was one in two for Maori women (58%), one in three for European/other women (34%) and one in three for Pacific women (32%). The number of family violence incidents continues to increase. The Clearing House advised in June 2017: "We don't know whether this is due to an increase in violence or an increase in people coming forward. However, it is clear that demand on services continues to increase".[19]

The *Pacific Living without Violence*[20] is a family violence prevention program, created by the Catholic Social Services (CSS) specifically to address violence within Pacific families. It weaves together teachings of the Gospel, insights from Western psychology and psychotherapy as well as Pacific cultural understandings, so that the program is tailored to meet the needs of Pacific people, especially those who attend church. It consists of six modules delivered by members of a congregation who are trained by CSS in terms of program content and facilitation skills. Two hundred and fifty facilitators have been trained and 52 groups have taken part in the program since 2016.

An evaluation of the program was undertaken, based on feedback from participants collected after each session, reports from participant groups, written feedback from some facilitators and face-to-face interviews with some facilitators and participants. The key findings of this evaluation are:

- All participants and facilitators who took part in the evaluation want the programme to continue.
- They would like the programme to have a strong family focus but with specific space for the 'voice' of young people.

---

19 Data are accessible from the New Zealand Family Violence Clearinghouse at nzfvc.org.nz and, specifically for June 2017 report, at https://nzfvc.org.nz/news/nzfvc-data-summaries-2017-family-violence-reports-reach-record-high.
20 Information on the program is available at www.nzcatholic.org.nz/2016/05/31/anti-violence-training-rolled-pasifika-communities/ and www.cs-sauckland.org.nz/family-violence/.

- The methodology of group sharing proved to be very popular. The programme improved the relationship between family members, deepened the relationship between participants, and helped participants to gain more self-awareness and to become less judgemental.
- The session on "Understanding Anger" elicited a strong response from participants, suggesting further emphasis on the issue of anger in follow-up programmes.
- There is a strong understanding of the need for young people to have a 'voice' within the family. It was highlighted that they have specific needs and that there should be space for the youth 'voice' in follow-up programmes.
- Men participants acknowledged that they do not talk about issues important to themselves or problems that they experience, but this programme clearly showed them that they do want to share their problems. The process of discussion and sharing met a deep need of the male participants.
- There should be space both for men-only discussions and for men and women to discuss and share together.

Game On, a parenting course for dads, was developed over 13 years ago in Dunedin by CSS. The course aims to support dads to be the best dad they can be for their children. As part of the group process in *Game On*, dads are helped to explore their goals for their children and themselves. Not surprisingly, their goals are for success and happiness for their children in all aspects of their lives, including relationships, and often it is said that they want their kids to have a better childhood than they did. They also want some tangible goals for themselves. The program then looks at how to achieve this, which includes recognising that their histories (how they were raised), their ideologies, their substance abuse and their lack of understanding and regulation of their emotions can get in the way. The next step is to consider how an understanding around communication, self-discipline and appropriate 'nutrition' (food, positivity, supportive friendships etc.) can help them achieve their goals and get through tricky situations.

When it comes to violence and attitudes to hitting and hurting, some of this has to do with their own childhood experiences with their parents, some of it being a false ideology around manhood. Some men talk about taking the hits from their partners, even to the point of having their bones broken; they can be bruised and battered but they will not call the police or 'nark' on their girlfriend/wife/partner because they are good mothers and they do not want the kids to miss out. Often the men talk about the way they feel that the system expects them to be violent and so, because of the way they are treated in the 'system' and are not being listened to, they end up 'acting out'.

At the end of the day, CSS spends quite a bit of time helping men to understand their feelings and how to manage these. Further support is offered after the course if men need it, either to manage themselves or the situations in which they find themselves.[21]

Conclusion

The domestic violence workshop addressed a key issue for our communities. Participants valued the comprehensive presentation on the reforms underway in the State of Victoria and the accounts of two successful New Zealand programs developed to address domestic violence. The learnings from the workshop will now be disseminated to a wider audience through this chapter.

---

21 For information on the course, see www.cathsocialservices.org.nz/raising-great-kids/.

Appendix 1 - Some Facts on Domestic and Family Violence

The data below are reproduced from the Our Watch website:[22]

- On average, one woman a week is murdered by her current or former partner.
- 1 in 3 Australian women (30.5%) has experienced physical violence since the age of 15.
- 1 in 5 Australian women (18.4%) has experienced sexual violence since the age of 15.
- 1 in 3 Australian women (34.2%) has experienced physical and/or sexual violence perpetrated by a man since the age of 15.
- 1 in 4 Australian women (23.0%) has experienced physical or sexual violence by a current or former intimate partner since the age of 15.
- 1 in 4 Australian women (23.0%) has experienced emotional abuse by a current or former partner.
- Australian women are nearly three times more likely than men to experience violence from an intimate partner.
- Almost 10 women a day are hospitalised for assault injuries perpetrated by a spouse or domestic partner.
- Women are more than twice as likely as men to have experienced fear or anxiety due to violence from a former partner.
- Almost one in 10 women (9.4%) has experienced violence by a stranger since the age of 15.
- Young women (18-24 years) experience significantly higher rates of physical and sexual violence than women in older age groups.

---

22 The data are reproduced from www.ourwatch.org.au/quick-facts/#key-statistics-on-violence-against-women-in-australia.

- There is evidence that women with disability are more likely to experience violence.
- 1 in 5 Aboriginal and Torres Strait Islander women aged 15 and over has experienced physical violence in a 12-month period. Over one-third of Aboriginal and Torres Strait Islander women who had experienced physical violence in the year preceding 2014-2015 identified an intimate partner as the perpetrator of their most recent experience of physical violence.
- There is a lack of comprehensive, population-wide data on violence experienced by LGBTIQ people; however, existing data and research suggest that rates of violence experienced by LGBTIQ people are at least comparable to that experienced by the wider female population. For example, one study has found that lesbian, bisexual and heteroflexible women are at least twice as likely to experience physical violence by a partner than heterosexual, cisgender women.
- In 2017-2018, the number of women making calls to elder abuse helplines across Australia exceeded men, with emotional and financial abuse most commonly reported.
- There is a lack of comprehensive, population-wide data on prevalence and impacts of violence against women from migrant and refugee backgrounds. Specific studies suggest high prevalence rates and specific issues of complexity, such as a partner using a woman's temporary migrant status as a means of violence.

SECTION 3
Catholic Social Services at the Margins

Parishes as an Integral Part of Social Services

Denis Fitzgerald with Alana Crouch, Cathy Hammond and Mark Phillips

At the *Hearing, Healing, Hope* Catholic Social Services conference in 2018, a workshop on parishes noted that "the parish environment remains a robust and active source of service and social justice",[1] and concluded that

> there is much to be gained from strengthened collaboration between parishes and Catholic social service agencies; such collaboration can deepen and broaden the work of the Church in reaching out to vulnerable and marginalised members of the community.[2]

The parishes and social services workshop at the 2020 Catholic Social Services conference followed up on those themes. It was a rich experience. As the earlier workshop had found, parishes are a vital part of the Church, where most of the Church's interaction with people occurs. They offer a wide range of services to their congregations, and they cooperate with Catholic social service agencies in a variety of ways. Participants in the 2020 workshop were largely from parish settings, from across Australia and New Zealand, with backgrounds in various aspects of parish engagement:

---

1 Gabrielle McMullen, Patrice Scales and Denis Fitzgerald, 2018. "Introduction", p. xix in Gabrielle McMullen, Patrice Scales and Denis Fitzgerald (eds), 2018. *Hearing, Healing, Hope: The Ministry of Service in Challenging Times*. Redland Bay, Qld: Connor Court Publishing.
2 Robert Dixon, 2018. "Love of Neighbour – What are our Parishes Doing?", p. 257 in *Hearing, Healing, Hope*, op. cit. n. 1.

members of the St Vincent de Paul Society, pastoral associates, clergy, parish council members and others. The workshop consisted of two presentations, followed by extensive sharing of experiences and discussion about the potential and the challenges of parishes playing their part in the tapestry of Church-sponsored social services.

The first presentation was led by Alana Crouch, Director of Catholic Early EdCare in Brisbane, and the second by Mark Phillips, CEO, with Cathy Hammond, Executive Manager of Mission and Outreach, with CatholicCare Sydney. Denis Fitzgerald chaired the session. This chapter draws on the input by these presenters, and on the accompanying discussion.

Catholic Early EdCare, Brisbane: Partnering with Parish Communities to Provide Early Education

Crouch has worked with Brisbane Centacare since 2001, in the childcare branch. Her presentation focussed on childcare and education, and their engagement with parishes. Crouch noted that, in addition to her Brisbane role, she was also in the process of creating a childcare agency under the Diocese of Townsville, thus adding to the dioceses that have already adopted a similar model to Brisbane.

Centacare Childcare Services[3] was formed in 2005, because then-Archbishop of Brisbane, John Bathersby, considered childcare to be very important within the worlds of family and parish, and parish and school. The program started by transitioning all of the childcare services that were then embedded in parishes and/or schools to Centacare ChildCare Services, and in 2019 the services were rebranded as Catholic EarlyEd Care.

Centacare manages around 128 childcare facilities across the

---

3 For further details on this program, see Centacare, n.d. "Child Care – Overview" at https://centacarebrisbane.net.au/child-care/overview-child-care/.

PARISHES AS AN INTREGRAL PART OF SOCIAL SERVICES

Archdiocese of Brisbane. Two-thirds of these are 'owned' by parishes, and managed on their behalf. They include nine stand-alone kindergartens, which provide pre-school education in the year before the first formal year of school. These were built as standalone facilities, and one of them is now parish-owned. There are 104 outside-school-hours (OSH) centres, 82 of which are managed on behalf of a parish. There are five hubs as part of a new initiative (which is touched on below). Approx. 26,900 children attended these services in 2019. They connect with a lot of children in our Catholic schools and parishes.

Centacare Brisbane has partnered its childcare services with Wollongong and Toowoomba over the past several years so that these other dioceses could establish local agencies to manage childcare. Brisbane has learnt from this experience how different dioceses work and how they each engage with parishes and school communities – "every diocese is incredibly different, as is every parish within every diocese", Crouch emphasised.

Eighty-four of the 128 Catholic EarlyEd Care services are parish-owned. Centacare engages with all parishes within the Archdiocese of Brisbane, and now also with those in the Diocese of Townsville. Administrative and service staff have regular meetings with parish priests and school communities, in which they talk about the program for the children in their schools and parishes. Staff also attend parish council meetings by invitation. Services have advisory groups that ask parents to attend so that there can be conversations about community needs and the provision of care.

Partnerships with local Catholic schools and parishes is a large element in Catholic EarlyEd Care's operating model – the fundamental way that Centacare positions itself within childcare services. "We don't sit there implementing independent childcare centres; we're embedded in these communities and we form part of them", Crouch explained. Because of this, all services are named after their school or parish. For example, there are eight St Joseph's OSH care centres because that is where they sit and where they belong.

Centacare provides parish-owned services with financial reports, and distributes surplus operational funds back to parishes, depending on the childcare agreements and policies that are in place. The parties work together on capital projects. This is of central importance for the service hubs, where Centacare needs to determine how they can best sit in the community and distribute additional services, rooms, consulting services and so forth. Couch related, "We're also able to support initiatives related to our other programs". Music groups, men's clubs, women's groups, mothers' groups and playgroups all use Catholic EarlyEd Care facilities.

In a similar vein and using symbols, prayers, reflection and engagement, programs also aim to reflect the charism of the parish or the school through the spirituality of the children and in the activities they undertake. Crouch provided some examples of this integration of spirituality into the daily operations of childcare. Grace at mealtimes is a moment to gather and reflect and it brings to life the charism of the parish and the school. The parish priests and other parish personnel often come to a centre to teach and work with the children. An example of this is 'Claire's Special Visits'. Claire is a member of the Graceville parish in Brisbane, and every Wednesday she pops across to the childcare centre for reading and other activities. The children just love her, and every year the next cohort of children comes through knowing that Claire will come. If the parish has a feast day or if the school has a saint's day, the centre will often be involved, and the parish priest might come to spend the afternoon with the children.

These linkages build familiarity between a parish and the children. Although they may not necessarily be in the Church on a Sunday morning, this is a way for them to be involved in the activities of the Church. Crouch told of a recent Ash Wednesday liturgy where the parish priest at a parish-owned kindergarten in Kenmore, Brisbane, was quite entertained by the number of questions that the children asked him. She reflected, "This is such a great opportunity for these three-year-old kids to be immersed in the mission of the Church and to be immersed in parish before they and their parents experience the formality of it in an educational institution. The children all had a cross on their forehead at pickup time, which gets the conversations happening". And through follow up visits to the centre and arranging to be there at pick-up time, the parents become familiar with the priest and feel as though they can build a safe relationship with him.

Another anecdote involved a couple of elderly members of the Gatton parish who regularly help the children with the OSH garden:

> They're very experienced gardeners and they want to pass on their legacy; the front of the Church is theirs and they want to make the kindergarten grounds the same. Again, this is a parish initiative – the parishioners approached us wanting to come and pass on their knowledge to the children. This is a wonderful way to create that intergenerational connection that is so vital in so many of our parishes.

Centacare is now working to create multi-care hubs when they develop and design new childcare facilities, with five already established. These bring together different types of care. For example, long day care and OSH programs at Springfield Lakes, Brisbane, have consulting rooms, meeting rooms and a commercial kitchen that are able to be used by various parish agencies and programs. They host a men's breakfast and mothers' group, for instance, and use the space for parish liturgy preparation. A recent hub in a fairly new suburb of Brisbane, Yarrabilba, is about to start hosting Mass on a Sunday in the hub's large meeting room.

Yarrabilba does not yet have a church, so the hub is a timely presence.

Being part of Centacare Brisbane also gives Catholic EarlyEd Care the opportunity to work with the other directorates of Centacare, which encompass community services in age and disability care, community and family relationships, counselling and parenting programs. These interrelationships enhance services for the communities supported by Centacare.

Crouch concluded that the most important thing about the role of Catholic EarlyEd Care is that it always works in partnership with communities: "We're invited into communities and our aim from day one is to form relationships with parishes and schools in order to support families and children and to enable them to grow as part of the Catholic community in which they live".

CatholicCare Sydney: Forming Parishes as Communities of Care

Mark Phillips commenced his presentation with a reflection on the variety of ways in which the Church offers its ministries. In the Archdiocese of Sydney early childhood services are managed by schools rather than by CatholicCare, because its Archbishop took the view that childcare was more of an educational experience rather than a social service. Moreover, CatholicCare's interaction with parishes has varied significantly over time – there was very little interaction three years ago, and it is now building up again.

He related this change to the teaching of the Church, and mentioned Pope Benedict XVI's first encyclical,[4] on love:

> He stated that the Church has three duties: the sacraments and the Word and then what you might call the ministry

---

[4] Pope Benedict XVI, 2005. Encyclical Letter: *Deus Caritas Est – God is Love*, Section 25; accessed at www.vatican.va.

of Charity, acts of love or mercy, or the welfare function. That's the third duty of the Church and it's inseparable from the other two. A parish doesn't make sense if doesn't have all three parts, interwoven together.

This was seen as a challenge for CatholicCare: "If we're the diocesan agency in charge of the ministry of charity then we've got to get into the parishes; we're called to do so", Phillips said. He then outlined a number of parish-focused programs that have been developed.

Three years ago CatholicCare established a team that was to be a permanent relationship point with parishes.[5] As there was no revenue associated with this initiative, it was quite a big step to take. The objective was to demonstrate that parishes could become "communities of care" – that was an interim formulation, but the same terminology is in use three years later.

Phillips then turned to how this concept of community care was given flesh, as CatholicCare worked to implement the initiative in Liverpool and Fairfield, two large Catholic parishes in the south-west of Sydney, which are both socio-economically and ethnically diverse. The pilot program, which has been in place for some months, puts a community care worker – a social worker – into the parishes on a regular basis for a year. It has been funded from a range of sources: the parishes, donations and the Archdiocese.

To date, the community care worker has worked principally with the parish priests who get approached regularly in relation to the needs of the community. Other members of the parish community, and people outside that community, can also make the worker aware of families and/or individuals who are in need of assistance. This is

---

[5] For further information on CatholicCare's parish focus, see CatholicCare, n.d. "Sydney Parishes" at www.catholiccare.org/catholiccare-learn-more/sydney-parishes/.

not detailed casework; the community care worker essentially runs a referral service in order to assist members of the parish to find the help that they need by pointing them in the direction of local services that they can access.

Phillips provided examples of issues that had come forward in the first few months.

> There was a young man who had been released from jail after serving a sentence for drink driving. He was homeless, desperate, cold and hungry, sleeping on a park bench in Fairfield. He was referred to our community care worker on approaching the parish for assistance with food and blankets. He was provided with support and also referred to the St Vincent de Paul Society as well as to some housing providers in the area. He returned to the parish over the Christmas break and told the priest that he was renting a unit with a flatmate and no longer sleeping in the park. The program was really helpful in terms of us getting to this person quickly so that he could be provided with what he needed.

Another example was also recounted:

> … an older parishioner in the Liverpool parish had recently moved into the area and she was basically on her own; she had three sons but they weren't necessarily visiting her. The community care worker contacted the lady on referral and the lady said that she was hungry and her fridge was just about empty. Again, we were able to assist her with the services that she needed and we also referred her to the local seniors' group and put her on the list for priority public housing. The only way that she'd actually considered seeking help was via the contact details for the local community care worker, which she'd seen on postcards put up in the local parish.

PARISHES AS AN INTREGRAL PART OF SOCIAL SERVICES

A number of other parishes in Sydney have expressed interest in participating in this initiative, which aims to locate services as close to the frontline as possible, with the parish often the first-to-know point for families and individuals in need. Schools can also play a part in this role and CatholicCare is planning to build on that relationship too. CatholicCare currently provides school counselling services into Sydney Catholic Schools but school counsellors in these schools have to limit their services to the students and are unable to reach out to the families. This leaves a gap, as so often the problems that students bring to school are tied to family issues. Bridging this gap is a target for a further pilot program.

Another relatively recent initiative at CatholicCare Sydney is CCareline. This single portal has replaced a range of CatholicCare phone numbers previously in place for contacting its services. Thus, CCareline is the phone number for accessing all CatholicCare services. There is also a CCareline app, which has a refer-a-friend function – by downloading the app, priests and members of parish communities have the means to refer someone else to CatholicCare. Once activated, the CCareline app sends the person relevant information. Then CCareline calls to offer support and refers the person to appropriate services so that they can receive the assistance that they need.

A further community of care initiative is addressing social housing. CatholicCare has engaged a General Manager who is knowledgeable and experienced in social housing and can go out with the Mission and Outreach team to the parishes. The aim is to identify spare and available property and optimise its usage. This requires significant effort, because the use needs to be affordable, and Church property dealings take time. Phillips gave an example:

> There is currently a three-storey building in North Bondi that

used to be used as a boarding house for priests, and which we're going to convert into six apartments as temporary accommodation for young mothers and their children for up to eighteen months. This will be in conjunction with an existing program that we have, to deal with young mothers and their needs. We have philanthropic funding as well as parish funding to support the capital works.

Other housing projects are in train. There is dialogue underway with the parish at Lewisham about converting an old convent into five bungalows as affordable housing for women over the age of 55 who are at risk of homelessness. CatholicCare is also working with another parish to convert an old school building, rented previously to some artists, into accommodation for 35 students, a third of whom will be at risk of homelessness.

Seniors' ministry is another area where it is planned that a parish base will be very fruitful. CatholicCare provides homecare services, and holds meetings to inform parishioners (and, indeed, anyone else who is interested) about the government-funded My Aged Care system. Bridging the large gap in awareness of these services has been successful in helping people get onto the waiting list for access to homecare. CatholicCare plans to grow the scope of the seniors' ministry to include planning for people as they age from about 60 years onwards. "It's not just about homecare, it's about planning all the way through to the end of life, linking in with services like palliative care. This will take a lot of work and development, but again, we want to base it in and around parishes", Phillips explained.

The list could go on. Pastoral supervision for priests is another recently introduced parish-linked service, covering for the first time all clergy members who are active in pastoral ministry. Another proposal is to build links between inner city parishes in Sydney and those further out that were affected by the 2019-2020 bushfires.

The idea is to create partnerships or collaborations in solidarity that will remain in place for as long as needed and provide prayer support, moral support and practical support to the parishes that are so badly in need.

Phillips concluded with a re-statement of his main theme: it is very important for us to connect all of this work to the life of the parish, to create community. Hammond complemented his remarks with an endorsement of Crouch's reflection that every parish is different. When her team goes into a parish to build relationships and to serve the parish, to help them build community, it has to be on their terms and in their own time: "We have to listen really carefully and try our best to give them what their community needs".

Open Forum

The workshop room was abuzz as participants shared their reactions to these case studies, and their reflections on the broader challenges of parish and agency engagement. Three themes emerged: the challenge to avoid detrimental bureaucratisation, the importance of focusing on value-add by agencies through means such as centralised information provision, and the importance of not losing site of smaller, local initiatives.

Might the employment of a social worker 'institutionalise' a parish, and move it away from the person-to-person service that is one of the great strengths of, for example, the St Vincent de Paul Society? Phillips recognised the risk, but did not think it was a major one. One feature of parishes that he identified was how busy the clergy are, and how little appetite there is to take on additional administrative responsibilities. CatholicCare can assist there, without adding undue complexity. However, the larger a set of services become, the more that risk increases, and Phillips could see the risk of a parish priest being pushed towards a CEO role if too many services were developed.

That led to a discussion of some very large parish endeavours, at St Agnes in Port Macquarie, and Sacred Heart Mission at St Kilda in Melbourne. Both have evolved in different ways, but both evolved from simple parish services and are now multi-faceted professional service providers for their local community.

A number of participants were very familiar with Sacred Heart Mission which, while maintaining a link with the parish, is no longer run by the parish. It started out more than 30 years ago when someone knocked on the presbytery door and said he was hungry, and Fr Ernie Smith invited him in for a meal. Today, the workshop was told, it is a strategic goal of the Sacred Heart parish council to maintain the links between parish, Mission and school: "We're always trying to keep those three elements together and to keep everyone involved". So, the risk of separation is present, and is actively managed.

Discussion turned to the other end of the scale, to parish services like a mums' group or the provision of meals for families experiencing illness. Those services are still being provided by parishioners across the country and, it was observed, you do not want them to be crowded out.

One participant, a parish pastoral associate, described her parish outreach. She and her colleagues visit homes of people who have been referred to them through the parish – frequently people who are older or lonely, or people with mental health issues. These visits often start by taking the Eucharist, which is a very intimate type of sharing, and in that context people will open up about issues in general. An important aspect is being aware of your limitations, and to refer a person on if it is beyond the visitor's capacity to assist. The parish priest is actively involved in the program: he also makes visits, he makes recommendations about people for others to visit, and he is kept updated on progress. It is very much a parish ministry, where the parish nurtures a relationship of care,

PARISHES AS AN INTREGRAL PART OF SOCIAL SERVICES

even if the person visited does not have other involvement with the parish.

A number of participants reflected on the value of centralised information and referral systems, along the lines of the CatholicCare Sydney's CCareline. One large service provider with a parish outreach goal noted that they offer information resources to many parishes, but:

> ... it's all paper and pamphlets with different phone numbers for various services. A centralised referral service would be absolutely fantastic for us because I often find it difficult to know what information to give out as a pastoral associate and the services and contact details change all the time.

The St Vincent de Paul Society's central phone service in Melbourne was mentioned as a valuable complement to other activities. For CatholicCare Sydney's CCareline, there are around twelve staff working the phones, and they take calls from anyone. Hammond related:

> We had a priest call up recently because he had a refugee family turn up on his doorstep and he didn't really know what to do. He called our central number and we were able to get a translator over the phone and get the family into emergency housing straight away and provide them with wrap-around services. The centralised phone service takes a huge amount of pressure off priests and pastoral associates.

Phillips also put the case for large scale organisations, necessary economies of scale being an important factor in many aspects of education, healthcare and also in social services. Crouch commented:

> I had a letter from a parish priest the other day that accused

us of becoming more and more like a bureaucracy because we've raised the administration fee for the running of childcare centres from 10 to 15 percent. I wrote back saying that we are a bureaucracy because that's the only way to run childcare ... If you had to [go through the Government registration requirements, etc. that we undertake] in each of the 104 parishes out there, the administration fee would be going up to 30 per cent.

A related point in favour of engaging with large scale activities is that we have a responsibility to work with governments to help them understand the community and its requirements. One participant shared as follows:

In my experience, their understanding of care and support and work on the ground is all but lost because they've sold it off to us ... Unless we continue to engage with government then there's no opportunity to make sure these services are run properly ... Even if we had our own money and we were doing all of these things off our own bat, someone would have come and regulated us by now. Bureaucracy is a challenge that we have to keep dealing with.

Conclusions

Closing reflections revealed the impact on all participants of the vibrant session.

Crouch led with the simple line: partnerships with parish are crucial. Service providers cannot reach the people unaided, nor can they go into a parish with the attitude that 'we can do it all better'. Agencies need to position themselves to support the community, school and parish, and all of those are complex environments. Parishes do not exist on their own anymore: school is a vital part of parish life, so too is childcare, and there is also a need there for aged care and disability support. An important challenge for agencies is to identify these service needs and to resource parishes so that together we can connect with them.

Hammond reflected on the value of sharing accounts of our experiences. She was energised by hearing the experience of Sacred Heart Mission: developments with parishes in Sydney have been messy, but hearing about Sacred Heart "gives me hope that what we're doing in Sydney is sowing a seed for the future".

Hope and humility were the key elements of Fitzgerald's conclusions. The Brisbane experience of a service model that empowers parishes, generates funds to run services there, and builds a real sense of ownership, speaks of hope and of humility – it is not all about the agency! And it has been exported to several other dioceses. Fitzgerald saw that as a very positive step towards a future in which services are an integral part of the Church at every level and parishes truly respond to the challenge set down by Pope Benedict. He also commented on the humility of the outreach program in Sydney. "The best that we have comes from the ability to interact humbly with others, to put our gifts at the service of others and to complement their gifts", he said.

Fitzgerald noted that, following the seminar, he would be working to impress on colleagues how the work of parishes can be better recognised and supported, and how the synergies between parishes and agencies can be better developed across the country.

Phillips had the final word. He revisited the discussion on bureaucracy, reminding the gathering of Pope Benedict XVI's challenge to the Church, as an organisation, to complement the loving service of individual Christians by organising itself around love and charity.[6] Phillips added, however, how important it is that this not duplicate services that are already available, but build on

---

6 *Deus Caritas Est*, op. cit. n. 4, Section 20.

and support the volunteer-based work that is the treasure trove of Catholic social services. Funding, he reminded everyone, important as it is, is only a means to an end. Pope Francis spoke at the beginning of his Papal ministry about being a poor church for the poor,[7] and under his direction part of the Vatican has now been turned into a home for the homeless.[8] Such action speaks volumes.

---

7 ABC, 17 March 2013. "Pope Francis wishes for a 'poor church'"; accessed at www.abc.net.au/news/2013-03-16/pope-francis-wishes-for-a-poor-church/4577724?nw=0.

8 ABC, 4 February 2020. "Pope Francis arranges for 19th century Palazzo Migliori to be converted into a homeless shelter"; accessed at www.abc.net.au/news/2020-02-04/vatican-palace-turned-into-homeless-shelter-pope-francis/11929828.

The Mission Alive in Regional and Rural Communities

Claire-Anne Willis with Meagan Giddy and Maryanne Stivactas

Introduction

Significant challenges face organisations that provide social services in regional and rural communities throughout Australia. They include finding and retaining qualified, skilled and experienced staff, providing services across vast geographic areas, and the significant costs of transport for both staff and clients. For some organisations, these challenges have fostered greater collaboration between services, at times with unlikely partners and across sectors, to develop innovative place-based solutions tailored to the specific needs of people in their local communities.

Over the summer of 2019-2020 much of regional and rural Australia was in the grip of drought. Unprecedented bushfires and floods then destroyed vast tracts of farming land and natural habitats and decimated many communities. The environmental and economic costs of these natural disasters brought climate change to the forefront of a national conversation about how we interact with our environment into the future. Subsequently, the COVID-19 pandemic changed our manner of work and the Australian economy in ways never seen before, placing additional burdens on regional and rural communities.

These crises impact severely on those affected. Relationships are under strain; and many people face problems regarding livelihood, income security and finances. A workshop at the Catholic Social Services conference, entitled "The Mission Alive in Regional and Rural Communities", examined how community services in regional and rural areas are responding to these immediate and long-term issues, to assist communities strengthen resilience and build hope for the future. The workshop was chaired by Rhonda Lawson-Street, Director of CatholicCare Sandhurst. Presentations were made by Maryanne Stivactas, Communities for Children Program Coordinator, CatholicCare Sandhurst, and Meagan Giddy, Team Leader and Family Worker, CatholicCare Wilcannia-Forbes. Their contributions are summarised in this chapter.

The presentations by Stivactas and Giddy each focused on initiatives in their own regions that strengthen specific communities through place-based responses. They include 'joined-up' service systems that develop capacity for prevention, early intervention and targeted responses. The programs demonstrate how passionate and committed staff and volunteers can shape the future of their communities as they serve them with courage and compassion. Such strong and dynamic webs of support that sustain individuals and families can build communities that are greater than the sum of their parts. They provide metaphorical examples of 'human future-proofing'!

Communities for Children Program – CatholicCare Sandhurst, Shepparton, Victoria

CatholicCare Sandhurst offers services across 4,000 square kilometres in the central, north-east and north-central part of Victoria. It is the facilitating agency for the federally-funded Communities for Children Program (CfC) in Shepparton, 200 kilometres from Melbourne.[1]

The CfC initiative aims to deliver positive outcomes for children aged 0 - 12 years and their families in disadvantaged communities throughout Australia. It uses a whole-of-community approach, which includes the engagement of service providers, governments, peak bodies and the community, to increase collaboration and integration across the children's and family service system. There are fifty-two CfCs around Australia. Each takes a place-based approach to respond to the specific needs of their community. For example, the CfC in Bendigo has different focus areas to Shepparton, based on different community needs.

The Shepparton CfC uses a family-centred approach to improve service accessibility, responsiveness and outcomes for vulnerable families and children. As the facilitating agency,[2] CatholicCare Sandhurst has subcontracted nine direct service delivery activities to seven community partners to achieve the outcomes of its strategic plan. The project outcomes so far are encouraging. The conference workshop was advised that an evaluation conducted in 2019 by an external evaluation consultant, Clear Horizon, found improvements in:

- knowledge and skills for parents and staff,

---

[1] For details of the Communities for Children program and its 2010 evaluation, see www.dss.gov.au/families-and-children/programs-services and Kristy Muir, Ilan Katz, Ben Edwards, Matthew Gray, Sarah Wise and Alan Hayes, May 2010. "The National Evaluation of the Communities for Children Initiative", *Family Matters*, No. 84; accessed at https://aifs.gov.au/publications/family-matters/issue-84/national-evaluation-communities-children-initiative.

[2] As facilitating partner, CatholicCare Sandhurst "brokers funding for place-based projects ... in the spirit of collaboration to improve service accessibility, responsiveness and outcomes for families and children in the Greater Shepparton region"; see https://ccds.org.au/kids-youth-services and https://sheppartoncfc.com.au/.

- parenting skills and accessing intervention programs,
- increased confidence in parenting and connection to the broader community,
- stronger relationships between organisations that have increased program effectiveness,
- greater collaboration between stakeholders which has reduced the duplication of services and increased the focus to address service gaps.[3]

Setting the CfC strategic direction involved the analysis of multiple data sources and community input to define the key needs. Six priority areas were formulated into a strategic plan. Importantly, the key priorities below do not operate in isolation, but have links with other priority areas to ensure a seamless experience for service users.[4]

Priority Area 1 – Smooth Transitions

The first strategy entails responding more effectively to critical transition points in the lives of children and their families. This is being achieved through a number of funded activities, including:

- The *Play to Learn Program*, delivered by Save the Children, provides a mobile playgroup for rural areas. The program acts as a soft-entry to engage families and strengthen referral pathways. The team includes a family support worker, a trained educator, and a maternal child health nurse. Some groups can transition to becoming a parent-led playgroup.
- The *Second Step Program* is provided through primary and secondary schools to help children at critical

---

[3] The 2018-2019 Clear Horizon's *Greater Shepparton Communities for Children* report can be accessed at https://sheppartoncfc.com.au/wp-content/uploads/2019/10/CfC-Evaluation-Report-2018-19.pdf.

[4] For details of the priority areas and CatholicCare Sandhurst's partners, see https://sheppartoncfc.com.au/.

transition points. This evidence-based program provides information to students about bullying, drugs and alcohol, and relationships and also facilitates referrals to school wellbeing teams.
- The *Future Parenting Program and Young Parents Group* meets weekly to build parenting capacity in a non-threatening environment and is delivered by the Bridge Youth Service. The group creates a safe environment for vulnerable young parents to access assistance programs such as Baby Makes Three, Bringing a Baby Home and Parents Under Pressure.
- The *Parent-Child Day Stay Program* assists parents with baby feeding, sleep and settling issues and operates in conjunction with other health professionals. The program is currently being evaluated by the Australian Institute of Family Studies.

Priority Area 2 – Cross-Cultural Focus

There are a high number of new arrivals to Greater Shepparton, many of whom are children whose first language is not English. CatholicCare Sandhurst promotes cultural competency through funding professional development for cultural reflective practice, foundations of cultural competency, and understanding domestic and family violence across diverse communities. All of its local community partners have Access Plans to promote equity and inclusion. Each plan details how culturally and linguistically diverse communities can access activities and programs. Specific cross-cultural CfC-funded programs include the following:

- The *Cultural Connections Plus Program,* delivered by Kildonan Uniting Care, builds the capacity of culturally and linguistically diverse families through the Parenting and New Culture Program and the Through the Looking Glass Playgroup. The latter is a trauma-informed playgroup model that includes transitional support – bicultural workers are available to facilitate smooth transitions for children entering kindergarten or transitioning into school.

- The *Seasons for Growth Initiative* is delivered by Primary Care Connect in local primary schools. This initiative assists children who have experienced trauma in association with migrating to Australia. There has been positive engagement from teachers which has increased consultations between local schools and improved the experience of newly arrived refugee families.

Priority Area 3 – Closing the Gap

The Closing the Gap priority area reflects the targets set by the Council of Australian Governments to reduce the gap in health and wellbeing outcomes between Indigenous and non-Indigenous Australians. Developing strong and meaningful partnerships with local Indigenous leaders and organisations has been key to establishing effective ways for the CfC to assist the local Indigenous community:

- *Strong Families, Smooth Transitions* is delivered by CatholicCare Sandhurst through a family support worker in Lulla's Children and Family Centre. The worker provides an holistic and culturally sensitive approach for children transitioning into kindergarten or school. In particular, the worker supports families with medical appointments, takes students to bush kinder, and conducts the Drumbeat program for children who attend the centre.

- The *Cultural Practice Series* involves training that focuses on inclusion. The sessions aim to build cultural awareness across the community. Participants have the opportunity to identify further training required. Workshops provided by Professor Gracelyn Smallwood have resulted in the provision of Indigenous cultural resource packs that are used by participating centres for children and families. Staff training sessions about the impact of trauma on families and how this affects the first thousand days in a child's life have also occurred.

An important evolution of this priority area has been the development of a steering group to address the under-representation of Aboriginal children and families in primary services such as maternal and child health services, kindergarten and playgroups. The cultural practice collaboration commenced in 2016. Deb Walsh, the former director of the Rumbalara Aboriginal Cooperative, was a key driver. The group has drawn in a wide range of providers to improve outcomes for local Indigenous children and their families. It has developed a Statement of Intent, signed by participating organisations, and has a shared action plan. A positive outcome is the inclusion of a family engagement worker, to work alongside the maternal and child health service, a need identified by the local community. The worker attends all the first home visits, providing an important opportunity to engage families and provide a familiar and safe service that emphasises the need for children to grow and thrive in a community that cares about them.

Priority Area 4 – Communication

The aim of the communication priority area is to ensure effective engagement with the local community and agencies, and to explore new ways to encourage families facing disadvantage to use the services available through the CfC program. This goal has been achieved through:

- active participation in family and children's events across Greater Shepparton,

- using the continuous Most Significant Change technique[5] to evaluate client access and experience of funded programs,
- community partners receiving training to ensure continuous quality improvement of service access and experience,
- cross-sectional learning across agencies and programs which has occurred as a result of the collaborations.

Priority Area 5 – Partnership

The relational and collaborative approach of CatholicCare Sandhurst as the facilitating partner has been critical to the success of the CfC program. The project adopted a 'no-wrong-door' approach in order to provide a seamless service experience for vulnerable families. This has required strong partnerships that recognise the importance of collaboration. The community partners have embraced a collective impact model and work to identify a common agenda and measures to achieve shared outcomes. This approach has involved:

- identifying key partners to deliver programs and meeting regularly with them,
- honest dialogue between services,
- promoting a culture of collaboration,
- committing to working flexibly between service providers,
- maintaining relationships to enable effective referral mechanisms.

Partnerships are supported through memorandums of understanding. In addition, evidence of previous inter-agency collaboration is a prerequisite for CfC funding of an activity or program.

---

5 "The Most Significant Change (MSC) approach involves generating and analysing personal accounts of change and deciding which of these accounts is the most significant"; see www.betterevaluation.org/en/plan/approach/most_significant_change.

The CfC collaborates across service sectors through a range of networks and collaborative projects – thus, there are collaborations of the community services sector with both the education and healthcare sectors. It is working with the Best Start Lighthouse to follow up the 2014 *State of Greater Shepparton Children's Report*,[6] by accessing a range of different data sets from across Greater Shepparton to assess how the children of the region are faring now.

Priority Area 6 – Evidence Base

At least fifty per cent of the activities funded by the CfC project are required to meet evidence-based requirements set by the Department of Social Services.[7] The CfC initiative has helped its community partners to get their projects recognised for this purpose. The conference workshop was informed that the CfC's most recent annual plan shows impressively that seventy-eight per cent of direct service delivery was allocated to evidence-based programs.

Training has been an important part of building local capacity. The CfC has funded ten evidence-based facilitator training programs for community partners and Aboriginal and Torres Strait Islander workers in the community. This training was tailored for local needs and has reduced the travel time for staff to attend training and costs to the organisation. The project's Theory of Change is a living document that is continuously reviewed and updated to reflect changing needs in the community. The project will shortly commence strategic planning in anticipation of seeking funding for the period after June 2021. The evidence-based practice that has been adopted will inform that planning.

Within the broader CfC Program, there is a strong focus on

---

6 See *State of Greater Shepparton's Children Report 2014*; accessed at www.gslp.com.au/wp-content/uploads/State-of-GS-Children-Report_Sept2014.pdf.
7 For details of the guidelines, see https://aifs.gov.au/cfca/expert-panel-project/communities-children-requirements/selecting-evidence-based-program.

monitoring, evaluating and learning. In Victoria, the various CfC programs meet annually to exchange ideas, experiences and progress. The development of consistent and meaningful benchmarking (pre- and post-service scoring by clients) and collecting meaningful data across CfCs is a challenging issue that is under active consideration. The strength of CfCs is their ability to respond to local needs, so benchmarking needs to maintain local specificity and should not unduly disrupt clients' engagement.

Conclusion

The CfC initiative allows for significant flexibility so that place-based responses can be developed locally in order to target specific local needs. However, as is the case for many community services, ongoing funding from Government beyond three-year service agreements remains a challenge. The CfC in Greater Shepparton has achieved increased and effective collaboration between service providers and more broadly with other sectors, such as health and education, to improve outcomes for vulnerable children and their families.

Wellbeing Mobile – CatholicCare Wilcannia-Forbes, New South Wales

CatholicCare Wilcannia-Forbes' (CCWF) response to the needs of drought-affected families who live in isolated locations in central and far western New South Wales is based on two simple premises: firstly, people know what they need, and secondly, people will access needed services and activities if they are available locally. This has been the approach that CCWF has taken to develop place-based responses to address the needs of small rural and remote communities in its region.[8]

---

[8] The following article provides further information on the situation in Wilcannia-Forbes and the work of CatholicCare: Kaitlyn Fasso-Opie, "Helping Struggling Farmers", *Australian Catholics*, 7 May 2019.

CCWF provides multi-disciplinary services across the western half of New South Wales. Most of the communities serviced are rural or remote, located more than four hours drive from regional centres. Further, they have high Aboriginal populations, averaging twenty-two per cent of the total population.

Farmers describe the 2017-2020 drought as the worst they have seen. It has exhausted their resources, their spirit and their hope. Many farms are completely de-stocked, leaving families without an income. Many families and communities suffer in silence and are reluctant to ask for help. Such communities are isolated and shrinking, the ongoing drought drawing people and businesses away to find other opportunities or employment. Much-needed community services do not exist or can only be accessed by driving long distances. In addition, transport and accommodation costs often make the latter option prohibitive.

Since the start of the drought, CCWF has raised awareness about mental health issues among farming families. When CCWF staff asked families around the Broken Hill region what they needed, their response was "distractions and strategies to keep positive". In response, CCWF has run events in the communities to offer people an opportunity to meet with neighbours and friends to socialise, check in with each other, and have fun. The people attending did not need to organise anything, no-one had to volunteer; they could just turn up. The events held from mid-2018 to early 2019 varied from football games, sausage sizzles and cinema nights.

As a result of the initial events, trust was built and families were able to say what they most needed: they wanted more counselling assistance. CCWF developed an outreach model that combined face-to-face meetings with video-enabled and phone counselling components. Funding through the Foundation for Rural and

Regional Renewal[9] enabled the counsellor based in Broken Hill to visit isolated farms and communities to provide face-to-face individual and group counselling. The counsellor conducted monthly visits to small centres, remaining for a week to conduct sessions. Local pubs played a significant role, providing a space for the counselling and getting the word out to the local community. Friends referring friends was also common. Priority was given to farming families. Individual sessions, consisting of counselling, relationship education and hypnotherapy, were quickly filled. Follow-up appointments were made available over Zoom video-conferencing or the phone. Evening groups with an emphasis on self-care and relaxation were also offered. CCWF also made use of existing events to provide wellbeing workshops; in one instance, CCWF collaborated with the School of the Air to provide the workshop to governesses who were attending an in-service. Over a twelve-month period the program reached fifty-eight individuals and the counselling service became a much-welcomed 'visitor' to these communities.

Key learnings from the program include:

- services need to become part of the community to be effective;
- building rapport through social events can help people to seek further assistance;
- local relationships are critical change agents; and
- technology can be very useful but needs to be used in conjunction with face-to-face interactions.

Regrettably, the Foundation for Rural and Regional Renewal was unable to provide funding beyond the twelve months to continue this initiative, but CCWF was able to build on the success

---

9 The Foundation for Rural and Regional Renewal seeks to strengthen rural, regional and remote communities in partnership with philanthropy, government and business; see www.frrr.org.au/.

of the initial work with further funding from the same body, under the Tackling Tough Times Together initiative, to develop the Wellbeing Mobile.[10]

Developing the Wellbeing Mobile

The Wellbeing Mobile initiative is an innovative approach to delivering adult-focused wellbeing services to farming families and remote communities. The goal of the program is to increase participants' ability to identify their own risk factors, such as poor emotional, mental and physical health, and to increase their capacity to find and apply protective strategies and solutions to address their problems or seek help from support services.

This service operates in conjunction with the already established children's service, the "Bush Mobile", for ten rural or remote communities within the Bogan Shire in central New South Wales. Each of the ten shire communities has been severely impacted by deterioration of stock and crops, financial hardship, loss of livelihood and family property, and isolation and relationship breakdowns. Many residents suffer poor emotional and physical health but have limited access to services. The Bush Mobile provides playgroups to farming families in these remote locations.

In collaboration with the Bush Mobile, the Wellbeing Mobile Coordinator is able to engage these established groups in the ten communities. A two-week consultation process enabled participants to identify their own wellbeing needs so that a package of services could be compiled. An important aspect of the model was building strong partnerships with local services, businesses and the farming community. Sub-contractors were engaged to provide the services. These included the engagement of a number of women within the

---

10 In May 2019, the Foundation for Rural and Regional Renewal distributed over $1.5 million to 61 drought-affected communities in rural, regional and remote Australia under the Tackling Tough Times Together grant program; see www.frrr.org.au/cb_pages/tackling_tough_times_together.php.

communities, who were able to start up their own businesses to provide financial counselling, life coaching, massage and yoga. These women were able to put their skills to use, earn some much needed income and have a role in helping others affected by the drought. They reported that being able to contribute to their family income built their confidence, increased their self-esteem, and has had a positive impact on their family life.

Once the sub-contractors were sourced, a roster was drawn up and sent out to farming families and remote communities to promote the service. Flyers advertising the service were distributed to local gathering places, such as pubs, schools, community hubs and Country Women's Association branches, to ensure everyone was reached. As the word spread, additional services were added to the roster: an exercise physiologist, a nutritionist and an occupational therapist, who each designed and offered a workshop. The model enabled the delivery of a range of wellbeing activities, predominantly for women, tailored to each community. These activities helped to enhance the emotional, mental and physical health of those attending and, where needed, created a pathway to other support services. Feedback from the women attending the sessions has been very positive, many saying that they feel revitalised.

The discussion has now turned to what can be done for the men in these communities. The overwhelming response from farmers has been: "Bring us a comedian, so we can have a laugh and forget about the drought for the moment". So that is the next goal!

An important aspect of this work is support for staff, many of whom are also adversely affected by the drought. CCWF has recently conducted a survey to check on the wellbeing of employees and to ask them for suggestions to address the impacts of stress on them and to enhance their wellbeing. The resulting strategy will include a range of simple low-cost activities such as providing exercise opportunities over lunchtime, while more demanding initiatives will require further planning.

Conclusion

The model of the Wellbeing Mobile is a valuable tool for combating stress, anxiety and depression, particularly during this time of unprecedented drought. Importantly, the early success of the Wellbeing Mobile indicates a model that can be replicated and used in other communities affected by the drought or other calamities, particularly for farming families and remote communities that are often poorly serviced.

Serving Rural Communities with Courage and Compassion

The workshop, "The Mission Alive in Regional and Rural Communities", provided two powerful examples of Catholic social service agencies serving rural and remote communities with courage and compassion. Significantly, their initiatives have also been imaginative and innovative as they have embedded community-informed approaches, strategic partnerships and new technologies. As Australia seeks to recover from the recent wave of natural disasters and the COVID-19 pandemic, more such programs will be critical to supporting the recovery of its rural communities and building capacity to re-vision the future and respond to the call of Pope Francis in *Laudato Si'* to care for "our common home".[11]

---

11 Pope Francis, 2015. Encyclical Letter, *Laudato Si': On Care for Our Common Home*; accessed at w2.vatican.va/.

Ecological Justice: How to Listen to the Cry of the Earth and the Cry of the Poor

Bronwyn Lay and Andrew Hamilton SJ

We have to realise that a true ecological approach always becomes a social approach: it must integrate questions of justice in debates on the environment, so as to hear both the cry of the earth and the cry of the poor – Pope Francis, *Laudato Si'*[1]

What is Ecological Justice? – The Jesuit Social Services Journey

Bronwyn Lay

The statement above from *Laudato Si'* framed the 2020 Catholic Social Services conference workshop on ecological justice, which was a collective enquiry into how to hear, listen and respond to the cry of the earth and the poor.

The workshop was presented as the intense 2019-2020 bushfire season was tapering off and a few weeks before COVID-19 dramatically changed our lives. We were in the midst of two crises, both of which can be seen as fundamentally environmental. The word 'unprecedented' was used about climate change impacts including the increasing ferocity of Australian bushfires. Over that summer 'unprecedented' became part of the vernacular and was sprinkled throughout our conversations. Now we can see that, for the community not directly impacted by the fires, this period prior

---

1 Pope Francis, 2015. Encyclical Letter: *Laudato Si' – On Care for Our Common Home*, Section 49; accessed at w2.vatican.va.

to COVID-19 was a much less intense version of where we are now. Futures that seemed invisible and difficult to imagine are now being seen and transitions are occurring at a fast rate. The year 2020 has tragically deepened our understanding of the social dimensions of environmental crises. Ecological justice is more important than ever before in these stressful times. The primary question of the workshop remains: How do we hear the cry of the earth and the cry of poor?

Jesuit Social Services[2] is a social change organisation. Our mission is to build a just society where all people can live to their full potential. We have over 40 years experience working at the hard end of social justice, working in solidarity with people experiencing disadvantage and working to change policies, practices, ideas and values that perpetuate inequality, prejudice and exclusion.

Since 2008 Jesuit Social Services has fostered an ecological culture where transformation starts with the personal, and the subsequent journey has been grounded in our Ignatian tradition. We have used our original Way of Proceeding[3] as a basis to develop our ecological approach. Our Way of Proceeding recognises three interconnected domains that must be considered in all aspects of the organisation's operations, namely:

- *Human Spirit* – Focusing upon essential anthropological and spiritual questions around what it means to be human and enquiries into the conditions within which humans thrive and have healthy relationships. This involves an informed and discerning process of understanding ourselves, our fellow humans and our relational context.

---

2 For background information on Jesuit Social Services, see https://jss.org.au/.

3 For background information on the 'way of proceeding', see Jesuit Social Services, 2018. *Foundation Document*, p. 14; accessed at https://jss.org.au/wp-content/uploads/2019/08/Foundation-Document-web.pdf.

- *Practice Framework* – Developing a relational way of being and acting that reflects and lives ecological justice. This promotes environmental awareness and ecological justice across our practice areas and our advocacy including justice and crime prevention, settlement and community building, mental health support and wellbeing, and education, training, and employment.
- *Business Processes* – Adopting environmentally sustainable business practices and processes. Discernment is adopted in relation to our financial and other resources so they respect and contribute to, rather than harm, efforts to build a just society.

The Jesuit Social Services approach is to encourage personal relationships with ecology and integrate an ecological justice perspective into all programs and advocacy. The acknowledgement of the interconnection between environmental and social issues has influenced our practice, policy and organisational identity, and shaped our strategy to ensure we are equipped to address the justice issues of the future. We are committed to achieving a just society that contributes to restoring healthy ecological relationships for all. The journey of incorporating ecological justice into our organisational culture and practice has been responsive, iterative and constantly evolving.

What is ecological justice? Ecological is commonly understood as being related to or concerned with the relations and interactions of living organisms to one another and to their environment and habitat. Integral ecology, as understood from the Encyclical Letter *Laudato Si'*, is an holistic paradigm resting on the principle that "everything is interrelated". Ecological justice asks us, personally and collectively, how we can hear cries that are not so obvious. The current dominant cultures that we have inherited have limited capacity or desire to hear the voices of the earth and the marginalised.

This involves thinking through how all the following are in relationship with each other: rivers, insects, local councils, trees, refugees, water, politicians, animals, roads, oceans, built environments. The ecological is about interdependent relationships between everything. And as we are seeing with COVID-19, this can be overwhelming.

What is justice that is ecological? Justice has many manifestations, definitions and histories. These include a non-exhaustive list of concepts and practices, such as distributive, procedural, retributive, regulatory, participatory and restorative justice, as well as concepts and principles such as accountability, recognition and equity. When viewed through an ecological lens, justice includes both social and environmental justice. Ecological justice acknowledges the interdependence and inter-relatedness of everything but the justice element amplifies hearing and responding to the cries of harm that emanate from social and environmental injustice: the cries of the earth and of the poor.

The integration of social and environmental justice allows us to hear what can be ignored in our systems of power. One way of hearing these voices is stillness. Can a process of listening and subsequently hearing also be a holistic, relational and restorative process of discernment? And what do we do with what we hear? If we hear cries where harm, injury, exclusion and suffering are occurring, how do we respond both institutionally and personally?

What does ecological injustice look like? The primary impacts of ecological injustice are social and ecological disasters, degradation, depletion, dysfunction, disruption and destruction. The secondary impacts are scarcity of essential ecological goods, infrastructure failures, governance fragility and financial risk or failure. The tertiary impacts are legal liabilities and regulatory crackdowns and increased compounded vulnerabilities in food, housing, labour markets, civic unrest and population displacements.

Radical and active hope underpins the realisation of ecological justice. In hearing the cries and seeing the harms being enacted against the poor and the earth, it is by entering genuine dialogue that we can learn from each other and from our relationships with the places we live in and are dependent upon. When Jesuit Social Services commenced trying to understand how ecological justice is relevant to our organisation, it was clear that a cultural shift in how we relate to the environment and each other was part of the journey. In *Laudato Si'* this is what Pope Francis refers to as an "ecological conversion", which is a transformation towards healing and healthy relationships personally as well as with our families and communities, public and private organisations, sectors and regions, our institutions and our governance structures:

> If everything is related, then the health of a society's institutions has consequences for the environment and the quality of human life ... Within each social stratum, and between them, institutions develop to regulate human relationships. Anything which weakens those institutions has negative consequences, such as injustice, violence and loss of freedom.[4]

To minimise the unfairness inherent in climate change and environmental degradation, increasing attention is being paid to the idea of a 'just transition'. This represents a proactive approach to avoid widespread disadvantage and inequity from poverty, social unrest, exclusion, alienation and marginalisation as a result of the transitioning of industries, economies and societies towards a healthy relationship between human communities and the ecosystems within which they live. Holistic social, economic and

---

4 Pope Francis, op. cit. n. 1, Section 142, quoting Pope Benedict XVI, 2009. Encyclical Letter: *Caritas in Veritate*, Section 51.

environmental transformation involves deep structural changes in social ecological systems in order to prevent harmful environmental and social impacts upon livelihoods and life and to regenerate and nourish these same systems.

Ecological justice could mean that all relationships, from interpersonal to national and international, need to undergo a just transition, to be more collaborative, based on a deep mutual understanding. This is a grand vision and, on a personal and organisational level, we need shared reflections and actions to rethink our lifestyles, to seek a simpler way of living and using natural resources wisely. It is evident that we all have different individual and national responsibilities, according to positions of power, our capacities and what resources are available. These also determine how we respond to hearing the cries of the earth and the poor: the cry of ecological injustice.

Joint actions alone cannot forge sustainable development if they are not rooted in actual dialogical processes where the voices of the powerless and the cry of the earth are truly heard. Community commitment and collective action are essential for integral ecology. How do we know what to do together?

In the workshop we turned towards each other and asked two questions of each other. How can I listen to the cry of the earth and the cry of the poor? How can my work, my community and/or my organisation contribute to the realisation of ecological justice?

Reflection on Hearing the Cry of the Earth and the Cry of the Poor

Andrew Hamilton SJ

In our workshop conversation we teased out many of the places where we have heard the cry of the poor and the cry of the earth, and how they come together. Here are a few key points that we can take away from reading this chapter.

First, in our reflection on the environment we must make central the connection between the cry of the poor and the cry of the earth. We recognise that if we pollute and neglect the earth and fray the relationships that keep it fertile and sustaining, we trigger the droughts in which poor people starve and pollute the waters that they drink. We recognise, too, that if we neglect and exploit the poor, there are consequences that impact on us: we can, for example, trigger illnesses that plague our cities and destroy our economies.

This point might be made vividly through the story of COVID-19. One of the smallest and simplest organisms on earth grounded planes, emptied city streets, crashed stock exchanges, broke economies and drove people out of work. Many consider that its origin lay, in part, in markets where impoverished farmers sold the meat of animals whose natural habitat had been destroyed. The cry of the poor and of the earth are a measure of the health of our world. Our conversations always need to return to them.

Second, to attend to the cry of the poor and of the earth requires attention. Attention begins by noticing the beauty and complexity of the world around us, the plant, insect and bird life and, for example, the complex harmonies involved in growing flowers and vegetables without insecticides. It also involves noticing the vast amount of plastic used for packaging and the way it enters our waterways and lies strewn by riverbanks, and the continuing pollution of the land caused by long abandoned mines. It involves making ourselves familiar with the causes, effects and ways of mitigating climate change. Flowing from all this attentiveness will be changes in our own lives and action to call for respect for our environment.

When we listen to the cry of the earth we are inevitably drawn to hear the cry of the poor. We notice the people sleeping on our streets, their lack of housing, food and care and their vulnerability to viruses and illness especially as winter draws on. We notice the dirt and lack of sanitation in the barrios where the poor live, and we notice the splendid houses of the rich. We notice tribal people driven out of forest areas in order to enrich further the already rich. Attention again breeds interest, interest breeds solidarity and solidarity breeds action.

Third, to rely on power, technology and undisturbed economic growth to address the cry of the poor and of the earth is disastrous. But governments, which do not hear these cries, continue to do so. When grave issues are forced on their attention, as in the case of the bushfires and COVID-19, they are always tempted to use their power to dictate a technological solution that does not impact on economic growth or people's wealth. This approach may be helpful for dealing with crises: by bringing in the army to help clear roads with heavy machinery during a bushfire, for example. But it is destructive when seen as a fully-fledged response to bushfires – there is much else that is also required. The multi-faceted response in Australia to COVID-19 gives hope that this temptation might be resisted more generally.

An adequate response must be guided by reflection on the factors that led to the fires and their destruction of the natural environment and of human life. These include both the inappropriate use of technology and an economic system that encourages exploitation of the earth and of people. We and our governments must ask what kind of economic framework and what kind of technology will enable us as a society to respond to the cry of the poor and of the earth.

Finally, a postscript: to attend to the cry of the poor and of the earth requires good words that enable good reflection. Stale words and images to do with war, markets and machinery are not up to the task. There is an ecology of words in which the complexity, depth and delicacy of the relationships that make our world are respected. If we care for the beauty, power and fragility of the world of which we are part we must also ensure that we find the right words to mirror them.

Mobilising Media for Mission and Advocacy

*Fiona Basile with Farah Farouque, Sam Patterson,
Andrew Yule and Barney Zwartz*

Effective engagement with the media is valuable for those working in Catholic social services. However, to have impact, fresh and innovative approaches to sharing news and information in a multi-faceted way are essential, as is a strategic and targeted manner in which to engage the media. With effective and well-communicated advocacy, Catholic social service organisations can be better agents for change, voices for the marginalised and 'voiceless', and instruments for influencing public and political discourse. With this in mind, how do we get our stories *out there?* How do we ensure that we are not just speaking to ourselves, within our own walls and silos of Catholic social services? How can your organisation effectively engage with the media to broadcast your stories, to enhance your work and mission, and to support your advocacy?

A forum, "Mobilising Media for Mission and Advocacy", was held during the 2020 Catholic Social Services conference to provide an opportunity for media and communications specialists to share their insights and wisdom on these questions. Sam Patterson, Director of Community Engagement at MacKillop Family Services was panel chair. The panellists were Andrew Yule, General Manager Strategic Communication and Engagement at Jesuit Social Services; Farah Farouque, then Principal Advisor Public Affairs and Policy at the Brotherhood of St Laurence (BSL);

and Barney Zwartz, journalist and Senior Fellow at the Centre for Public Christianity. Each of the panellists shared their 'top tips' and 'strategies' for effectively engaging with the media in the current climate. Yule closed the session with a case study, which demonstrated how Jesuit Social Services had effectively engaged with the media on the issue of youth justice, in order to change the public and political narrative. What follows is a summary of the presentations and ensuing discussion.

Influencing the Broader System

In opening, Patterson outlined a set of criteria for high-impact not-for-profit entities, developed by two Harvard researchers and detailed in their book, *Forces for Good*:[1]

> The big insight in our original work was that high-impact nonprofits focus on mobilising forces beyond their four walls, rather than worrying only about internal management or scaling up their organisations ... The most successful nonprofits, we found, spend most of their time trying to change entire systems by advocating for government policies, tapping into the power of free markets, nurturing nonprofit networks, and building movements of evangelists—individual volunteers and supporters who advance their cause. And to be effective at influencing external systems, they share leadership internally and adapt quickly to changing conditions. These then were the six practices that great nonprofits use to have markedly more impact than their peers.

While some Catholic social services are set up purely for advocacy, most aim both to advocate and to serve. The commitment

---

[1] Leslie R. Crutchfield and Heather McLeod Grant, 2012. *Forces for Good: The Six Practices of High-Impact Nonprofits*. San Francisco: John Wiley & Sons Inc.

to, and resources for advocacy can be difficult to achieve, given the practical need to focus energies on those being served. For instance, MacKillop Family Services in Melbourne works with some of the most vulnerable people in the community. Patterson explained:

> We need to be constantly asking ourselves how we can influence the system rather than just continuing to work in the way that we always have. This can be a challenge because we're conscious of not wanting to 'bite the hand that feeds', which can prevent advocacy by organisations heavily dependent on government funding. But advocacy is critical for an effective not-for-profit. We need to not only keep these kids safe through our frontline staff, but we also need to use our knowledge to influence policy and ensure that the system is better for kids in the future.

This highlights the need for good communication systems to be utilised by those working in the sector. Patterson stated:

> You can't serve and advocate without telling stories. You can't engage corporates, inspire the community to get involved or nurture networks without telling stories. We need to not only tell stories but to access the channels that can get our stories out to the broader community.

Am I Providing Something of Value?

Yule shared his experiences: "One of the main things I've learned working for organisations that are trying to get issues-based stories in the media is that it's always a negotiation, it's always an agreement. You provide something of value to them and they provide something of value to you". If you have an event coming up, or a media release that needs to go out, when approaching a journalist, always consider what you are offering the media organisation. Think about:

- What is it about my offer that would make a journalist, in particular, want to follow up this story?
- How will it benefit what I am trying to achieve for the organisation, for the people at the centre of the issue, or the issue itself?

These questions are important to keep in mind, otherwise we can fall into the trap of trying to get media for the sake of media. Only send out a release when you really have something pertinent to say. If you are sending something every day, without something new to say, you will be seen as a nuisance, and your media releases will often be deleted unread. Zwartz, formerly a journalist at *The Age* for 32 years, the last 12 years of those as religion editor, suggested: "One of the best advantages is to be counter-cultural, not to fail what I call the 'they would say that' test. If a news editor's first response is, 'well they would say that, wouldn't they?', your chances plummet".

Often the best way to get a story 'up' is to provide some fresh news and facts, an expert voice and a human interest aspect. If you can tick off those three things, there is a good chance that you will get some coverage. Think like a journalist, and not an advocate. Provide text that is written in a news style, which is easy for media outlets to republish. In the current media climate, more and more journalists are sourcing stories from media releases, rather than from contacts or their own research. "You probably have ten seconds or less to hold the attention of a news editor or whoever is the point of entry for the media organisation, so be direct and stick to the point. If there is a strong human-interest angle or a photo opportunity, make that information prominent", stated Zwartz.

Know Your Purpose

What are you trying to achieve by approaching a journalist or media outlet to obtain coverage? There can be very different reasons for trying to generate media coverage on a story. It might be:

- to give a platform to someone who does not otherwise have their voice heard,
- to pressure government to adopt certain policies or stances,
- to create an alternative narrative where there otherwise has not been one, or
- to stand up for an issue simply because it is the right thing to do.

By stopping for a moment and considering the outcome that you are hoping to achieve, you can determine how you are going to pitch the story, to whom you are going to target the story, and who you are going to use as the 'voice' for the story. There is no point engaging with the media for no outcome – that is critical to understand. In calling for a new narrative when engaging with the media, it must be a new narrative of purpose.

Human Interest Stories

It is important to share the lived experience of people who have been affected by the issues that we want to talk about. Human interest stories can be a difficult issue, particularly when you work with vulnerable people or people with complex pasts, even though they might now be in a position to be a spokesperson. We have a duty of care and we need to be aware that they may not want to be known for the same issue in two or three years time. They may not want to have that on the public record. These are decisions that we need to consider and discuss with them.

Jesuit Social Services work with a lot of young people in the criminal justice system who are also dealing with many other issues. The agency wants to give these young people the opportunity to be part of change, which is really empowering for them. Further, it knows that their stories connect well with the general public. Similarly, MacKillop Family Services has recently been working with some young people who are in their mid-twenties and seven or eight years out of the child protection system. "Many of them feel really empowered and proud to have the opportunity to share their stories and influence change", said Patterson.

With this in mind, when trying to find the right 'talent' or 'spokesperson' for your media story or advocacy campaign, panel members suggested that we consider the following:

- Do your due diligence with the people you put forward. You have to judge their suitability for the public telling of their stories. It is a huge balancing act.
- Give them training and support while also giving them the opportunity to speak for themselves – to have agency.
- While there can be a tendency in the social services sector to assume that you know what is best for these people, young people are very media-savvy. They have grown up communicating in such different ways, so be aware that they may already be advanced communicators.
- In doing your due diligence, also engage with trusted and responsible journalists. For example, you would not choose to put a vulnerable young person onto *A Current Affair*, but you might consider another show like *The 7.30 Report*. Use your judgement.
- There is a variety of ways of capturing lived experience, and this does not always have to take place in a live media environment.

- Be conscious of not overusing a particular story that is stuck in the worst part of the narrative. We do not want a young person retelling a traumatic experience over and over again because the retelling keeps them in that moment and does not allow them to grow and to move past it. We should either have a limited amount of time for someone to tell this sort of story or we ensure that the narrative matures and changes as the young person has some form of 'success'. The young person might achieve employment or re-engage with education, family or community, for example, so their story needs to evolve with them, and they need to have the opportunity to progress the narrative.
- In choosing the talent, be careful not to reinforce any stereotypes. For example, when Jesuit Social Services launched its campaign around youth justice and changing the public and political narrative, it had several young people speaking from their lived experience. The agency specifically chose not to engage young speakers of African descent or Aboriginal Australians (who are shamefully overrepresented in youth justice), in order to make the campaign about the value of young people rather than focusing on specific cohorts within the justice system. In doing the latter, Jesuit Social Services would have risked the conversation getting caught up on those issues. In advocacy, we always need to keep a key eye on perception and framing.
- Choose someone who is authentic and has a real connection with the issue on the ground. For example, Julie Edwards has been a social worker and is now the Chief Executive Officer of Jesuit Social Services. She spans both worlds, that of CEO and that of a worker on the ground, really well. With this background, she knows the issues inside out and can prepare herself well, before presenting to the media. Consider who in

your organisation will relate well to the media, and who can present the facts in a warm, informative and engaging way.

Heads of organisations need to empower their media and advocacy teams. There needs to be a culture of trust and openness in the organisation that encourages the sharing of stories in order to advance the organisation's advocacy. Similarly, communications and media staff need to foster relationships and trust with their service delivery staff, whom they rely upon heavily to put forward suitable clients who have the ability to represent themselves and the issue. In so doing, we know that our spokespeople will be well supported and in a good place to be able to tell their stories.

Video and the Power of Storytelling

In this age of so many competing messages, what distinguishes Catholic social service organisations from the Institute of Public Affairs (IPA) or the Grattan Institute? What do we offer? We work with people and we represent their voices. Statistics are key and certainly part of the packaging but a powerful voice, an empowered voice (usually with some coaching), makes all the difference.

Farouque showed a video clip of 'Troy',[2] who helped the BSL launch its youth employment campaign. "It's a very simple video but it's highly effective. The handheld camera gives the video an unpolished style and shows that we're not the IPA, we don't have those resources", she said. On the day that BSL launched the video, Troy and the then head of BSL, Tony Nicholson, went to Canberra and held a doorstop in the Senate courtyard. Despite thinking they were taking their chances and that no-one would show up, there was a large array of media representatives, which demonstrates that the idea of "Mr Smith goes to Washington"[3] or 'Troy goes to Canberra'

---

2 For access to the video clip, see www.bsl.org.au/media/video-gallery/.
3 "Mr Smith Goes to Washington" is a 1939 American comedy-drama film about a recently appointed American Senator taking on the fight against a corrupt political system.

is really powerful, particularly when linked to a larger advocacy campaign. Many people in the environs of Parliament House, be it state or federal, do not hear much from people like Troy.

Farouque stated:

> The power of the storytelling is the agency of a young person, someone who is informed and who knows their rights, someone who knows that they can withdraw if a question is not to their liking, someone with the support to have their voice heard. That's the power of this sector and I think it should be deployed more frequently.

That power has been the success of the BSL's campaign for youth employment, which was launched in March 2014. It did not succeed immediately when the 2014 budget came down, but rather in 2015 with a $331 million youth employment strategy announced.

The Media is Not Our 'Enemy'

It can be difficult to break into mainstream media, especially for religious organisations and for the Catholic Church more than most. Zwartz stated:

> Many Catholics believe the media is hostile to the Catholic Church, and it's easy to see why they feel that. There has been some really unfair and ignorant criticism, and I think there is a strong anti-Catholic bias in wider Australia in 2020. Of course, clergy abuse and cover-ups and the Church's poor record of redress are a serious problem, but it's more than that. Let us be honest, the Church leadership is also seen as hypocritical and moralising, not welcoming, and patriarchal. However unfair this is, it happens to be what many people think. And it is easy for social service organisations to be caught up in the general opprobrium, but I still think there is a lot of respect for what community

service agencies are doing in the community and these judgments do not necessarily apply to you.

These issues are institutional. The people in the parishes don't pay much attention to the bishops; they pay attention to their local community. Social research shows that 88 per cent of Australians who are not Christians want a church in their neighbourhood because they recognise the benefits that a church brings, the stability and community-mindedness and so on. I've always said in speeches and in print that the Catholic Church is an overwhelming force for good and we're much the better for it being here, despite the well-documented problems.

This can be some welcome relief for those working in Catholic social services. We can be confident that we have many 'good news' stories and individual actors or 'heroes' to draw upon and highlight to provide interesting content for media outlets. "Brigidine Sister and activist Bridget Arthur, for instance, was a hero of mine when I was a journalist and I was constantly trying to make contact with her", stated Farouque.

Journalists have a job to do; they need to produce content. If we work strategically, we can help them do their job. Farouque shared an example:

> Andrew Yule and I had one of these 'relationships' when I was social affairs editor at *The Age*. Although I'd never met him, I liked him because he was very prompt at providing me with case studies and other things I requested. Particularly around budget time, journalists are often looking for someone who is struggling financially, and they do a ring around of the agencies. I would urge you to develop a revolving list of people who can speak to these sorts of issues so that you can provide links to journalists and build relationships from there.

Unfortunately, this is often not the case. Farouque said that it is not uncommon for journalists to feel frustrated by the social services sector, as it was often 'very slow'. "When I used to offer people within the sector an opportunity to say something or to critique an issue, the offer often went untaken", she said.

Panel members offered some tips to consider when building relationships with journalists and those working in the media:

- Do not just send your media release to the news editor. Be really targeted in what you do. Consider what the issue is – refugees, prisons, homelessness, government welfare policy – and focus on who in each media organisation specialises in the issue you are dealing with and could advance it in the most effective way, and send the release to these people also. They are much more likely to see the point immediately and press your case with the news editor. There is nothing better than an advocate from within.
- There are tools that can help you determine who is the best journalist to contact. Jesuit Social Services uses Meltwater,[4] which allows you to search through articles that have already been published about a particular issue. This gives you a good idea of which journalists have covered the issue and therefore who might have knowledge and understanding about it. You can then tailor your pitch to them while referencing the fact that they have covered the issue before.
- Journalists now are younger and less experienced, and they cannot make the same time commitment to a story anymore. Younger journalists also do not engage on the phone like the older generation of journalists – they love text messages and emails.

---

4 For information on Meltwater, see www.meltwater.com/au.

- Do not leave what journalists might perceive as annoying messages on their voicemail, unless you are returning their call.
- On a practical level, network where journalists network. It might be worthwhile attending media awards or one of their regular events so that you can start networking in the forums where journalists congregate. That includes online forums like Twitter.

The Media Landscape

The media landscape has changed a great deal. It is important to consider the media landscape within which we now work. Today, there are still some big players whom we need to attempt to contact if we want broad coverage, in particular our national and/or state-based newspapers and radio and television stations. However, there are many more outlets that create a range of different options for reaching niche audiences. Generally, these smaller outlets allow you to have more control over the story and how the story is presented. Often community newspapers and radio are interested in community news for which the bigger media do not have room. If the release is professional and already reads like a news story rather than a press release, they are quite likely to utilise it. Again, think like a journalist rather than an advocate.

Today, we also have our own media channels and can build a following with social media, allowing us to reach an audience with the messages that we want to convey. Zwartz referred to the United States President Donald Trump and his use of Twitter as an example: "Tell 15 lies a day in the certainty that some will be believed? No, that's not it. It's his masterly use of social media to bypass the mainstream media and communicate directly with his supporters. Social media is, as it were, unmediated, and you have total control of the message and how it is presented".

Be aware, however, that in so doing, your own audience is

probably already engaged with you as an organisation so they are likely to have similar values when it comes to the issues you want to promote. Remember, we want and need to go beyond our own four walls and the social services sector. It is worth taking the time and effort to be strategic, and to reach out to broader media outlets so that we can influence different audiences. Farouque stated:

> It's a big win to get on talkback radio with one of the commercial stations. If I were going on commercial radio about the issue of youth employment, for example, I'd say to the Sydney talkback commercial radio host, 'John, do you remember how difficult it was to get your first job?' And then he'd go on and on and feel that he's an important part of the issue. I have a lot of little strategies like that.

Twitter

We need to use the new media tactics. Twitter is an important positioning medium because the politicians and journalists are there. Journalists, in particular, use Twitter, more than Facebook, to disseminate and find stories, and to engage in public debates. CEOs of Catholic agencies are encouraged to build social media profiles so that they too can be part of the public debate.

Social media relies on personality, and that is why it is much more powerful to have your CEO or another leader of your organisation present and speak about the issues with an editorialised voice, rather than utilising an organisation-wide outlet, like the media office. Fr Bob Maguire, community worker and media personality, is one of the most popular religious communicators in Australia on social media. While he may not be embraced by everyone, he is a Catholic voice and he has a huge following. He is known for being very generous on Twitter in terms of retweeting news and information. Try tagging him: @FatherBob.

Audience

It is important to know the audience of the media channels you might be approaching. Have a good idea of the people who will be reading, listening or watching whatever media outlet to which you are pitching a story. Are these the people you want to reach out to, to hear your message, to take action, or to have a different conversation? We do not want just to be talking to people in our own backyards!

With this in mind, it is important to be aware of and speak to the current public debates. "You need to bring a tabloid eye to your communications", stated Farouque. Monitor social media, watch TikTok,[5] understand what people are talking about. "Take, for example, the so-called 'avocado generation'. If everyone is talking about kids and avocados, then find a way to talk about that, use that, and turn that around. The language is important. It is not about 'dumbing down'; it is about speaking to the current conversation and debates", she said.

Be Creative – Think Outside the Square

When it comes to content, think outside the square in terms of how to present information. "For instance, we need to use video creatively", stated Farouque. "I recently saw the power of TikTok. There was a physician in America who was juggling and dancing with fruit and talking about the need for vaccination. That video became a huge social media sensation. It was a new way of presenting very serious information. Take some inspiration from that kind of thing".

Even when it comes to news reporting, think outside the square in terms of presentation. Following on from its youth employment campaign, the BSL created a document called the

---

5 For background on TikTok, see https://www.tiktok.com/.

Youth Unemployment Monitor, which combines the elements of a data report, a compelling story and other material repackaged from the public domain. Farouque said, "Although the statistics we used were essentially in the public domain, our team in the research and policy centre of the Brotherhood refined and repackaged them, and then my public affairs team plucked out some choice phrases". Try using colourful and engaging infographics to present what otherwise might be a list of dull and complex statistics.

Philanthropic Partnerships to Fund Media and Advocacy Campaigns

It is worth considering who or which philanthropic organisations might be interested in partnering with or funding a media or advocacy campaign. As part of the detailed case study outlined below, Yule indicated that the #WorthASecondChance[6] campaign received substantial philanthropic funds, which allowed Jesuit Social Services to hire a staff member to work on the campaign full-time for a year and run focus groups and produce extensive materials. In fact, a range of philanthropic organisations approached Jesuit Social Services because they knew there was a need for this campaign.

Similarly, a group of philanthropists wanted to support the Home Stretch[7] campaign, which aims to extend the age of support for children in care from 18 to 21 years. Patterson stated, "Getting the campaign up and running took a lot of work but once the message was out a group of philanthropic organisations came together to offer significant support. Philanthropists want to be part of these advocacy programs aimed at changing the system".

---

6 Details of the campaign are available at www.worthasecondchance.com.au/.
7 For details of the Home Stretch initiative, see http://thehomestretch.org.au/.

#WorthASecondChance – A Case Study in How to Mobilise Media Effectively for Mission and Advocacy

Jesuit Social Services works 'deeply' in the youth justice space and has hopes and dreams for the young people in the criminal justice system. The agency's staff have been very concerned by the framing of related issues by the media, particularly from around 2016 onwards, and they were aware that bad decisions were being made in policy and practice as a result of the dominant negative media narrative. Jesuit Social Services decided it wanted to lead an advocacy campaign to change the narrative around youth criminal justice in Victoria completely, and in so doing, change the media, public and political discourse around this issue.

Background

Statistics indicate that the youth offending rate in Victoria from 2008-2009 to 2017-2018 had been on a steady decline. At the same time, the youth detention rate, which mirrored the decline in youth offending for the first few years, rapidly and starkly increased from about 2013-2014. Rather than celebrating the fact that the youth offending rate was dropping and that we must have been doing something right, we started to have an emergence of media coverage that framed this issue in a reductive and concerning way. There were headlines like, "Blunders clear path for Victorian teenage thugs",[8] "Premier vows to deal with nasty youth crime",[9] and "The violent youth gangs terrorising Melbourne's streets".[10] This was the only real narrative that anyone in the community was receiving about the issue. It was all about thugs, and how bad and dangerous they were, which drove up fear in the community.

---

8 For the article, see Gavin Brown and Rick Morton, "Blunders clear path for Victorian teenage thugs", *The Australian*, 26 January 2017.

9 For the article, see www.abc.net.au/news/2018-01-11/victorian-premier-daniel-andrews-youth-crime-african-gangs/9319802.

10 For the article, see "The violent youth gangs terrorising Melbourne's streets", *Daily Telegraph*, 5 January 2018.

This well-established media frame was not only driving public opinion; it started impacting policy and legislation. Political parties, on both sides, were also ignoring the facts and not implementing evidence-based practices because they were stuck in a battle to implement changes based on public opinion. Following riots by young people at the Parkville Youth Detention Centre in Melbourne, Premier Daniel Andrews stated, "Those inmates will be going to adult prison and I make absolutely no apology ... Highly trained prison officers have been deployed to keep the facilities secure and Victorians safe. These thugs will be brought to order".[11] The Government also proposed a new 224-bed facility at Cherry Creek, more than doubling the capacity of the current system. It introduced tougher laws including mandatory sentences, new offences such as intimidating a prison officer, and the uplifting of a number of charges to the adult court. As it got closer to the 2018 election, the opposition was also putting out ideas about punitive and restrictive measures such as policing schools and shops, increasing bail restrictions, implementing boot camps and so on.

Jesuit Social Services decided that it wanted to introduce an alternative narrative in this space. It set about creating a different conversation in the community, one that would hopefully lead to different outcomes. Essentially, the agency wanted to create an authorising environment in which the newly elected government would have an opportunity to deliver different policies with confidence that the public would be calling for them.

Having received some funding from philanthropic sources to undertake this advocacy campaign, Jesuit Social Services conducted a number of focus groups to determine what members of the community were thinking and feeling. The focus groups expressed strongly that participants wanted young people to be held

---

11 The Premier's statement is available at www.premier.vic.gov.au/restoring-order-to-youth-justice/.

to account and to understand the impact of their actions, although they did not necessarily believe that sending offenders to prison was the best option. Those consulted called for early intervention and prevention and they expressed a strong desire for pathways to education and employment: "They need guidance, they need assistance, they need help". One focus group participant said, "Their whole world has been negative and that's why they've been acting out this way. Change the way they see the world and give them positive experiences". The focus group feedback demonstrated that participants wanted a different narrative in which to talk about these young people.

Starting a New Conversation with #WorthASecondChance

Armed with this information, Jesuit Social Services decided to focus on values and solutions and launched its #WorthASecondChance campaign (Figure 1).

Figure 1: Image Promoting the #WorthASecondChance Campaign

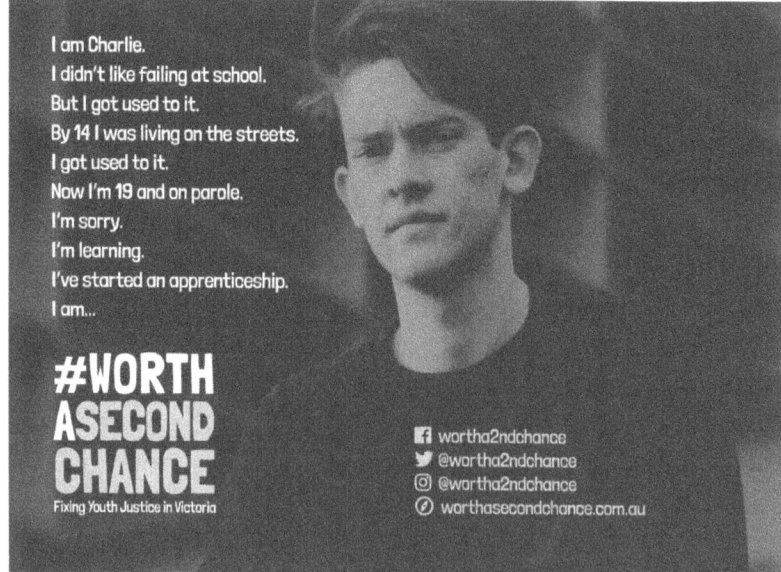

Instead of entering into the then current debate, and talking about crimes, incidents and the technicalities of legislation, this campaign wanted to create a completely new conversation about values and solutions, and highlight that these young people were worth a second chance. It wanted to mobilise the community and media narrative around another conversation with lived experience at its centre.

Jesuit Social Services introduced key ideas about disconnection from school and family, having accountability for actions, and moving towards a positive path. Highlighting the transformational nature of what can happen with young people was key for the campaign. Jesuit Social Services hosted a media launch, which had good attendance, including young people who could speak to the issue. In fact, young people were involved in every related event. They wanted to be part of the campaign and really embraced it. The media interviewed one of the young speakers at the launch and another had an opportunity to go with CEO, Julie Edwards, to speak live on air. Significantly, a film from the launch was embedded on the websites of *The Herald Sun* and *The Australian*. While, as anticipated, the ABC was covering the issue well, Jesuit Social Services was very pleased to get coverage by those other mainstream media outlets that had largely been responsible for running the negative headlines and framing the narrative which they wanted to change.

Diverse Range of Speakers and Media Platforms

When formulating the #WorthASecondChance campaign, Jesuit Social Services brainstormed to identify different people who could deliver the key messages. Over an extended period, they had a range of diverse speakers on the issue, providing a new perspective and narrative. Examples included:

- Rosalinda, who worked as a nurse at the Parkville Youth Detention Centre. Though she had been assaulted by one of the young people there, she came out as a very strong advocate for young people in detention because she had a lot of sympathy for what they had been through,
- Ron, a Jesuit Social Services staff member with his own history of incarceration in both youth and adult detention,
- Pat Allen, a lawyer who spoke eloquently about the young people whom he represented,
- fiscal conservatives who talked about how much money would be wasted in building new prisons.

Jesuit Social Services took a multi-faceted approach when it came to disseminating information, utilising a range of mainstream media outlets and platforms including Twitter, Instagram, Facebook and YouTube. The agency engaged with the mainstream media at the launches, as well as hosting a number of panel events with the young people, which were well attended and covered by the media. Jesuit Social Services brought out Vincent Schiraldi from the United States, a key spokesperson on youth criminal justice issues, who received good mainstream coverage. An op-ed piece penned by CEO Julie Edwards was published in the week leading up to the Victorian State election.

Videos with the voices and stories of some young people, who did not want to be identified, were very moving. They were filmed anonymously. Some young women who were in the criminal justice system came together in a structured way to provide Jesuit Social Services with feedback about their experiences. They allowed Jesuit Social Services to make use of their stories through social media. The agency was also able to quote other people who were vocal about the campaign. For example, a tweet by Indi Clarke from the Koori Youth Council[12] had fantastic engagement, with

---

12 The quote can be accessed at https://twitter.com/KYC_Vic.

614 responses and 108 comments. Another tweet from the above-mentioned Rosalinda, which talked about Jesuit Social Services' op-ed, was shared 67 times.

Such support proved that people wanted to engage with the issue. The comments and contributions to these discussions were overwhelmingly positive and there was a whole community on social media who would argue the point in the face of negative or dissenting viewpoints. This was a massive shift within the public realm. There has also been a shift in Premier Daniel Andrews' language since the 2018 election. Upon winning the election, he stated: "We're the most progressive government in the nation. We're the most progressive state in the nation. Victorians have resoundingly endorsed our positive and optimistic plan for the next four years. I'm also very proud and pleased that the Victorian community has comprehensively rejected the negativity, the fear, the spite, that small brand of nasty politics that was on offer and was rejected in record terms".[13]

Although this quote is not directly related to youth justice, the outcome of the election saw a shift in language from the Australian Labor Party. Further, when the Coalition did a review of its campaign, it also admitted that its negativity around social justice issues had not worked. Fortunately, Jesuit Social Services is seeing a bit of 'clear space' in this area at the moment and it intends to continue engaging the community around this improved, positive narrative.

Conclusion

At the time of writing this chapter, the world is being deeply impacted by the COVID-19 pandemic. As we come to terms with

---

13 The Premier's statement is quoted in Tom Minear, Matt Johnston and Monique Hore, "Melbourne Metro tunnel, North East Link among projects to take shape in weeks, amid Cabinet shake-up", *Herald Sun*, 26 November 2018.

this new reality of lockdowns and self-isolation, unemployment and loss of income, and living our lives in a very different way for an indeterminate amount of time, we can use this opportunity to 'take stock'.

Social change takes time; we will be 'in the trenches' for the long haul. It is worth reviewing, modifying and refreshing our tactics and methods. We need to be proactive and to have the courage of our convictions. We can be confident that, within our field of endeavour, Catholic social service organisations have some of the best-informed and courageous professionals of all. Their contributions are underpinned by excellent research, hands-on experience and important insights. We have much good news to share and much to contribute to building the future. Importantly, there are many vulnerable Australians, for whom a better future will depend on our effective engagement with media to provide a platform for their voices to be heard, and to empower them to be positive agents of change.

Collaboration Enhancing the Church's Disaster Response

Gabrielle McMullen with Janet Cribbes, Jack de Groot and Ursula Stephens

As the 2020 Catholic Social Services conference was in the final stages of planning, the country was in the midst of a very challenging summer. Much of Australia was in extreme drought, devastating bushfires were widespread, parts of Queensland and New South Wales were recovering from severe flooding and, with soaring temperatures and fierce winds and dust storms, the community was increasingly aware of climate change. Short-term aid was required, as were medium-term recovery and rebuilding initiatives, and long-term action to save the planet.

Across the country Catholic social services agencies were playing their part in assisting with emergency aid and recovery initiatives. There were many demonstrable instances of our people "serving communities with courage and compassion". The conference offered an opportunity to share experiences, identify effective practices and acknowledge the contributions of the Catholic agencies.

Further, in February 2020 a number of Church agencies announced a new initiative, Catholic Emergency Relief Australia (CERA).[1] In seeking a more coordinated response within the Catholic Church to disaster recovery, it brings together key peak national

---

1 For information on CERA, see www.cera.catholic.org.au/.

organisations: the Australian Catholic Bishops Conference, Catholic Religious Australia, Catholic Social Services Australia and the National Catholic Education Commission, with other organisations expected to join. Church ministries that have contributed to emergency relief encompass parishes, social services, education facilities, health and aged care providers, aid and advocacy bodies, and religious congregations. Church-wide collaboration of Catholic agencies has the potential to serve the Australian community more effectively at times of local or national calamity.

In light of these developments, a session on the role of Catholic agencies in disaster recovery was built into the conference program. Three speakers, who have each had key roles in meeting challenges arising in the aftermath of bushfires and other catastrophes, were invited to share their experiences:

- Janet Cribbes coordinated the Victorian Bushfire Community Recovery Service in 2009-2011, an initiative of Centacare Melbourne (now CatholicCare Melbourne and Gippsland). Her input provided lessons from the so-called Black Saturday bushfires to inform recovery from the 2020 inferno.
- Jack de Groot is CEO of the St Vincent de Paul Society in New South Wales. In this role he was actively engaged in the contemporary bushfire response there. Previously, as CEO of Caritas Australia for 13 years, he gained international experience in disaster recovery.
- Dr Ursula Stephens is the CEO of Catholic Social Services Australia. She was instrumental in putting together the CERA framework and, in the months before the conference, was keenly supporting Catholic social service agencies responding to the summer's crises.

The following sections summarise their presentations as members of the "Collaboration Enhancing the Church's Disaster Response" panel at the conference. These provided insights into the Catholic sector's contributions to disaster recovery and learnings for future involvement. A further section captures contributions from the open forum following their presentations.

Lessons about Recovery from the 2009 Victorian Bushfires

Janet Cribbes

My experience centres on the Victorian Black Saturday bushfires of 7 February 2009, which at the time resulted in the largest loss of life due to a natural disaster in Australia's history. One hundred and seventy-three people died, and an estimated 7,662 people were displaced.

To put this into context, 25 people (five of whom were in Victoria) died in the 2020 fires, 414 people were injured, 109 towns and 33 communities affected, 2,400 properties destroyed and 1,400 damaged. In New South Wales 2,439 homes were lost, with 396 in Victoria. To take another perspective, 420 hectares were burnt in 2009, whereas 1.5 million hectares were burnt in Victoria and 5.4 million in New South Wales in recent months, and over 55 businesses and 3,500 agricultural facilities were ruined, 60,000 people lost electricity, and 70 national parks and 950 local parks were damaged or destroyed. Whereas the affected wildlife was not counted in 2009, we know that well over one billion animals died during the 2020 fires.

At the time of the 2009 fires, Australians and some Catholic institutions overseas donated over $4 million to the Archbishop of Melbourne's Charitable Fund Bushfire Appeal (ACFBA), which was launched on 9 February 2009, within days of the bushfires. It was set up specifically to address recovery for those affected by the Black Saturday bushfires, whose reach included communities located in the Archdiocese of Melbourne and the Dioceses of Sale and Sandhurst.

The Catholic response was comprehensive, and targeted not only at Catholic communities, although these were engaged with and, in many cases, provided initial points of engagement with local areas. Some Catholic churches were destroyed, but no Catholic schools or Church or school personnel were lost. These Catholic communities, though, were severely impacted, and support from many points within the Church, and from within the Catholic education system, was prompt and strong: St Mary's Parish in Whittlesea, for example, was inundated with help from other schools. The Catholic Education Office in Melbourne provided financial support in the form of waiving fees and helping with uniform purchases. Counselling and pastoral services were made readily available. The St Vincent de Paul Society also launched an appeal and was very active in the provision of material aid and relief.

In this complex context, the ACFBA was intended to enable longer-term responses. There were other initiatives too in the general community, including the Government Bushfire Reconstruction and Recovery Fund, so that it was critical for the ACFBA to develop a strategic approach to realise its vision and, in particular, following the emergency responses, to identify service gaps and provide recovery initiatives for the long term. Denis Fitzgerald, then Executive Director of Catholic Social Services Victoria, and Fr Joe Caddy, then Chief Executive Officer of Centacare Melbourne, were instrumental in developing ACFBA's long-term recovery vision.

An Initial Response Team was established to give life to this vision, and also an inter-agency committee with major Catholic service providers from the Melbourne metropolitan area. The latter agreed that Centacare Melbourne and the regional services in Gippsland and Sandhurst would take the lead in implementing the disaster recovery response.

An early project was the bushfire recovery chaplaincy. The initiative was well-publicised, and personnel were equipped to assist. Fr Greg Bourke initiated workshops for priests, pastoral associates and teachers on disaster recovery, which were presented by child-adolescent psychologist Olivia Kean and Fr Peter Hoskins from Jesuit Social Services. The chaplaincy was particularly critical in the first three months.

I was engaged to perform a rapid needs analysis and to recommend the service model to be funded by the ACFFA. The needs analysis began in March 2009. I recommended a recovery service led by the community and serving the five municipalities affected by the fire. I also recommended the integration of the bushfire recovery teams into existing services in the Dioceses of Sandhurst and Sale. Subsequently on 1 April 2009, I was appointed Manager to establish and coordinate the Bushfire Community Recovery Service. Centacare opened its services in the most impacted areas: Kinglake, Marysville, Whittlesea, Strathewen, Alexander, Flowerdale, Nillumbik, Buxton and Yea, which are all on or just beyond the north-eastern outer fringes of the Melbourne metropolitan area.

Due to the long-term nature of recovery for the affected communities, it was planned that our services would be funded for up to three years. The utmost care was taken not to duplicate services that were being funded through other initiatives. As there were many, many players in the space, it was important to identify and provide for the service gaps.

Importantly, we set up long-term counselling services and became involved in capacity-building community partnerships. Overall, our team provided 2,280 counselling sessions and 4,400 hours of staff time in community partnerships, helping communities to help themselves. We originally started with seven employees and ended up with fifteen through partnerships with the community.

One of the things that we noticed was that each of the communities had projects that they wanted to get off the ground and initiatives they wanted to implement to promote healing. We established what we called the Small Poppy Fund, which had $100,000 from the ACFBA and $150,000 donated directly to Centacare by the Whitehall Foundation in Queensland. The Small Poppy Fund enabled a range of initiatives. Let me give you the example of the Bemm River project, which nobody else wanted to fund.

The Bemm River community in East Gippsland had proposed a fishing trip for local men; other agencies saw this project as an excuse to have a good time, but our team persevered in getting funding for it. One of the workers from Centacare joined the excursion with the men, who were allowed time to grieve, cry, bond and tell stories to each other without being judged. The participants came back transformed. This catalysed a monumental turn-around in that community. It addressed what was seen as a major risk of increased family violence, given the pressure that the men were under and their vulnerability if they had no avenue to express their anguish other than through anger.

Professor Ruth Webber and Dr Kate Jones of Australian Catholic University were engaged from the outset to undertake a three-year study of the Catholic response to the 2009 bushfires so the Church would be better prepared for such engagement in future. Their report, *The Catholic Bushfire Recovery Response*, was presented in 2012 and provided critical information to equip the Church to respond more effectively to future catastrophes. As well as in the report,[2] the findings were also made available in a publication released by the Archdiocese of Melbourne and

---

2 Ruth Webber and Kate Jones, 2012. *The Catholic Bushfire Recovery Response: Final Report*. Melbourne: Australian Catholic University.

CatholicCare Melbourne[3] and academic papers published by Webber and Jones.[4]

Let me conclude by highlighting that the needs at the time were complex, but we were convinced that recovery was best led through the community – by listening to what the community needed and by walking beside them. One of the things we did as a Catholic organisation was to go to areas where there had previously been no services or Catholic presence. Centacare had not only to work across a vast geographic area, but also to establish new services in spaces where there were not a lot of players. Within the first year, we quickly became one of the most trusted agencies because the community had confidence that we were working with them. That was the major difference between us and other agencies.

The St Vincent de Paul Society and Local and National Responses

Jack de Groot

The 2020 Catholic Social Services conference brought together several St Vincent de Paul Society CEOs from various States and our National Council, and others who serve, or who have served, in Vinnies. If you ask how we actually work together, the answer is slowly. And always with love (although the love can be hard to win).

---

3 *Beyond Black Saturday 2009-2012: A Report Prepared on Behalf of the Archbishop's Charitable Fund Bushfire Appeal by the Catholic Archdiocese of Melbourne and CatholicCare Melbourne*; accessed at https://engonetccam.blob.core.windows.net/assets/uploads/files/Assets/Reports/Beyond-Black-Saturday-report.pdf.

4 For example, Ruth Webber and Kate Jones, 2011. "A Catholic Community Response to the 2009 Bushfires", *The Australasian Catholic Record*, 88(3), 259-270; 2011. "After the bushfires: Surviving and volunteering", *The Australian Journal of Emergency Management*, 26(2), 35-40; and 2013. "Rebuilding Communities After Natural Disasters: The 2009 Bushfires in Southeastern Australia", *Journal of Social Service Research*, 39(2), 253-268.

In December 2019 in New South Wales, we had a $2 million bushfire response program implemented in response to the bushfires in Queensland and New South Wales over the period September through to December 2019. Seven weeks into the new year, we had a $30 million bushfire response. So, things moved very quickly. The St Vincent de Paul Society's involvement began back in September 2019 with the rainforest fires in Queensland, in an area which had not known such burning since the arrival of Europeans to this country.

One of the curious things about Vinnies is that we are not technically a 'first responder', but this does not matter because people often decide that we are. People come to us. The community of Wytaliba in north-west New South Wales came to the Vinnies conference in nearby Glen Innes the Saturday morning after the fires, within sixteen hours of their onset. Wytaliba had a population of 100 before the fire, which destroyed 25 houses along with its school.

The community 'decides' who the first responder is. Technically, it may be the Office of Emergency Management or its equivalent in any state or territory which has the official designation, or Australian Defence Force personnel deployed, or agencies such as Anglicare, the Red Cross or the Salvation Army, but I think we need to understand that the community decides. In our case and in the case of the Society in Canberra-Goulburn and Bairnsdale, Victoria, people very quickly came to Vinnies and we were involved in emergency centres from the beginning. This meant that we had to decide whether to stay or to get out because we are not formally set up for a first responder role like the Red Cross, Salvos and Anglicare agencies in these centres. For a time in Canberra-Goulburn, the Society stayed in the emergency centres and in other centres we operated from our traditional base of the shops.

Our focus moved to a national level response at the beginning of January 2020. Just before Australia Day, the Commonwealth's Department of Social Services (DSS) announced emergency relief funding for bushfire households. This certainly changed the nature of the work – what had been a $20 million Vinnies fundraising campaign then gained $10 million additional DSS funds, and there was a clash of very different models of care.

Commonwealth funding regulations only allow a maximum payment of $1,000 per client, which gets you nowhere. As members of corporate Australia lent their resources and support to a business taskforce to respond to the bushfires, one of them said, "One thousand? Is that it? What does that do for any householder?" So, there is a real issue about how the Government and the community sector engage. Our model of support is focussed on partnerships with the people whom we serve as opposed to a transaction to the 'deserving poor', which seems to be ever-more the Government model of care.

For example, I met a woman in Sussex Inlet, on the New South Wales central coast, who was a former Warrant Officer in the Royal Australian Navy. With another five Vinnies conference members, she made up the only community organisation that partnered with the Australian Defence Force to take care of 500 people over three days. They fed them, clothed them and provisioned them with toiletries and other non-food items – they did it in three days, then closed up and went back to re-building their own lives.

Many of our members were people who had lost their own properties. Another St Vincent de Paul Society CEO told me the story of one of his members who signed up to volunteer on the far south coast of New South Wales the day after she lost her own home. One volunteer's house was looted during the crisis.

In this context, it was a moment of extraordinary offence when Government Ministers and local Members of Parliament attacked charities, including Vinnies, for not responding quickly enough to the needs of their communities. When they attack Vinnies, in fact, they are attacking the constituents who elected them because these are the local Vinnies people. They are not attacking those in the head office; they are attacking their own constituents – that is who constitutes the St Vincent de Paul Society. The Society's leadership makes decisions in collaboration because we are not a command-and-control organisation; that is not how it works. We collaborate and we co-ordinate and, with goodwill, we get there.

About a third of the funds that came into the Society were allocated to the initial response across New South Wales. We then had to focus on not just relief but also recovery and rebuilding. That was the next challenge. Importantly, in such situations, it must be about the community's decision to rebuild, and community engagement must be from Day One.

We have been working with the Government and other NGOs, which does not come naturally in Australia. As noted above, I worked with Caritas Australia for some years. To be frank, there is better coordination and communication between community-based organisations in the United Nations' international responses to emergencies than there is between such bodies here in Australia. That includes responses in cases that were incredibly difficult, such as in Myanmar after Cyclone Nargis in 2008 or even after the Indian Ocean tsunami of 2004 some years before. There is much to learn out of that – we need a cultural shift towards cooperation around these matters in Australia. The various parts of the Catholic Church must be part of this, and I think that the laypeople will be leading this rather than the hierarchical and geographically determined jurisdictional Catholic entities in Australia.

There is a lot that we are doing in going forward but let me speak of a particular challenge of governance in the community sector. The attacks of the media and of parliamentarians (both at state and

Federal level) that interrogate the integrity of our organisations mean that our governance needs to be reviewed. The challenge of media scrutiny has changed significantly since the 2004 Indian Ocean tsunami. Journalists always used to ask, "How quickly were you able to spend the money?" Now journalists never ask; they simply accuse you of not spending the money. There is no dialogue and we must be better at shaping the narrative. We have to be far better with community engagement and, in particular, with telling the story of community-based responses.

Introducing Catholic Emergency Relief Australia

Ursula Stephens

What happened in Australia over the summer did not just start in 2020. The fires in New South Wales on the Central Coast, on the North Coast, up in New England and then in Western Sydney and the Blue Mountains all happened before Christmas but the nation and the world only really started to respond in January.

The Government has created the National Bushfire Response Agency and Catholic Social Services Australia is participating in conversations with that agency, which represents a whole-of-government response. One of the big challenges we have seen is that the communities who were affected so significantly before Christmas feel completely forgotten and left out now.

Because of the shock and the national trauma in response to the bushfires at Christmas time that we were being confronted with every day in the media, I had a conversation on Boxing Day with Archbishop Mark Coleridge, President of the Australian Catholic Bishops Conference, about the need for a pastoral message to the nation. We wanted to convey that the catastrophe was something that affected all of us. Even if we were not in a bushfire-affected area, we were all traumatised by what we were seeing and by the stories that we were hearing.

Facebook has a function whereby you can record yourself as 'safe'. So, all of us on social media platforms were getting messages that friends somewhere were safe and we were thinking, "Well thank God for that, but what can we do to help?" The notion of a whole-of-Church response was informed by the idea that it is not just about the communities in the bushfire-affected areas; it is about all of us. We wanted to know how best to mobilise Catholics to demonstrate faith in action. How we can prepare ourselves, knowing that this climate change emergency is not a one-off event, knowing that this is what we are going to be enduring regularly in the future?

Whether it is fire or famine or flood or pestilence or drought, we know that we must find a way to work alongside Government but also to think of ourselves as an ecosystem outside of Government. The Catholic Church has the biggest non-government footprint in Australia. We touch every community across aged care, health care, schools and community services. With that comes the responsibility to respond to a challenge like this. The notion of a whole-of-Church response came about because of this. In the first week of January 2020, Archbishop Coleridge prepared a statement on behalf of the Australian bishops, outlining what the Church would do and we are now responding to the call to action.

We came up with CERA, Catholic Emergency Relief Australia. Gavin Abraham from the Australian Catholic Bishops Conference and I were trying to arrive at a name for this new entity and I 'Googled' for a relevant saint and actually found one; I could not believe it. Saint Cera, the female equivalent of Kieran, was a sixth-century Irish abbess. Saint Brendan instructed some people who were challenged by an obnoxious fire to ask Saint Cera to intercede on their behalf. She did and the fire was put out. You could not make it up! We needed an acronym that fitted with her name, so we came up with Catholic Emergency Relief Australia.

Catholic Social Services Australia had been having weekly interactions with Catholic Health Australia, the National Catholic Education Commission, Catholic Religious Australia, Vinnies, Catholic Earthcare Australia and the Australian Catholic Bishops Conference to keep each other informed about what was happening in the various parts of the Catholic sector in response to the bushfires. We were also hearing from our membership and bringing those reports back each week to share with each other. What we heard, for example, was that western New South Wales was still ravaged by drought and that communities there felt completely forgotten in all of this.

As January and then February rolled on, we had the first meeting, in Brisbane on 10 February 2020, of the CERA National Advisory Council, which is chaired by Susan Pascoe AM. As one of the members of the 2009 Victorian Bushfire Royal Commission, Pascoe has an extraordinary knowledge of the aftermath and the lived experience of those bushfires. On the Council, we also have Fr Joe Caddy AM, who worked very closely with the Centacare response to the 2009 Victorian bushfires, described above. We have closely considered the outstanding work that was done and the evaluation report, *The Catholic Bushfire Recovery Response* by Ruth Webber and Sandra Jones,[5] provided in that context, in order to determine how we could scale up our response to the current national emergency.

Now that the Advisory Council has met, we are looking to develop a taskforce that will come up with a blueprint for mobilising Catholic institutions and organisations in response to national disasters. We do not want to duplicate anything; we are trying to align with the same challenge that the Australian Government faces. Their representatives are seeking to work this through themselves and we are trying to walk with them, to advise and influence the decisions they make. The biggest message that

---

5 Webber and Jones, op. cit. n. 2.

we tell them every time we meet is the importance of the long-term recovery process.

Currently, we are also thinking about the COVID-19 pandemic, which is unfolding as a national disaster. What will the Catholic institutional response be to a pandemic? It is an ongoing piece of work. We are working closely with and learning from other agencies.

In conclusion, let me return to the bushfire recovery efforts. I live in Goulburn, just outside of Canberra, and I know the work that is being done and the services that are being delivered into the south coast of New South Wales by CatholicCare Canberra-Goulburn, Marymead, MacKillop Family Services and Vinnies. We all know that we are going to be there for a very long time. It is, indeed, a privilege to be part of such a responsive and community-focused network.

Other Learnings

Following the panel presentations, the forum was opened for wider input. A key issue identified was support for a Catholic agency's staff providing services on the ground after a calamity. From her Bushfire Community Recovery Service experience, Cribbes advised:

> We were cognisant of the fact that there was vicarious trauma and we put in place a psychologist to work with the staff. Over time, vicarious trauma became an issue for all of our employees and the communities, so we ran workshops and other sessions. Putting in place debriefings, formal workshops and informal activities was important in terms of our team but also extended into our community support. The whole community was impacted because everybody had lost someone. There was no escape from the trauma of supporting grieving community members

and families. You could not just go next door to get a bit of space. Everyone had to deal with that trauma the whole time.

de Groot added:

A lot of the people who work for Vinnies in this context are volunteers from the community. Genuine guidance – and sometimes confrontation – is needed to maintain self-care and to ensure that experience and support are shared. It is quite an issue and it needs a community response.

It was noted that lessons from the 2009 bushfires have been learned in terms of deaths directly related to the bushfires. However, we still have a long way to go in dealing with the health impacts of the heat waves now associated with climate-change-impacted summers. Many Catholic agencies are associated with people who are the most vulnerable – the poor, the elderly, the homeless, etc. It was suggested that CERA might have a mandate in terms of advocating for change to the combined carbon footprint of our Catholic institutions.

Stephens responded that major Catholic agencies and the Government are acutely aware of the significant health and other impacts of the changing climate. In fact, there have been discussions about Government and CERA incorporating these considerations into blueprints for their future action. The CERA taskforce has set itself a timeline of November 2021 to develop a blueprint. This will outline a decision-making matrix that will mobilise the Church's response to emergency events.

CERA aims to develop resources that can be accessed by Church organisations across the board and to make recommendations about the most effective way to inform the Government on these issues. One of the key members of its Advisory Council is Justice Terry Sheahan, a former judge in the Land and Environment Court in

New South Wales, who has a deep interest in the environmental impacts of community recovery and future planning.

Stephens highlighted that Catholic Social Services Australia is currently undertaking a major research project focussing on entrenched disadvantage.[6] It includes case studies about bushfire-affected communities to ensure that we re-imagine those communities that are recovering and rebuilding and not just recreate their entrenched disadvantages. Catholic Social Services Australia wants to ensure that these factors are considered as part of the bigger picture.

de Groot noted that he remembered living in Melbourne during the 1983 Ash Wednesday bushfires and also being there on the Monday after Black Saturday 2009. There was, however, something very different about the impact of the 2020 fire crisis, in particular on the people of Sydney and Canberra:

> In Sydney, between 28 November and about 12 December 2019, there were three weeks of smoke haze that prevented you from seeing anything. This was all day, every day. There were outbreaks of respiratory illnesses and a marked decline in wellbeing. Canberra went through the same thing for six weeks. This experience was in every household in those areas and it has 'twisted a different dial' in the public imagination about the impacts of climate on their health, especially in the context of drought and bushfire. I think there is a lot for us to tap into. We need to leverage this experience in moving forward to the change now required.

Cribbes highlighted a difference in the 2020 fires because of

---

6 Brenton Prosser and Gabriel Helleren-Simpson (eds), 2020. *Mapping the Potential: Understanding persistent disadvantage to inform community change*. Canberra: Catholic Social Services Australia; accessed at https://mappingthepotential.cssa.org.au/.

their impact on the environment and wildlife. These factors add to the issues impacting on effective responses. She emphasised that "communities are complex and diverse, which means that a community response is never homogenous. There are always fractures and splinters in human behaviour and you just have to adapt and respond and work through it each day".

Conclusion

The panel session on disaster recovery at the 2020 Catholic Social Services conference was timely as participants and their agencies were in the midst of the many challenges of late 2019 and early 2020. The forum provided an opportunity to share experiences and learn from and support one another.

This summer brought some learnings for the Church as well as the challenges of the drought, fires, floods and now the COVID-19 pandemic. At the time of CERA's launch, Archbishop Coleridge said: "Our response to the bushfires, and the drought that has exacerbated the fires, has demonstrated once again the collective power of the Catholic Church to respond to disasters in all sorts of ways". He emphasised: "At its core, the Catholic Church is about people, about families, about parishes, about school communities, about ministries that proclaim and live out the Gospel of Jesus. Most of those ministries are local, but there is a national – and universal – dimension of the Church that can sometimes be under-utilised".[7]

With the establishment of CERA and initiatives like the formal evaluation of the Church's 2009 Victorian bushfire response, we are better able to 'harness' the Church's capacity to service its communities at the time of a disaster. Stephens has highlighted: "One of the Church's key social teachings is about 'subsidiarity',

---

7 CERA, 28 January 2020. "Collaboration Will Enhance Church's Disaster Response", media release; accessed at www.cera.catholic.org.au/news.

which means that we empower local communities to respond to their realities as they best see fit. Alongside that, though, sits 'solidarity', which compels us to see the needs of others and work collaboratively to respond to those needs. That response can be most effective when it's coordinated and focused".[8] Such embodiment of Catholic social teaching in CERA's planned blueprint and its future endeavours will throw open the doors of the Church and take it to the margins, as has been entreated by Pope Francis.[9]

---

8 Ibid.
9 Pope Francis, 2013. Apostolic Exhortation: *Evangelii Gaudium*. Sections 46-47; accessed at www.vatican.va/.

Mission at the Margins: The Call to Uncommon Courage

Debra Zanella

As I address the theme of "Mission at the Margins", let me introduce Joan Chittister. It was her recent book, *The Time Is Now: A Call to Uncommon Courage*, which inspired the title of this chapter.[1] Chittister, a Benedictine nun, is one of my prophets of hope. This chapter is based on the keynote address that I presented at the 2020 Catholic Social Services conference in Melbourne.

On Being a Prophet

One of the key things that I want you to reflect on is this: As people of faith, what will you do here and now, in this world, in our time? Chittister asks: Will you simply stand looking in? As people of faith, as faith-based, mission-driven organisations, is our role to be prophetic? Are we to be prophetic organisations? Are we asked to walk the prophetic road?

Chittister describes a prophet as an inspired teacher or proclaimer of the will of God, someone who advocates or speaks in visionary ways. She speaks about prophecy as advocacy, about the rich Catholic tradition of prophets and prophecy, and of the prophet as one who speaks the truth to a culture of lies. In particular, she refers to Daniel Berrigan, an American Jesuit priest, who was highly

---

1 Joan Chittister, 2019. *The Time Is Now: A Call to Uncommon Courage.* New York: Convergent Books.

active during the Vietnam War and who created an alternative to the war narrative of his time.

Chittister suggests one of the key understandings that we must recognise is that we have divided the spiritual life between Christian practice and Christian witness. She claims that Christian practice has been reserved for our personal Christianity, tucked away nicely in our going to Mass on Sundays, or whatever other form of practice that we might follow. She talks about the decline of Christian witness, saying that although not everyone is called to be prophets in the classical sense of the word, we are all called to be carriers of the prophetic message in our time.

Prophets call out not just the act of injustice and violence, which is critical, but also the underlying structures, beliefs and systems that feed injustice, even within the traditions that espouse a prophetic role. I think this is perhaps the most important and uncomfortable element of prophecy. The prophet is the person who says no to everything that is not of God. Chittister writes:

> The problem is that we have lost all consciousness of the biblical prophets and so of our own spiritual birthright. In fact, we might not even recognize them if we saw them. Yet it was precisely for times such as ours that God sent these prophets of old to wake up the world around them to its distance from Truth. It is surely time for this generation to rediscover them.[2]

I think another of our contemporary, modern-day prophets is Francis Sullivan. I was struck by his words in his opening address at the Catholic Social Services conference, when he spoke about our current Catholic reality, one in which "we bleach the Gospel of its radical nature".[3] We have bleached the Gospel – that is a very

---

2 Ibid., p. 30.
3 Francis Sullivan, 2020. "Margin Call: The Risk of Integrity" in this volume.

strong image of what we have done to the radical words of Jesus. So, the call for us is to reignite, to bring colour back to, the radical nature of the message of the Gospel.

Are We Prophetic?

Let us ask what we can do that is prophetic as individuals and as faith-based mission organisations in this world at this time. What have you chosen? What does it mean for you and your organisation? Does the prophetic word or prophecy have a role in your organisation? How is your organisation a prophetic witness of God's word in the world?

Chittister talks about qualities that are important in the work of the prophet or organisation engaged in prophecy. One of the areas she talks about is risk. She quotes T. S. Eliot, who said: "Only those who will risk going too far can possibly find out how far one can go". The clear, important role of the prophet is to hold a restless and unyielding vision of what tomorrow might be.

Ruah Community Services[4] in Western Australia conducts a day centre, an engagement hub for people who experience homelessness. As a CEO, you are at times somewhat remote from the frontline service delivery. In my leadership I make a deliberate effort to go down there to meet with the people we serve. I went recently and my head was full of things that were annoying me. I am a bit of a dog lover and there was a little grey Staffie in the office, so I had ten minutes of unadulterated love from this beautiful dog.

Then the owner came to collect his dog, so I was speaking to this gentleman, whom I shall call John. We had a bit of a chat about the dog and about how beautiful and loving Staffies are, and then I said to John, "How are you? How are you going?" And he said to me, "It's really tough living on the streets". And I asked him how

---

4 For information on Ruah Community Services, see www.ruah.org.au.

long he had been living on the streets, knowing that the average period for someone who is chronically homeless is five years. And he said, "The hardest thing for me is that, when I go to sleep at night, I am frightened that someone is going to steal my dog. And it's the one thing I have that unconditionally loves me".

So I was, as usual, put back into my place about what was concerning and worrying me. But that was not enough for John. He then, in prophetic words, said to me, "But listen, CEO. Don't worry. I have hope that things will get better". The transformative power of hope is something we sometimes deride in our society as akin to wishing for unicorns. But, as Sullivan recounted from his experience, the transformative power of hope creates a vision to which prophets talk.[5] And that is what I think we are mandated to do as Catholic organisations.

Chittister talks about prophets then and prophets now as those who look at life as hard of heart for many and unfair for most, and who set out to respond. Prophets refuse to accept a vision of tomorrow that is limited to the boundaries of yesterday and empty of God's word for today.

Three years ago, a group of seven CEOs in Western Australia got together; five of us were from Catholic organisations, all of us from faith-based organisations. We said that we did not want to be in the business of managing homelessness anymore. We said that people have a human right to housing and that surely this is solvable. Fast-forward three years to the creation of the WA Alliance to End Homelessness[6] and the State Government's decision in December 2019 to inject $32.4 million into a housing-first approach that ends homelessness, with a $112 million investment into social housing

---

5 Sullivan, op. cit. n. 3.
6 For details of the WA Alliance to End Homelessness, see www.endhome-lessnesswa.com/.

and the building of two 'Common Ground' facilities.[7] What I want to highlight about this initiative is that when we change the narrative, when we change the language, a shift in our community and a shift in our society happens. I really believe that this is one of the key roles of prophets today.

The Risks of Prophecy

Chittister also says that the risk for prophets, of course, is exclusion. They call out not just the acts of injustice but the underlying structures, beliefs and systems that feed those injustices. In what I think others might view as a controversial book, James Carroll in *Toward a New Catholic Church: The Promise of Reform* calls for Vatican III. He writes:

> Here is the lesson: a power structure that is accountable only to itself will always end by abusing the powerless. Even then, it will paternalistically ask to be trusted to repair the damage. Never again. Not only the discredited bishops who protected abusive priests must go; the whole system that produced them must go. Full democratic reform is the Catholic Church's only hope. If we can take the Body of Christ in hand, we can take the Church in hand too.[8]

The risk of addressing underlying structures, beliefs and systems is that it will cause us to be excluded, to walk closer to the edge of marginalisation. This we have seen over and over again. In seeking to address clericalism and male privilege and power, the risk of prophecy is that, when you speak out, people will attempt to silence you. Whether in the work of *The Boston Globe* reporters who broke the story of systematic cover-up in Boston, made famous by the

---

7 For details of the Common Ground concept, see www.communities.wa.gov.au/strategies/homelessness-strategy/common-ground/.
8 James Carroll, 2002. *Toward a New Catholic Church: The Promise of Reform*. New York: Mariner Books, p. 15.

movie *Spotlight*. Whether in the *Four Corners* report aired on 17 February 2020 about St Kevin's College in Melbourne and athletes coach Peter Keogh, who was charged with sexual grooming. Whether in naming gender stereotyping and structural gender inequality, which are the core root drivers of violence against women, where one woman dies every week in this country and yet we do not call it a national crisis.

There is also the example of John Lawrence, a child migrant from Britain placed in a Christian Brothers orphanage in Western Australia. He suffered years of sexual abuse. As lawyers currently engage in negotiations, those representing the Christian Brothers mount the 'salt in the wound' argument. This argument says that the abuse and educational neglect of the children, coupled with their "already poor prospects", because they were orphans or had been separated from their parents, should somehow be reflected in lower compensation than that to which they would otherwise be entitled.

The barrister representing the Christian Brothers opened her case by noting that the judge would need to determine the extent to which Lawrence's psychological trauma was driven by various factors, including the abuse that he suffered. She pointed to the emotional trauma suffered by Lawrence when he was separated from his family years before he was sent to Australia, as well as his subsequent alcohol and substance abuse and other issues that impacted upon his life. In the proposition that she put to the judge, the barrister said that it could not be overlooked that many of these migrant children had very poor prospects simply because of the lack of care of their society.

My service and many Catholic social services are full of these children. Children who were abused at the hands of people whom we should be able to trust. The question of risk is whether we are courageous enough to accept full accountability and what that means, rather than attempt to create a reduced margin in that space.

The other quality that Chittister talks about is paradox, a seemingly absurd or contradictory statement or proposition. She says that we often define as holy those who work with people who experience suffering, discrimination and poverty. We define people like me, perhaps, as difficult and we denounce them when they challenge, question or name the structures that keep those same people suffering. Chittister cites Dostoyevsky who wrote in *The Brothers Karamazov* that people "reject their prophets and slay them, but they love their martyrs".[9] Chittister writes that charity is laudable and seldom dangerous but, without prophecy, it makes the world safe for exploitation. Doing and advocacy are interdependent and accepting one without the other is like accepting half of the Christian message. I often think that the question for us as organisations is: Which half of the message have we accepted?

Embodying the Gospel Message

Chittister talks about the quality of awareness. She quotes Mary Oliver, who writes, "Pay attention. Be astonished. Tell about it".[10] She says that prophetic people need to move from practising religion towards embodying the Gospel message, and not a bleached version. To be spiritually aware, we must each be about something greater than ourselves. We are required – I would suggest that we are mandated – to think and study the causes as well as the consequences. It is our responsibility and nobody else's to understand the root cause of injustice and, as Chittister says, to be the herald in the camp. We cannot hide behind a life of prayer as an excuse for doing nothing or for staying quiet. We

---

9 Chittister, op. cit. n. 1, p. 33.
10 Ibid., p. 40.

must take on the responsibility to spread the word, to name it, and to call out the issue. We are to identify with the issue, and we are to live the issue.

The rate of homelessness in our country has increased five per cent over the last five years. Just four per cent of all properties have been affordable and appropriate for households on government support in the last five years. One property in 69,000 is affordable if you are on a youth allowance; 3.2 million people in our country live in poverty; 15,000 children in Western Australia go to school without breakfast. Aboriginal children are five times more likely to be reported to child protection. In Western Australia, Aboriginal women are 32 times more likely to experience family violence. As I stated above and as has been my mantra for the last five years, one woman dies every week in this country from family-related violence. We need to pay attention. We need to understand the core drivers and we need to name them.

Bravehearts was founded in 1997 by Hetty Johnston AM.[11] She has a section on her website that talks about the plight of children in Australia. In 2016, there were about 5.7 million children in Australia. She says that it is difficult to know how many children are sexually abused, but the best estimates put it at roughly eight per cent of boys and 20 per cent of girls. Staggeringly, if you put all those numbers together, you will fill the Melbourne Cricket Ground eight times over with children living in Australia right now who have been or will be sexually abused.

Chittister talks about audacity, the willingness to take bold risks. She quotes Catherine of Siena, one of my prophets, who urged: "Proclaim the truth and do not be silent through fear". All of us can acknowledge the level of fear with which we live

---

11 For information on Bravehearts, see http://bravehearts.org.au/.

when we proclaim the truth. She says that proclaiming truth is an audacious act that takes courage and discipline, and we must ensure that there is no judgement in proclaiming truth, there is no attack upon the other, there is no violence. Proclaiming the truth does more than denounce just the evil. The prophet speaks to the development of an alternative vision that speaks the truth.

The Call for Reform

When I think about audacity, I think about the voices of faith organisations in the Catholic Church who call for reform, for Vatican III, a prophetic Catholic Church where women's voices count, where they participate and lead on equal footing with men. It is heartening to hear that the issue of leadership, governance and gender in our Church are high on the agenda for the forthcoming Plenary Council. The Council must be a place where we advocate for and empower women's leadership in the Catholic Church.

When audacious people claim the truth, there is no judgement in that truth. I quote Carroll when he says:

> ... the answer to Pilate's question, 'What is truth?', matters. If truth is the exclusive province of authority, then the duty of the people is to conform to it. That answer to the question fits with the politics of a command society, whether a monarchy, a dictatorship or the present Catholic Church. But if truth is, by definition, available to human beings only in partial ways; if we know more by analogies than syllogisms; if, that is, we 'see in a mirror dimly,' then the responsibility of the people is to bring one's own experience and one's own thought to the place where the community has its conversations, to offer and accept criticism, to honour the positions of others, and to respect oneself, not in isolation but in this creative mutuality.

The mutuality, in this community, has a name – the Holy Spirit.[12]

Two audacious women are Joan Chittister and Mary McAleese. Both women have spoken with incredible respect, discipline and fierce courage. They have spoken motivated by love for their people and for their Church. I will quote from the March 2018 speech given by McAleese at the Voices of Faith International Women's Day Conference at the Jesuit Curia in Rome:

> The Israelites under Joshua's command circled Jericho's walls for seven days, blew trumpets and shouted to make the walls fall down. We don't have trumpets but we have voices of faith ... and we are here to shout, to bring down our Church's walls of misogyny. We have been circling these walls for 55 years since John XXIII's encyclical *Pacem in Terris* first pointed to the advancement of women as one of the most important 'signs of the times'.
>
> '... they are demanding both in domestic and in public life the rights and duties which belong to them as human persons' (*Pacem in Terris*, Section 41).[13]

Chittister speaks about proclamation, saying, "In every period the prophetic task was the same: to interpret the present in the light of the Word of God so that new worlds could be envisioned and new attitudes developed that would eventually make the world a better place".[14] What is it that we need to be proclaiming as a prophetic voice in the twenty-

---

12 James Carroll, 2 November 2002. "Enhancing Democracy: The Key to Religious Reform", address at Call to Action conference, Milwaukee; see Carroll, 15 November 2002. "To Reform Church, Embrace Democracy", *National Catholic Reporter;* accessed at www.natcath.org/NCR_Online/archives/111502/111502d.htm.

13 Mary McAleese, 8 March 2018. "The time is now for change in the Catholic Church", address at Voices of Faith conference; accessed at www.irishcatholic.com/the-time-is-now-for-change-in-the-catholic-church/.

14 Chittister, op. cit. n. 1, p. 103.

first century, as a Church, as individuals, as Catholic organisations? Carroll would suggest that we need Vatican III. He writes:

> ... the twenty-first century desperately needs an intellectually vital, ecumenically open, and morally sound Catholicism, a Catholicism fully itself – that is, a Catholicism profoundly reformed. The world needs a new Catholic Church.[15]

He goes on to suggest that a proclamation of reform and repentance is needed:

> ... with Karl Rahner, who wrote generally of the 'sinful Church of sinners,' the confession must be made that the failures that bought Catholicism to the present crisis are 'the actions and conduct of the Church herself.' The culture of the Church itself – its clericalism, its triumphalism, its absolutism – must be renounced, as the culture that has kept the structure of victimization of the other so firmly in place, even now.[16]

The Archdiocese of Sydney has an Anti-Slavery Taskforce and the Archdiocese and its various agencies are implementing the Taskforce's recommendations to help to eradicate human trafficking. In an address to the Select Committee of the Legislative Council of New South Wales on Human Trafficking, Archbishop Anthony Fisher OP of Sydney said: "... it is not enough for groups such as churches to lecture or exhort the rest of the community in such matters: we must demonstrate our own willingness to act where we can".[17] I would call on our institutional Church to act on the place and full participation of women in the Church.

---

15 Carroll, op. cit. n 8, p. 18.
16 Ibid., p. 109.
17 Anthony Fisher OP, 29 March 2017. "It's not enough for us to lecture on trafficking, so here's what we are going to do", *The Catholic Weekly*; accessed at www.catholicweekly.com.au/.

A Vision for the Future

Chittister also talks about vision. She quotes Helen Keller, who wrote: "The only thing worse than being blind is having no vision". Prophets point us to what is and what is not vision. As Paul Vallely notes, Pope Francis made quite a revealing comment in his book on mercy. Valley writes:

> ... the Church had got too wrapped up in itself. It was too navel-gazing. It had become 'self-referential' which had made it sick. It was suffering a 'kind of theological narcissism'. When Jesus said: 'Behold, I stand at the door and knock' people assumed he was outside, wanting to come in. But sometimes Jesus knocks from within, wanting to be let out into the wider world. A self-referential Church wants to keep Jesus to itself, instead of letting him out to others.[18]

This is the vision that Pope Francis has seen for the Church, although he is perhaps not always free to enact and enable it.

When I first became a CEO ten years ago, I was talking to a man called John, who told me about his life as a person who had used and misused drugs and alcohol. I was profoundly touched by his story. About a week later someone sent me a sermon by Archbishop Rowan Williams, the previous Archbishop of Canterbury who stated:

> The reverence I owe to every human person is connected with the reverence I owe to God's creative Word, which brings them into being and keeps them in being. I stand before holy ground when I encounter another person – not because they are born with a set of legal rights which they can demand and enforce, but because there is a dimension of their life I shall never fully see; the dimension where

---

18 Paul Vallely, 2013. *Pope Francis: Untying the Knots*. London: Bloomsbury, p. 155.

they come forth from the purpose of God into the world, with a unique set of capacities and possibilities ... It means that there are no superfluous people, no 'spare' people in the human world. All are needed for the good of all.[19]

These lines opened my heart. Human failure is tragic and terrible because it means that some unique and unrepeatable aspect of God's purpose has not been allowed to flourish. We have no room to allow even one human being to fail. There are none for whom it is not worth fighting.

Chittister talks of faith, the single gift that makes prophecy real. She quotes Rabbi Abraham Heschel who said: "There is no choice now. Something must be done and someone must do it. Somebody must do something – and that leaves us – leaves me ... faith leads us from the dregs of despair to trust again in possibility ... faith in God takes us from the fear of public recrimination to the courage it takes to do God's will for the public good".[20]

I am very interested in Chittister's reflections on confidence. She says that lacking faith in an invisible God during difficult times makes a lot of sense. We have all experienced the dark night of the soul, moments in time when we cannot really believe that God exists. She says, however, that to lack confidence is to deny the abilities that we have been given. It is a virtual sin against creation.

She refers to the story in which Moses asks, "Who am I that I should go the Pharaoh?" And God says, "I will be with you. This will be your sign". Yet Moses objects, saying, "Suppose they do not listen to me". So, God shows him that he will be saved if the

---

19 Rowan Williams, 12 May 2007. "Christianity: Public Religion and the Common Good", presented in St Andrew's Cathedral, Singapore; accessed at aoc2013.brix.fatbeehive.com/articles.php/1165/christianity-public-religion-and-the-common-good.
20 Chittister, op. cit. n. 1, p. 113.

pharaohs remain obdurate. But Moses is no fool; he is rather canny. "If you please, my Lord", he says, "I have never been particularly elegant. I am slow of speech and tongue. Please, Lord, send someone else". The scripture tells us that God becomes angry with Moses and instead sends his brother Aaron, the one with the public speaking skills.[21]

Consciousness of God's disappointment at Moses' reluctance is a warning that we should take seriously. As Chittister suggests, to lack confidence in this way is to deny the abilities that we have been given.

Prophets in our Midst

Confidence has a modern face: the confidence to speak out. This will be familiar to those who have followed the Harvey Weinstein story and read Jodi Kantor and Megan Twohey's writing on sexual harassment that helped to ignite a movement. It was manifest in Christine Blasey Ford, who came forward about the behaviour of Justice Brett Kavanagh when he was about to be (and has subsequently been) appointed to the Supreme Court of the United States. We also have the example of Malala Yousafzai, who defied the Taliban in Pakistan and demanded that girls be allowed to receive an education. She was shot by a gunman in 2012, and in 2014 she became the youngest person to receive the Nobel Peace Prize.

We may not be called to be prophets, but we and our organisations are called to walk the prophetic road. We may not always feel or know the presence of God, but we have God-given talents and abilities that must be used: Joan Chittister, Mary McAleese, Dr Christine Blasey Ford, Australian Indigenous land-rights activist Eddie Mabo, American feminist Gloria Steinem, Moses, American civil rights activist Rosa Parkes, environmentalist

---

21 *Exodus*, Chapters 3-4.

Greta Thunberg are those from whom I have heard the prophetic voice, today and yesterday.

There are prophets in our midst. Recently I saw a statement issued by six faith-based religious organisations, Anglicare Victoria, Good Shepherd Australia New Zealand, Jewish Care, Uniting, Sacred Heart Mission and McAuley Community Services for Women. The statement, in response to the proposed Federal Government anti-discrimination bill, was written by services that are committed to the common good and see all people as equal. They accept all humans as they are. These are prophets in our own time, organisations that have taken the prophetic road and spoken out.

And you, what will you do, here and now in the world, in our time? Will you simply stand looking in? I take my final words from Mary McAleese's speech on International Women's Day that I quoted earlier. She proclaims:

> We are entitled to hold our Church leaders to account for this and other egregious abuses of institutional power and we will insist on our right to do so no matter how many official doors are closed to us.
>
> At the start of his papacy Pope Francis said, 'We need to create still broader opportunities for a more incisive female presence in the Church', words a Church scholar described as evidence of Francis' 'magnanimity'. Let us be clear, women's right to equality in the Church arises organically from divine justice. It should not depend on *ad hoc* papal benevolence.
>
> Pope Francis described female theologians as the 'strawberries on the cake'. He was wrong. Women are the leaven in the cake. They are the primary handers on of the faith to their children. In the Western world the Church's cake is not rising, the baton of faith is dropping. Women are walking away from the Catholic Church in droves, for those

who are expected to be key influencers in their children's faith formation have no opportunity to be key influencers in the formation of the Catholic faith ...

Yet Pope Francis has said that 'women are more important than men because the Church is a woman'. Holy Father, why not ask women if they feel more important than men? I suspect many will answer that they experience the Church as a male bastion of patronizing platitudes to which Pope Francis has added his quota.

John Paul II has written of the 'mystery of women'. Talk to us as equals and we will not be a mystery! Francis has said a 'deeper theology of women' is needed. God knows it would be hard to find a shallower theology of women than the misogyny dressed up as theology that the magisterium currently hides behind.

And all the time a deeper theology is staring us in the face. It does not require much digging to find it. Just look to Christ. John Paul II pointed out that:

... we are heirs to a history which has conditioned us to a remarkable extent. In every time and place, this conditioning has been an obstacle to the progress of women ... Transcending the established norms of his own culture, Jesus treated women with openness, respect, acceptance and tenderness ... As we look to Christ ... it is natural to ask ourselves: how much of this message has been heard and acted upon?[22]

Women are best qualified to answer that question but we are left to talk among ourselves. No Church leader bothers to turn up not just because we do not matter to them but because their priestly formation prepares them to resist treating us as true equals.

---

22 McAleese quoted Pope St John Paul II, 1995. *Letter to Women*, Section 3; accessed at www.vatican.va/.

... in 1995 the Jesuit Congregation asked God for the grace of conversion from a patriarchal Church to a Church of equals; a Church where women truly matter not on terms designed by men for a patriarchal Church but on terms which make Christ matter. Only such a Church of equals is worthy of Christ. Only such a Church can credibly make Christ matter.

The time for that Church is now, Pope Francis. The time for change is now.[23]

Conclusion

In conclusion, let me return to my questions: What will you do, here and now in this world, in our time? Will you simply stand looking in?

---

23 McAleese, op. cit. n. 13.

Serving Communities with Courage and Compassion – A Reflection

Mark Monahan

The purpose of my engagement is to provide some closing remarks, trying to touch on trends that I noticed in the *Serving Communities with Courage and Compassion* conference presentations and now in the chapters of this book. I will not pretend to think I have captured all trends, so alongside my reflections I invite you to consider: what are your key impressions, what connections did you make, or what emotional response are you having upon reading some chapters in the book?

At the pre-conference Indigenous forum, Elder Dave Wandin welcomed us to Country and outlined a very important point for the start of our gathering: that Aboriginal people are guardians of the land; they are not owners. To me, this relates to something about power, service, right relationship, respect and equality. I heard many conference presenters interact with these words in different ways.

Misogyny, consciously or unconsciously, exists within our Church, our religious orders, our politics, many of our educational environments, our social services and our general community. I think we need to shift to the message of guardianship; no-one owns or carries the power but rather we are guardians of Earth, of the Catholic faith, of Catholic social teaching and a model of social service which is relied upon by many thousands of people.

Furthermore, while some within our eco-system hunger for control and top-down management, I have heard we are ready for a new paradigm – one of consultative leadership, one that values the voice of the child, people with a disability, the non-English speaking community member or the volunteer unpacking the dishwasher. It is up to us to find ways to hear their voices, not for our community members to assume a certain long-established style of leadership.

I hear a calling for us to do things differently and that there is a thirst to explore this difference. But we must be deeply truthful about this desire for difference. More of the same with a few tweaks is not what is on the lips of many. I hear and see possibilities for different leadership models and structures, I hear exploration of what our mission really could be, I hear our sense of welcome needs to grow wider and not just through words but through actions. Executive Director of Catholic Social Services Victoria Josh Lourensz displayed this leadership when facilitating the opening morning of this conference by inviting the attendees into a simple gesture, after they had heard the powerful presentation from Francis Sullivan.[1] Lourensz invited everyone to take a moment and place their feet on the floor, grounding them to Mother Earth. A meditative moment to ensure they were grounded in Sullivan's provoking presentation but also sturdy enough to hear the next voice and begin to wonder, what next?

At the Catholic Social Services conference four years ago, I felt that the attendees were a group sitting and waiting in anticipation for the final recommendations of the Royal Commission into Institutional Responses to Child Sexual Abuse[2] – I felt a heavy cloud hovered over us, and quite rightly so. Two years ago, I heard, es-

---

1 Francis Sullivan, 2020. "Margin Call: The Risk of Integrity" in this volume.
2 The Royal Commission into Institutional Responses to Child Sexual Abuse ran from 2013-2017; see www.childabuseroyalcommission.gov.au/.

pecially from Robert Fitzgerald, one of the Royal Commissioners,[3] advice that Catholic organisations can only say that they have the trust of the community that they serve, once their community says so – it can no longer be presumed. I now hear an expectation that we should have, and always should have had, the understanding that we must earn trust and never presume it exists.

As the 2020 conference progressed and in the book's chapters, I continued hearing the need for new models of operation:

- I heard relief that the rights of LGBTQI+ people are recognised and they must be welcomed and given equal consideration as part of our Catholic family.
- Policies and procedures are not enough, cultural change is what is significant.
- How can we have Cultural Leave as part of our workplaces?
- Boards must be diverse in membership.
- In the response to natural disasters, such as bushfires and floods, a community may gravitate to particular first responders. Afterwards the community should play a key role in determining its own recovery. Encouraging examples were recounted of responses by Church agencies after bushfires.
- Community members with whom we work, take for example, Jocelyn Bignold of McAuley Community Services for Women,[4] have courage and strength that we need to draw upon to inspire us and move us out of this time of questioning our resolve.

---

3 Fitzgerald's presentation at the previous conference is summarised in Maria Harries, 2018. "Responding to Abuse, Ensuring Safety and Dedication to Service" in Gabrielle McMullen, Patrice Scales and Denis Fitzgerald (eds) *Hearing Healing Hope: The Ministry of Service in Challenging Times*, Brisbane: Connor Court Publishing, Brisbane, 82-103.

4 Bignold's presentation at the conference is summarised in Jocelyn Bignold, Vincent Long Van Nguyen OFM Conv and John McCarthy with Patrice Scales, 2020. "Putting Courage and Compassion into Action" in this volume.

- Global injustices, such as slavery, can be responded to, even with the smallest deeds, like choosing which coffee we buy.
- We are too easily cajoled into "a palatable consumption of outrageous injustice". We need to stick our necks out and engage with "risking as an act of love".[5]
- We must pursue revenue streams and methods where we share resources to ensure we can resource our Catholic mission, rather than rely just on Government funding which 'tones down' our approach.
- We have friends in Catholic Social Services in New Zealand so we should ensure that we think beyond the shores of Australia.

I have picked up a real sense that many individuals and organisations are keen to work together. I have heard queries about how partnerships could work and how we could share resources to ensure maximum community outcomes. In the past I have felt different Catholic social services have prioritised their own delivery of mission over what might be best for community benefit. This correlates back to a sense of control and narrow-mindedness.

I felt so alive when I was speaking with a delegate from the St Vincent de Paul Society who suggested the establishment of a portal for all Catholic organisations to access and which would provide social service learning opportunities for young people in the sector. She said by doing this we could have more young people informed and involved and increase our community impact. Furthermore, she explained that we could assist each other with training and formation. It could be that simple. While some might focus on the problems associated with such a possibility, whereas this emerging

---

[5] Donna McAuliffe, Charlotte Williams and Linda Briskman, 2016. "Moral outrage! Social work and social welfare", *Ethics and Social Welfare*, 10(2), 87-93.

leader has a vision for maximising community impact. She knows the 'gold' of Vinnies, but equally respects others in ministry and sees that it would be even better working alongside Don Bosco, Marist, Edmund Rice, Jesuit and other ministries. The leaders of tomorrow are here and ready.

The importance of formation has emerged many times. Formation will be a key ingredient to enable us to discover the new way for the Church and our social services mission, as it identifies our personal gifts but also helps expose our weaknesses, supports our child safety efforts and helps to build a stronger Catholic social services community.

In relation to formation, I invite you to consider the following thoughts in reflective mode. What has your Catholic social service journey been? When did it begin? Did it begin at your school, a local parish, a sporting club connected with your parish, with a teacher, your first volunteer experience, your first food van or volunteering on a camp? Did it begin or evolve with an overseas immersion, a job, a member of a religious order who mentored you, a contribution you made by being a committee or board member?

What filled your heart about these Catholic social service experiences, and how much did they relate to where you are right now? Was there anyone significant that walked this journey with you?

Where might this journey go? What fills your heart full of love as you seek to imagine the next part of your journey? Will it continue on the trajectory it is on now, or can it gain 'wings' and explode with passion and enthusiasm for a new trajectory, one that we have been called to by this conference?

Grounding ourselves in our formation journey helps us to remain authentic to mission. It keeps us aligned with the true worth of being involved in Catholic social services. It evolves our commitment to be a community that demands prophetic justice for all.

A quote from John Maxwell, an American writer on leadership, is very relevant in this context. He says:

> Every test you face as a leader begins within you. The test of courage is no different ... 'All the significant battles are waged within self'. Courage isn't an absence of fear. It's doing what you are afraid to do. It is having the power to let go of the familiar and forge ahead into new territory.[6]

In the same volume, Maxwell also quoted civil rights leader Martin Luther King Jr: "The ultimate measure of a man and woman is not where they stand in moments of comfort and convenience, but where they stand at times of challenge and controversy".[7]

I think that one of the most important elements of the conference, at least for me, was what Helen Christensen, an Indigenous Education Officer with Catholic Education Melbourne, shared as one of the speakers at the Indigenous forum, "Beyond Surviving to Truthfully Thriving: Continuing our Journey of Listening in Truth and Justice". Christensen spoke very powerfully about trauma and how she feels when she is amongst raised voices. I can amplify her honest sharing with a personal story of my own.

Eighteen months ago, my wife and I invited a good friend and her daughter to stay with us for as long as they required because of their need to escape serious family violence. Throughout their time with us, I noticed the daughter, aged seven, would always watch over her shoulder to be sure of where I was and what I was doing. Often, I would read my youngest daughter, Evie, a book before bed. The daughter wanted to join us but felt extremely unsure about

---

[6] John C. Maxwell, 1999. *The 21 Indispensable Qualities of a Leader: Becoming the Person Others Will Want to Follow.* Nashville, TN: Thomas Nelson, p. 40.

[7] Ibid.

being with me while I was reading the book. Throughout the day I kept my distance and I did my best to ensure she could see me. I would check with her regarding many things. I would ask her questions: if she would like her mum to stay with us while I read a book, or where I should sit in relation to her and Evie. I was conscious of everything I did. She would never talk to me; she was just so scared of me, an adult male. I did all I could to create a safe space for her.

One morning our house was chaotic and I was struggling to get my kids organised for school. At one point, I found myself losing my patience and yelling at my son. Immediately afterwards, I realised my friend's daughter was right beside me; the fear in her eyes spoke of having to hear another male yelling. Our friend hugged her daughter like she had had to do so many times before. I walked outside and felt so ashamed of myself. I eventually left for work. As I drove to work, I heard a man ring into ABC Melbourne radio to speak to broadcaster John Faine. He spoke of the fact that the previous night he had perpetrated male verbal violence. He advised that he rang up because he realised he needed to own his loss of control and his lack of capacity to respond to his emotions in a more productive and in a non-violent way. I found this very hard to listen to because I was in the same boat, but I had to listen. Regardless of how much I had tried to advocate for women with regard to gender-based violence in the past, that could not extinguish the fact that I had exposed a young girl to another moment of inappropriate male violence.

This was a moment in time for me to recognise I needed to do better, and I have done so subsequently. I have seen this girl again since she left our home after staying for four months and now she talks briefly to me and I do not see the fear in her eyes that I remember seeing in her each day while she was staying with us.

I heard many times in the conference presentations that before anything can change in our organisations, systems or structures, we need to change ourselves and that we need to be more critical of ourselves. We need to hear the diversity of the voices that are oppressed, we need to look into the eyes of the vulnerable and see what they mirror back and we need to be brave enough to change. We need to educate ourselves to improve our cultural competence. We need to face up to some difficult self-realisations, perhaps that is where the word 'courage' in the conference and book titles seeks to lead us. I see this as a wonderful opportunity for our own growth and therefore our ministry.

In a conference workshop which focused on child safety[8] it was mentioned, significantly, that we probably would not have had such a 'conversation' five years ago due to lack of organisational maturity, strength or leadership. But we are now having these conversations which we must see as progress. The "Governance for Mission" workshop[9] presented the challenge that, if we continue with more of the same, being Catholic may be the greatest risk to our integrity; on the other hand, being Catholic could perhaps be our greatest opportunity if we are willing to be a radically new Church and Catholic social services.

Our challenges are to embrace consultative leadership, to work with others, to work from grass roots, to shift the cultures of our organisations, and to be authentic.

This conference explored many topics deeply and now is the time for action, to resolve that we can move forward in a new direction of being Church and of social service delivery. Perhaps we need to look around our workplaces and our parishes to see the

---

8 For a summary of the workshop, see Maria Harries and Robyn Miller, 2020. "The Centrality and Challenge of Child Safety" in this volume.

9 For a summary of the workshop, see John Warhurst and Katherine Juric, 2020. "Governance for Mission" in this volume.

extraordinary gifts that we are blessed with right now and move into the new paradigm. In part, this book seeks to 'catalyse' the action required for a new way of doing things.

I wonder when will waves stirred up by the Royal Commission into Institutional Responses to Child Sexual Abuse actually end, will they ever end, will we allow them to end? Or can we let them be a part of us as a strength that helps guide us to a new reality. I think the richness of words spoken at the conference and flowing out of these pages are trying to say to us to keep going, to be brave, that it is definitely worth sticking at it and to be courageous as we serve our communities with compassion.

Acknowledgements

The development of a book such as this requires the contribution of many people and organisations, to whom the editors and readers alike are indebted. Cooperation on this scale reflects the practice of dialogue and collaboration that is a feature of Catholic social services in Australia, and of its collaboration with the many parts of the Church and society on which they rely for their full effectiveness.

This is the fourth in a series of books that have documented biennial Catholic Social Services conferences. This book, entitled *Serving Communities with Courage and Compassion*, builds on a conference of the same name held on 26-28 February 2020 at the Catholic Leadership Centre in Melbourne. All papers from the conference included in this volume have been revised for publication, and some chapters – Sr Joan Healy's *Preface* and the *Introduction* – have been written in light of discussion at the conference.

We are in the debt of those who have written specifically for this book. Deep thanks is also owed to the many authors who presented at the conference, and to those presenters whose work was incorporated into chapters that have been written by others. Special thanks is extended to those who coordinated the writing of chapters by multiple authors, or who worked with a number of others to integrate a range of material on a particular topic into a coherent narrative. In addition to the editors, Fiona Basile, Peter Hudson, Netty Horton, Josh Lourensz and Claire-Anne Willis all contributed in this way.

ACKNOWLEDGEMENTS

Anthony Cappello and his colleagues at Connor Court Publishing facilitated the development of the book, as they did with earlier publications in this series. Their support is deeply appreciated. The conference out of which the book emerged was organised by Catholic Social Services Victoria in partnership with Catholic Social Services Australia. We are grateful to the conference participants and session leaders from across Australia and Aotearoa New Zealand who contributed to the delivery and discussion of the ideas that were presented at the conference and are now offered to a wider audience through this volume. Prominent among these are Uncle Dave Wandin, who warmly welcomed us to Wurundjeri country on the opening evening, and Esmae Manahan whose workshop on culturally informed trauma-informed practice from an Aboriginal perspective formed part of the Indigenous awareness that permeated the whole conference.

The conference organising committee was chaired by Denis Fitzgerald and included Peter Hudson, Gabrielle McMullen, Jenny Glare, Mark Monahan, Fiona Basile, Josh Lourensz and Aileen Martin, with Lucia Brick joining at various times. Committee members all contributed to the event in many ways. Lucia Brick, now well practiced in the field, again led staff and volunteers in conference administration, supported in particular by Huong Nguyen and staff of the Catholic Leadership Centre. Josh Lourensz managed post-conference arrangements, including administrative support for the development of the book.

Communications for all stages of the conference were coordinated by Fiona Basile of Catholic Social Services Victoria, with highly valued support from *Melbourne Catholic*, Jesuit Communications and *Eureka Street*, with the latter the official media partner for the conference. Some of the chapters in the book include material that was first developed for *Eureka Street* as part of its focus on conference themes.

Sponsors made it financially feasible for the participation of a number of presenters and others, including emerging leaders, who added to the dialogue and overall experience; and their generosity thus made this book feasible too. Many of these also supported the earlier conferences. We thank:

- Australian Catholic University
- Catholic Church Insurance
- Catholic Development Fund, Archdiocese of Melbourne
- Catholic Education Melbourne
- Christian Brothers Oceania Province
- Marist Brothers Province of Australia
- Sisters of St Joseph of the Sacred Heart

Ultimately, this book is about contributing to a more just and equitable society through advancing the Gospel-inspired work of service and work for justice of the Church in Australia. The editors, on behalf of Catholic Social Services Victoria and Catholic Social Services Australia, express their thanks to all those mentioned here for their part in bringing this book to fruition, and advancing that over-arching objective.

Contributors

Sherry Balcombe, Coordinator, Aboriginal Catholic Ministry Victoria

An Olkola/Djabaguy woman from Far North Queensland, Sherry Balcombe has worked for Aboriginal Catholic Ministry for 16 years, for the past four years as its Coordinator. She is passionate about her work and enjoys supporting her local community on a state and national level. She is actively involved in advocacy, visiting children in detention, liaison with schools and extensive committee work.

Fiona Basile, freelance writer and photographer

Fiona Basile is a freelance writer and photographer based in Melbourne. She provides regular communications assistance to Catholic Social Services Victoria as well as to the Missionary Sisters of Service, various agencies of the Archdiocese of Melbourne and other community and commercially-based clients. As part of her own creative writing and photographic endeavours, Fiona is the author of a children's book, *Shhh ... God is in the Silence*, published by Loyola Press in the United States, for which she is a regular contributor to its spirituality outreach work, www.ignatianspirituality.com.

Jocelyn Bignold OAM, CEO, McAuley Community Services for Women

Jocelyn Bignold has been CEO of McAuley Community Services for Women since 2008 and, under her leadership, McAuley has had a track record of innovation, especially in recognising and responding to the needs of children affected by family violence. She oversaw the concept, design and building of McAuley House, Victoria's first purpose-built facility offering women safe accommodation and support to get their lives back on track. Jocelyn gave expert evidence before Victoria's Royal Commission into Family Violence, and has chaired the Western Integrated Family Violence Committee and been a member of the Victorian Government's Family Violence Housing Assistance Implementation Taskforce.

Helen Burt, policy adviser

Helen Burt has worked for over 30 years in the community sector, mostly in faith-based organisations. In that time her roles have included program development, policy work and management. Due to a progressive illness, Helen now uses NDIS services and, at times, undertakes advocacy around disability-related issues.

Monica Cavanagh RSJ OAM, Congregational Leader, Sisters of St Joseph

Monica Cavanagh is the Congregational Leader of the Sisters of Saint Joseph and previously served as the President of Catholic Religious Australia. Originally from Queensland, she has spent most of her religious life serving people across its five dioceses. She began her years in ministry as a primary teacher. This was followed by experiences in parish pastoral roles, adult education, facilitation and spirituality. Monica was involved in providing resources and presentations in preparation for World Youth Day 2008 and the canonisation of St Mary MacKillop.

Helen Christensen, Indigenous Education Officer, Catholic Education Melbourne

Helen Christensen was born and raised in Darwin in the Northern Territory before settling on Wadda Wurrung Country in Victoria. Through her mother, she has inherited her Tiwi identity and obligations as a member of the Miyartiwi skin group. Her father was a member of the Stolen Generation and his cultural connection is with the Anmatjere skin group. Through her current role at Catholic Education Melbourne, Helen is able to educate the wider community in Catholic schools about Aboriginal and Torres Strait Islander peoples.

Belinda Clarke, Executive Manager Social Impact, CatholicCare Tasmania

Belinda Clarke is committed to driving change in complex environments, in particular for individuals and communities experiencing entrenched disadvantage. She has had diverse leadership experience across the not-for-profit, healthcare, community, social services, education and business sectors, with a particular motivation to advance the social teachings of the Catholic Church, and is currently the founding director of CatholicCare's Social Impact Project. Belinda has held a range of board roles, including inaugural Chair of All Round Health and Community Care, a not-for-profit holistic healthcare service supporting marginalised and homeless Tasmanians.

Daniel Clements, General Manager, Justice and Crime Prevention Programs, Jesuit Social Services

As General Manager, Justice and Crime Prevention Programs for Jesuit Social Services in Victoria, Daniel Clements heads a large team of staff and volunteers in the State-wide delivery of support programs for children, young people and their families caught up in the criminal justice system, and for men and women exiting Victorian prisons. Included in his portfolio is responsibility for programs using restorative practice including the Youth Justice Group Conferencing Program and Community Conferencing Programs. Daniel has a keen interest in building strong organisational cultures for change, a passion for practice development and social justice, and a commitment to partnerships to advance these goals.

Janet Cribbes, consultant, facilitator and mentor

Janet Cribbes' career spans three decades, encompassing roles in State government, community services, the private sector and, more recently, not-for-profit bodies. Her community involvement saw her elected to Port Phillip Council in 2004-2008 with a term as mayor in 2008. After the Black Saturday 2009 bushfires, she established and managed the Archdiocese of Melbourne's Community Bushfire Recovery Service. Janet is currently a consultant, facilitator and mentor, working mostly in local government, as well as Chair, Wellsprings for Women Board and Director, St Kilda Community Housing Board.

Alana Crouch, Director, Catholic Early EdCare

Alana Crouch has pursued a career pathway in education, working in schools, early learning centres, outside school hours care and kindergartens, and now with Catholic Early EdCare. After being called early in her career to establish an Outside School Hours Care service for a parish in Brisbane, she commenced her leadership journey with the Archdiocese of Brisbane in 2005, moving into her role as Director in 2011. Her passion for supporting families and recognising the importance of the Church and communities working in partnership has given her the opportunity to lead and support many wonderful projects and staff, witnessing mission in action.

Trudy Dantis, Director, National Centre for Pastoral Research

Dr Trudy Dantis is the Director of the Australian Catholic Bishops Conference National Centre for Pastoral Research. She is the author of *A Handbook for Building Stronger Parishes* (2016) and has co-authored several books and research reports, including the recent *Listen to What the Spirit is Saying: Final Report for the Plenary*

Council Phase 1. Trudy is an Honorary Research Associate of the University of Divinity and a board member of the Christian Research Association.

Deanna Davis, General Manager, Family and Community Services, Centacare Catholic Diocese of Ballarat

Deanna Davis joined Centacare Catholic Diocese of Ballarat in April 2007. Her current role as General Manager, Family and Community Services has responsibility for a wide range of services. Previous roles encompass 22 years with the Department of Health/ Human Services, including as General Services Manager, Lakeside Psychiatric Hospital and in Mental Health Policy and Program development, facilitating implementation of both state and Federal Government initiatives. Deanna has long-standing involvement in sector networks and various committees across the health and community services sector.

Jack de Groot, CEO, St Vincent de Paul Society NSW

Jack de Groot is CEO of the St Vincent de Paul Society NSW. Previously, his roles have included CEO of Caritas Australia and Group Mission Leader at St Vincent's Health Australia. He currently serves on the boards of St John of God Healthcare, the University of Notre Dame Australia and Caritas Australia, and was until recently Chair of the Implementation Advisory Group that monitored the Catholic Church's implementation of the recommendations of the Royal Commission into Institutional Responses to Child Sexual Abuse.

Linda Di Sipio, Mission Education and Formation Lead, St Vincent's Hospital Melbourne

As Mission Education and Formation Lead at St Vincent's Hospital Melbourne, Linda Di Sipio is responsible for facilitating the formation program *Inspired to Serve* as well as creating bespoke formation experiences for hospital staff. A focus and research area for Linda is staff formation in Catholic schools and hospitals using an adaptation of the Ignatian Spirituality Exercises.

Janene Evans, General Manager, Safety and Resilience, Good Shepherd Australia New Zealand

Now General Manager, Safety and Resilience, Good Shepherd Australia New Zealand, Janene Evans has worked in the community sector for over 20 years, predominantly in family violence, homelessness and child, youth and family services. She has held senior roles in the not-for-profit agencies Berry Street, Hanover (now Launch), Emerge Women's Refuge, Wesley Mission Victoria/ Uniting Vic Tas, Women's Domestic Violence Crisis Service (now Safe Steps) and The Salvation Army.

Farah Farouque, Director of Community Engagement, Tenants Victoria

A strategic communicator, policy analyst and advocacy specialist, Farah Farouque has been leading the community engagement portfolio at the peak body for renters, Tenants Victoria, since April 2020. She was previously Principal Advisor Public Affairs and Policy at the Brotherhood of St Laurence where she shaped political advocacy and strategic communications for the agency, including directing its high impact campaign for youth employment. She joined the community sector in 2012, after an award-winning career as a senior writer at *The Age* spanning social and legal policy, Victorian and Federal politics, and the creative arts. Her toughest reporting assignment was covering the 2004 Boxing Day tsunami out of coastal Sri Lanka for *The Age* and sister paper *The Sydney Morning Herald*.

Denis Fitzgerald, ministry and governance adviser

For 12 years until October 2019, Denis Fitzgerald was Executive Director of Catholic Social Services Victoria, where his focus included reflection on mission and its practical implications in Catholic social service providers and parishes. Earlier careers were as an Australian diplomat and a senior executive with the Victorian Government. Among his current engagements are governance and advisory roles with several social service organisations, volunteer service in prison ministry and local parish roles.

Andrew Gardiner, Chief Executive Officer, Dandenong and District Aborigines Co-operative Ltd

Andrew Gardiner, a descendent of the Wurundjeri clans of the Woiwurrung people of the Kulin Nation and since 2006 accepted as an Elder, has been Chief Executive Officer at Dandenong and District Aborigines Co-operative Ltd since 2009. His service in other significant roles includes Co-Chair of the DHHS South Division Aboriginal Governance Committee, 'Respected Person' to the Koori Court which is a part of the Magistrates Court of Victoria, and membership of the Board of the Wooroondjeri Woi-wurrung Cultural Heritage Aboriginal Corporation, the Victorian Aboriginal Health Service and the Metropolitan Partnerships and Community Advisory Committee of Ambulance Victoria. In December 2019 Andrew was elected to the First Peoples' Assembly of Victoria and occupies the Wooroondjeri RAP Reserved Seat on this Assembly.

Cath Garner, Group Director Mission and Cabrini Outreach, Cabrini Australia

Cath Garner is a member of the Cabrini Australia executive with responsibility for vision and leadership in Catholic identity and mission integration across the group. She also heads up Cabrini Outreach, a health-focused community development organisation working with people seeking asylum and those experiencing intergenerational disadvantage within Australia and overseas. Starting her career as a registered nurse, over the last decade she has held a variety of leadership and voluntary governance roles within the Catholic health and social services sectors.

Meagan Giddy, Team Leader and Family Worker, CatholicCare Wilcannia-Forbes

Meagan Giddy is a Team Leader and Family Worker for CatholicCare Wilcannia-Forbes. She has a background in counselling and social work. Meagan has recently taken on a two-year project, Wellbeing Mobile, a counselling and wellbeing outreach service providing regular visits to families living on drought-affected properties around Nyngan, where she is situated.

Sarah Jane Grove, Mission Integration Manager, St Vincent's Hospital Sydney Network

As Mission Integration Manager in the St Vincent's Hospital Sydney Network, Sarah Jane Grove engages staff in formation and assists them to make meaningful connections, across their divergent roles, with the shared mission and values of St Vincent's Health Australia (SVHA). This role allows her to contribute to Inclusive Health projects at SVHA and the work of various committees. Her previous professional background was in religious and pastoral leadership in the education sector.

Andrew Hamilton SJ, senior writer, Jesuit Communications

Andy Hamilton, a Jesuit priest, is a senior writer at Jesuit Communications and works in media and advocacy at Jesuit Social Services. For many years he taught theology and church history at the United Faculty of Theology. He continues his long-standing work with refugees and writes on issues connected with them.

Cathy Hammond, Executive Manager Mission and Outreach, CatholicCare Sydney

Cathy Hammond leads the Mission and Outreach Team at CatholicCare Sydney, promoting and building relationships and partnerships that enable the growth of care and support services for the most vulnerable in the community. Prior to her work with parishes and schools at CatholicCare, Cathy worked and served in the Church in the areas of mission formation, youth and young adult ministry, and marketing and communications for agencies such as Caritas Australia, The Cardoner Project, Broken Bay Institute, and the Diocese of Broken Bay.

Maria Harries AM, Chairperson, Catholic Social Services Australia Board

Professor Maria Harries is Senior Honorary Research Fellow in the School of Population Health at The University of Western Australia and Adjunct Professor at Curtin University's School of Occupational Therapy and Social Work. She runs her own consulting practice and continues to undertake research and research supervision. Maria works with state and national organisations involved with people who have experienced 'care'. She was inaugural Chair of MercyCare WA, has held many leadership positions within the mental health and broader social services sector, and in 2014 assumed the role of Chair of Catholic Social Services Australia Board.

Sr Joan Healy RSJ AM, Life Member of Catholic Social Services Victoria

Sr Joan Healy's focus has always been to support the growth of communities of faith and of service. When a book she wrote attracted publicity and literary recognition, response from many readers convinced her that story-telling is a powerful way of provoking reflection on life and on spirituality, and she continues to mentor and to write. Joan is a life member of Catholic Social Services Victoria.

Netty Horton, CEO, CatholicCare Melbourne and Gippsland

In 2017 Netty Horton joined CatholicCare as CEO. Previous positions have included Territorial Social Programs Director for the Salvation Army, General Manager of Community Services for the

St Vincent de Paul Society's Aged Care and Community Services, and CEO of the Council to Homeless Persons. Netty's career has focused on advocacy and working with disadvantaged people and she has served as chair of the Ministerial Advisory Committee on Homelessness and a member of the Prime Minister's Council on Homelessness and the Federal Aged Care Sector Committee.

Peter Hudson, Professional Services Support Officer

Peter Hudson has been involved in the Catholic sector in education, community development and spiritual formation roles for the past forty-five years. Most recently he was Network and Member Support Coordinator at Catholic Social Services Victoria for seven and a half years. In early 2020 he commenced a new role, returning to Catholic secondary education as Professional Services Support Officer.

Katherine Juric, Risk Consultant, Catholic Church Insurance Limited

As Risk Consultant for Catholic Church Insurance Limited, Katherine Juric delivers strategic and operational risk management consulting for clients across the health, aged care and education sectors, parishes and religious orders. Key assignments include work health and safety (WHS) reviews, risk control reviews, and introduction of automated risk management databases for clients. She has 13 years experience in WHS, return-to-work and risk management in the healthcare, pharmaceuticals, and warehousing, distribution and logistics sectors.

Helen Kennedy, Chief Operations Officer, VACCHO

Helen Kennedy is a proud descendant of the Trawlwoolway and Plairmairrener clans from North East Tasmania and is currently the Chief Operations Officer of the Victorian Aboriginal Community Controlled Health Organisation (VACCHO), the peak body for Aboriginal health and wellbeing in Victoria. She has worked in

Aboriginal Affairs for over 25 years in senior capacities across the Aboriginal community-controlled sector as well as government, health, mental health, education and community services. Helen has been Director of several organisations, including the Yappera Aboriginal Children's Centre, Victorian Aboriginal Child Care Agency and Indigenous Leadership Network of Victoria.

Anne Kirwan, CEO, CatholicCare Canberra and Goulburn

A registered psychologist with over 20 years experience in the social services sector, Anne Kirwan has held the position of Chief Executive Officer of CatholicCare Canberra and Goulburn since 2014. She commenced her career working in homelessness services, and has overseen youth, employment, mental health, disability and aged care services during her time with CatholicCare. Anne has held various board positions, including President of Alcohol, Tobacco and Other Drug Association of the ACT, and is currently on the Catholic Social Services NSW/ACT Association Executive.

Bronwyn Lay, Ecological Justice Project Officer, Jesuit Social Services

Dr Bronwyn Lay is the Ecological Justice Coordinator for Jesuit Social Services and Climate Justice Coordinator at RMIT University's Climate Change Exchange. With a background in criminal and family law, Bronwyn has worked as a legal consultant for international NGOs and expert organisations on environmental crime, was the Director of the Caux Dialogue on Land and Security in Geneva, and has published in a wide variety of forums on the subject of ecological justice.

Sheree Limbrick, CEO, Catholic Professional Standards Ltd

Sheree Limbrick has been inaugural CEO of Catholic Professional Standards Ltd (CPSL) since July 2017. She has led the CPSL team to develop and publish the National Catholic Safeguarding Standards and to develop and roll out a national training and development program for Church personnel to support their implementation. She also has overseen the development and commencement of safeguarding audits in Catholic entities. Sheree has more than 25 years experience in child, youth and community services, including in senior executive roles.

John Lochowiak, Manager, Aboriginal Services, Centacare Catholic Family Services and Head, Aboriginal Catholic Ministry, Adelaide

Uncle John Lochowiak was born in Coober Pedy and is an initiated Man with strong ties to many language groups throughout Australia, including Pitjantjatjara, Kaurna, Ngarrindjeri and Arrernte. He is Manager of Aboriginal Services at Centacare Catholic Family Services, Head of Aboriginal Catholic Ministry in Adelaide, and Chairperson of the National Aboriginal and Torres Strait Islander Catholic Council. He has previously been a Vice-President of the South Australian State Council of the St Vincent de Paul Society and is now the State Council Consultant on Indigenous matters.

Bishop Vincent Long Van Nguyen OFM Conv

Bishop Vincent Long Van Nguyen came to Australia as a boat person in 1981 and joined the Order of Friars Minor Conventual in 1983. After ordination, he served as a formator and pastor in different parishes. He was elected Superior of the Order in Australia in 2005 and from 2008-2011 was Assistant General in Rome. He was appointed an Auxiliary Bishop of Melbourne from 2011-2016, and was installed as the fourth Bishop of Parramatta in June 2016. Nationally, Bishop Vincent serves as Chair of the Bishops Commission for Social Justice, Mission and Service. He is the first Vietnamese-born bishop to lead a diocese outside of Vietnam and the first Vietnamese-born bishop in Australia.

CONTRIBUTORS

Joshua Lourensz, Executive Director, Catholic Social Services Victoria

Joshua Lourensz was appointed Executive Director of Catholic Social Services Victoria in 2019. Previously, he was the coordinator of the Catholic Alliance for People Seeking Asylum for a number of years. Josh is a member of the Board of the Brigidine Asylum Seekers Project and a Director of the Arena Foundation.

Sr Cabrini Makasiale, psychotherapist, Catholic Social Services Otara, New Zealand

Sr Cabrini Makasiale is of Tongan and English background, and was born and raised in Fiji. She lives in a community of Catholic women with religious vows in South Auckland. She has extensive experience as a psychotherapist, counsellor, tutor, supervisor, spiritual director and group facilitator.

John McCarthy QC, Chair, Sydney Archdiocesan Antislavery Task Force

John McCarthy was Australian Ambassador to the Holy See from 2012-2016. During his diplomatic service, he was closely involved with human rights issues, particularly the eradication of modern slavery and human trafficking. Upon returning to Australia, he has remained engaged in the anti-slavery cause and, since May 2017, been Chair of the Sydney Archdiocesan Antislavery Task Force. In 2019 he chaired the Eradicating Modern Slavery from Catholic Supply Chains Conference which recommended the formation of the Australian Catholic Antislavery Network (ACAN), for which he currently serves on the Executive.

Lisa McDonald, Group Mission Leader, St Vincent's Health Australia

As Group Mission Leader of St Vincent's Health Australia (SVHA), Dr Lisa McDonald has a broad range of responsibilities including leading a national mission team to deliver formation to all staff, animating SVHA's Inclusive Health program which outreaches to those on the margins of society, supporting excellence in pastoral care, leading pilgrimage and retreat experiences, and ensuring that SVHA's mission, values and ethics remain central in all that it does. She has worked in numerous church and other leadership roles and especially appreciates the opportunities these have afforded her to share stories to inspire continued love for mission.

Gabrielle McMullen AM, Emeritus Professor, Australian Catholic University

Professor Gabrielle McMullen joined the Faculty of Medicine at Monash University and was appointed Dean of its Catholic residence, Mannix College, in 1981. She was then Rector of Australian Catholic University's Ballarat campus and its Pro- and Deputy Vice-Chancellor (Academic). From 2011-2017 she was a Trustee of Mary Aikenhead Ministries. Aside from her academic work, Gabrielle's community contributions have included membership of education, healthcare, theology and community service boards. She is currently Deputy Chancellor of the University of Divinity.

Robyn Miller, CEO, MacKillop Family Services

Dr Robyn Miller, social worker and family therapist, has over 30 years experience in the community sector, government and child protection. She was a senior clinician and teacher for fourteen years at the Bouverie Family Therapy Centre. From 2006-2015 Robyn was the Chief Practitioner within the Victorian Department of Human Services. She was a consultant for the Royal Commission into Institutional Responses to Child Sexual Abuse and currently serves as Deputy Chair of Catholic Social Services Australia and a board member of Catholic Professional Standards Ltd and the Association of Children's Welfare Agencies in NSW.

CONTRIBUTORS

Mark Monahan, Executive Officer, Edmund Rice Services – Mount Atkinson

For the past five years, Mark Monahan has been the Executive Officer of Edmund Rice Services – Mt Atkinson, a community-based service in the growth corridor of Melbourne's western suburbs. He brings 20 years experience to his role of striving to foster partnerships between land developers, local government, community agencies, schools and the neighbourhood to respond to community concerns such as social cohesion, isolation, strengthening families, migrant and refugee settlement, and trauma. Mark convenes the Catholic Social Services Victoria Emerging Leaders group.

Tony Nicholson, leading social advocate

Tony Nicholson has been a front-line social worker and a senior executive in the social services and policy sector and has 30 years experience in leadership of diverse and complex community organisations.

Sam Patterson, Director of Community Engagement, MacKillop Family Services

Sam Patterson brings a balance of legal and communications experience to his role as Director of Community Engagement at MacKillop Family Services. He worked as a litigation lawyer and communications consultant for twelve years, before his passion for social justice and the rights of children led him to Save the Children. He has since led teams responsible for marketing, communications, stakeholder engagement and fundraising at Cancer Council Victoria and the Alannah and Madeline Foundation, and has been a board director at the Victorian Deaf Society.

Sally-Anne Petrie, Pastoral Coordinator, CatholicCare Melbourne and Gippsland

A pastoral coordinator at CatholicCare Melbourne and Gippsland, Sally-Anne Petrie coordinates a program that offers transitional housing, welcome and simple practical supports to vulnerable asylum seeker families, through partnerships with local parish communities. It has been a blessing to witness how these housing and hospitality experiences enrich the lives of all involved. This work offers Sally-Anne diverse learning opportunities, to reflect and draw on her own postgraduate study in faith leadership, her previous work experiences as a primary school teacher and parish pastoral associate, and her lived experience as a mother of four young adults.

Mark Phillips, CEO, CatholicCare Sydney

CEO of CatholicCare Sydney since 2016, Mark Phillips has a broad background in international financial markets and a proven track record in establishing, managing and growing businesses. His executive roles have included Managing Director of ASX-listed companies and senior positions with a major Australian bank. He currently has governance roles in not-for-profit organisations as the co-chair of End Street Sleeping Collaboration, chair of Cancer Council NSW, director of Cancer Council Australia and director of AccessEAP.

Felicity Rorke, Executive Director, Good Samaritan Inn

Felicity Rorke, Executive Director of Good Samaritan Inn, has been working in the community services sector for over 25 years and has experience in local government, state government and both local and international not-for-profit organisations. Most of her work has been in providing practice, policy and management in the area of responding to family violence.

Patrice Scales, not-for-profit consultant

Patrice Scales is a former Chair of Catholic Social Services Victoria. She has had a long career in the private, public and not-for-profit sectors in communications, publishing and senior executive roles, as well a decade as a management and communication consultant. She has over 15 years experience on Catholic governance boards including MacKillop Family Services, Catholic Care Victoria Tasmania, Sacred Heart Mission and Caritas Australia, and as a member on grant-making committees of several philanthropic organisations.

Ursula Stephens, Chief Executive Officer, Catholic Social Services Australia

Dr Ursula Stephens has a long personal and professional commitment to the social services sector and is a passionate advocate for social inclusion and the not-for-profit sector. She served in the Australian Senate for twelve years, including as Parliamentary Secretary to the Prime Minister for Social Inclusion and the Voluntary Sector. Ursula has been an adult educator, senior public servant, small business owner and social entrepreneur. She chairs the Code Authority of the Fundraising Institute Australia and is a Visiting Fellow and Director at the Australian Centre for Philanthropy and Non Profit Studies at QUT.

Maryanne Stivactas, Coordinator, Communities for Children, CatholicCare Sandhurst

Maryanne Stivactas, Program Coordinator for the Greater Shepparton Communities for Children initiative, is passionate about her local community and believes that an early intervention and prevention approach will lead to positive sustainable change. She has endeavoured to maximise the program's impact by identifying key health and wellbeing issues and rallying other services to join in creating change for children and families.

Francis Sullivan AO, Chair of the Board, Mater Group

Francis Sullivan, as Chair of the Board of the Mater Group, is playing a leading role in its One Mater Project. Prior to this, he was

Chief Executive Officer of the Truth Justice and Healing Council, Secretary General of the Australian Medical Association, and Chief Executive Officer of Catholic Health Australia. He is committed to equity and justice and has been highly successful in bringing a social conscience to the political debate on health and aged care issues. In 2008 the Australian Catholic University awarded him an honorary doctorate for his work in public health advocacy.

Michael Tonks, Director, Catholic Social Services Dunedin, New Zealand

Director of Catholic Social Services Dunedin Michael Tonks is 'Dad' to four amazing adult daughters and 'Pop' to three grandkids. He has worked to support positive family life through most of his career and developed the Game On parenting course and services for fathers to support families.

Lana Turvey-Collins, Plenary Council Facilitator

In November 2017 Lana Turvey-Collins began working with the Australian Catholic Bishops Conference to facilitate a three-year process of listening, dialogue and discernment about the future of the Catholic Church in Australia. Prior to this appointment, she worked as Program Manager for Mission Formation and Professional Development at Catholic Mission. Previously, Lana worked in corporate businesses in roles focused on leadership, implementation of vision and values, and organisational culture, both in Australia and overseas.

Claire Victory, National President, St Vincent de Paul Society National Council

Claire Victory lives in Adelaide and started volunteering with the St Vincent de Paul Society from 10 years of age, including helping in Vinnies shops, visiting elderly people in their homes, and later assisting with youth camps. She joined the National Council in 2011 and, in March 2019, became the first woman, first South Australian and youngest person elected Australian National President. She is a solicitor who has worked in private practice for 12 years, mostly in the areas of employment and workers compensation.

John Warhurst AO, Chair, Concerned Catholics Canberra Goulburn

John Warhurst is Emeritus Professor of Political Science at the Australian National University and Chair of Concerned Catholics Canberra Goulburn. He was a member of the Governance Review Project Team attached to the Catholic Church's Implementation Advisory Group, and co-author of its 2020 report, *The Light from the Southern Cross: Promoting Co-Responsible Governance in the Catholic Church in Australia*. He is a delegate of the Archdiocese of Canberra Goulburn to the forthcoming Plenary Council.

Henry Williams, Reintegration Team Leader, Centacare Kimberley

Henry Williams, Reintegration Team Leader, Centacare Kimberley, was born in the Torres Strait. His language groups are Kala Lagaw Ya and Meriam Mir. He was the first Indigenous male health worker in the Douglas Shire Multi-Purpose Health Service in Mossman. Other roles have included Senior Officer in Alcohol Tobacco and Other Drugs Services in Cairns, service at Kimberley Mental Health and Drug Service, Red Cross Programs Officer in Derby and Senior Aboriginal Programs Officer in the Department of Justice.

Claire-Anne Willis, senior policy advisor

With over 25 years experience working in the Victorian State Government and the community sector, Claire-Anne Willis has a commitment to social justice in the provision of high quality social services for people facing disadvantage and marginalisation. As Senior Policy Officer at Catholic Social Services Victoria from 2017, she drew on her experience in direct service delivery, development of programs and services, and policy development across the human services sector.

Andrew Yule, General Manager, Strategic Communication and Engagement, Jesuit Social Services

With more than 17 years experience working for social change organisations, Andrew Yule is passionate about connecting the lived experience of vulnerable and marginalised Australians with sound policy and research to advocate for long-term change. He has taken a senior role in campaigns to improve youth justice, child protection, mental health services and affordable housing using traditional media, social media and other public engagement strategies to deliver success. He has previously worked as a freelance journalist, radio presenter and short-film maker.

Debra Zanella, CEO, Ruah Community Services and President, Western Australian Council of Social Services

With more than two decades experience in the health and community service sectors, Debra Zanella is a passionate advocate for practical and decisive action to disrupt cycles of social disadvantage. She is currently Chief Executive Officer of Ruah Community Services, President of the Western Australian (WA) Council of Social Services and on WA's East Metropolitan Health Service Board. A founding member of the WA Alliance to End Homelessness, she is now a member of the Australian Alliance to End Homelessness.

Barney Zwartz, journalist and Senior Fellow, Centre for Public Christianity

Barney Zwartz was a journalist with *The Age* for 32 years, and worked in roles including letters editor, opinion editor, chief sub-editor and religion editor, the latter for the last 12 years of his time with Fairfax, winning several awards. He retired in 2013, but still

CONTRIBUTORS

writes about classical music and opera for *The Sydney Morning Herald* and *The Age*, and has a regular faith column for *The Sunday Age*. Barney is also Senior Fellow of the Centre for Public Christianity and the media consultant to the Anglican Archbishop of Melbourne.

www.ingramcontent.com/pod-product-compliance
Lightning Source LLC
Chambersburg PA
CBHW050834230426
43667CB00012B/1990